Reforming a Theology of Gender

"This lucid and timely book is a profound gift for the Christian church. With great wisdom and skill, Patterson guides readers into a genuine encounter with one of the seminal thinkers of our age. . . . This book challenges our fear, disrupts our categories, and jolts our theological imaginations out of tired ruts. Most of all, this book models a posture of humility worthy of the gospel of Christ."
 —Sarah C. Williams, Regent College

"Patterson offers a unique, creative, and boundary-breaking engagement with the avant-garde gender theorist Judith Butler; yet he remains thoroughly biblical and Christocentric. . . . This is a generous book, a boundary breaker and a bridge builder. . . . It is full of wisdom for scholars and advanced students of theology open to new ways of conceptualizing what it is that they believe."
 —Lisa Sowle Cahill, Boston College

"Judith Butler is far and away the most important queer theorist of the modern world, and her practical influence cannot be underestimated. Most Christians have responded with withering attacks or uncritical embraces. Daniel Patterson offers the first patient, probing, and detailed theological analysis of her work. This biblically and philosophically astute study usefully introduces Butler's difficult body of work and is critical reading for any church seeking to faithfully engage the turbulence of our newly gender-fluid age."
 —Brian Brock, University of Aberdeen

"If theological accounts of gender will succeed, they must be characterized by at least two traits: first, they must engage a complex set of interlocutors with patience, charity, and nuance; and second, they must be sensitive to the rich ways the Christian story of creation and redemption implicate our understandings of the topic. Patterson's book exemplifies both of these traits brilliantly in its interpretation of Judith Butler's work and in its constructive theological proposal."
 —Fellipe do Vale, Trinity Evangelical Divinity School

"A persistent searching analysis of Judith Butler's influential queer theory inspires the deepest reflections on subjectivity, desire, violence, law, and embodied life. Patterson articulates here a Christian vocation of gender that is transformed by her critique whilst, in return, witnessing to another

transformation made possible in unity with Christ. This is an exemplary study in discipleship in a contemporary context."
—SUSAN F. PARSONS, editor, *Studies in Christian Ethics*

"Patterson's meticulous book demonstrates a core Christian virtue in action—how creative listening can be. Having heard Judith Butler with charity, he returns to Christians and poses critical questions that will press our contribution on this contentious cultural issue into useful new spaces. This is the best theological account of these issues I have yet encountered."
—KEVIN HARGADEN, Jesuit Centre for Faith and Justice

Reforming a Theology of Gender

Constructive Reflections
on Judith Butler and Queer Theory

Daniel R. Patterson

CASCADE *Books* • Eugene, Oregon

REFORMING A THEOLOGY OF GENDER
Constructive Reflections on Judith Butler and Queer Theory

Copyright © 2022 Daniel R. Patterson. All rights reserved. Except for brief quotations in critical publications or reviews, no part of this book may be reproduced in any manner without prior written permission from the publisher. Write: Permissions, Wipf and Stock Publishers, 199 W. 8th Ave., Suite 3, Eugene, OR 97401.

Cascade Books
An Imprint of Wipf and Stock Publishers
199 W. 8th Ave., Suite 3
Eugene, OR 97401

www.wipfandstock.com

PAPERBACK ISBN: 978-1-6667-3149-1
HARDCOVER ISBN: 978-1-6667-2405-9
EBOOK ISBN: 978-1-6667-2406-6

Cataloguing-in-Publication data:

Names: Patterson, Daniel R.

Title: Reforming a theology of gender : constructive reflections on Judith Butler and queer theory / Daniel R. Patterson.

Description: Eugene, OR: Cascade Books, 2022 | Includes bibliographical references and index.

Identifiers: ISBN 978-1-6667-3149-1 (paperback) | ISBN 978-1-6667-2405-9 (hardcover) | ISBN 978-1-6667-2406-6 (ebook)

Subjects: LCSH: Butler, Judith, 1956– | Butler, Judith, 1956-—Religion | Queer theology | Gender nonconformity—Religious aspects—Christianity | Gender identity | Social ethics | Liberation theology

Classification: BT708 P38 2022 (print) | BT708 (ebook)

To my mum . . .

Contents

Preface xi
Acknowledgments xv
Abbreviations xvii

Introduction 1

1. Re-forming the Subject as Desire 15
   Introduction 15
   A Power Operation 18
   Desiring the Other 23
   Conclusion 42
2. Departing Adam and Eve 44
   Introduction 44
   Seeing in the World 46
   Created Intersubjectivity 55
   Desiring to Be What I Am Not 76
   Conclusion 90
3. Diagnosing Gender Violence 92
   Introduction 92
   Observing Normative Violence 93
   Weapon of Violence 100
   Inscription or Description 105
   Conclusion 114
4. Eden's Seduction 116
   Introduction 116
   The Fall of Sex 118
   A Seductive Image 128
   Conclusion 138
5. An Ethics of Gender: Finding Hope in Desire 141
   Introduction 141

        God, Desire, and Hope 144
        Vulnerability and Nonviolence 151
        Democratizing Gender 159
        Conclusion 166

6. The Vocation of Gender: Vulnerability in Union 169
        Introduction 169
        Resisting Idols, Iconoclasm, and Transcendence 171
        A Body of Hope 180
        The Image of God: A Vocation of Conformity 192
        A Body Not My Own: Gender as Becoming 201
        Conclusion 215

Bibliography 219

Subject Index 229
Scripture Index 243

Preface

THIS BOOK IS THE result of a journey that began in May 2013 in Wisła, Poland. Over a casual beer in the lobby of a hotel, Professor Glynn Harrison encouraged me to take up doctoral research at the intersection of theology and queer theory. Before that time, I had not read any of Judith Butler's works, and I did not realize that she had been one of the most influential philosophers shaping the moment in which we live, and not only on questions related to gender.

I slowly began to make my way through Butler's corpus, beginning with her published doctoral dissertation and through this reading I came to understand that her thought on gender was more open to theological interaction than I first imagined. This was obvious because Butler's gender theory did not allow me to interact with her thought without simultaneously interrogating the theological coherence of my own views. The methodology and structure of this book reflect this confronting realization.

For some, the idea of induced theological reflection by a powerful thinker like Butler is a scary proposition, which is in part my motivation for writing this book. I want to offer a resource that explores Butler's thought in a slow and sustained theological manner to invoke reflection on one's own theological views that inform one's idea about gender.

From an academic standpoint, my intention with this theological reading of Butler's gender theory is to create fresh avenues for thinking about Butler's theory of gender in theological discourse. Butler is no stranger to theology. Theologians have been drawing on Butler's thought since her early work. Since that time, the discipline of queer theology, which Butler's thought heavily influenced, has cemented itself as an influential voice in the development of Christian theological method and content. In recent times, however, Butler's thought has faded into the background, not because it is no longer relevant, but because many have "moved on" from Butler. In a sense, Butler's thought operates as an assumed foundation for much queer theology and theologies of gender and sexuality more broadly, manifesting only sometimes as a footnote. In short, in terms of theological discourse, Butler's gender theory is "old hat."

Yet for all of Butler's influence, no one has attempted a sustained interaction with Butler from a theological position, let alone a conservative theological position. No doubt, this is because her conclusions about gender are assumed to be in radical opposition to more conservative points of view. But to begin with this conclusion before the work is done to ascertain whether this is the case results in fleeting dismissal and one-sided critical interactions. Consequently, many reject Butler as liberal nonsense. This book fills this lacuna by providing a sustained and interactive theological engagement with Butler's thought to reveal her "theological" commitments, and to grasp the theological and ethical implications for Christians who reject *or* accept her thought. My desire is that this theological interaction might draw Butler's thought into conscious theological reflection again, and in so doing provide new avenues for theological engagement with Butler in the future.

From the outset, I would like to confront a critique of this book: that my theological convictions and view of Scripture impact my reading of and response to Butler. I think, however, that my *response* to Butler should not be confused with my *reading* of Butler. Reading Butler means taking the time to understand Butler's complex prose to decipher her theoretical emphases, mode of operation, and conclusions, while showing sensitivity to her own desire for life. In this way, my reading of Butler seeks theoretical accuracy and faithfulness to Butler's intentions. My *response*, on the other hand, seeks to give not only theological expression to Butler's theory but a theological reflection from my viewpoint.

This book is a substantial revision of my doctoral thesis that I submitted in October of 2018 at the University of Aberdeen, Scotland. Since then, I have had some time away from the content, which has allowed me to see my research on Butler and gender with fresh eyes. Turning to this book, I have sharpened explanations of Butler's more difficult ideas for the sake of clarity, but where the most change has occurred is in my theological chapters (2, 4, and 6). I purged many peripheral discussions, which enabled me to see the theological content differently and in a more streamlined manner, and thus where reordering of component parts of my overall argument was needed. In contrast to my doctoral thesis, this book represents a major recrafting of my theological interaction with Butler, which reaches a climax in a final chapter that comprises entirely new material.

Acknowledgments

MANY PEOPLE HAVE BEEN instrumental in helping me get this book to the point of publication. I must begin with Professor Brian Brock, who took the lead role in supervising my doctoral research at the University of Aberdeen, Scotland. I cannot express how thankful I am to Brian for the patience, wisdom, and hospitality he showed me throughout my time in Aberdeen. Brian's care for each person he encounters, careful reading, rigorous thinking, pinpoint questioning, and love for God are not easily disentangled. Professor Stanley Hauerwas was also my doctoral supervisor and was instrumental in shaping my early approach to reading Butler. Furthermore, and as we have come to know well, Stanley has a keen eye for hairline fractures in arguments, as well as a sensitive nose for the kind of paper that conceals cracks. I thank Stanley for his commitment over decades to take the lead in sensitively facing up to stiff cultural and church assumptions on all manner of issues, but importantly in the service of those who find themselves not justified by norms that dictate who can be human. I am grateful for Brian and Stanley, who have, in their own ways, modelled clearly to me what it takes to be a faithful servant of God and the church in the academy.

I am also grateful to many others who have helped me to iron out poor word choices, incomprehensible sentences, clumsily framed paragraphs, and what seemed at the time to be cogent, robust, and persuasive ideas but which were exposed under their critical gaze to be somewhat inadequate. First, Marcia Patterson has read and reread this book many more times than any other constructive critic. I am grateful for the time she committed, as well as her attention to the detail of English grammar that has helped me to make this book readable and flow well despite the complex content. She has not only edited this book thoroughly, but in the process taught me how to write in a way that is more readable and concise. I am also thankful for Allan Chapple, Rory Shiner, Michael Morelli, Jacob Marques Rollison, Fletcher Creelman, and Josie Rivett, who offered critiques and suggestions to develop my ideas in fruitful ways. Of special note is Kevin O'Farrell, who drew my attention to a number of critical issues at crucial moments throughout the book. One of these resulted in a substantial revision. In addition to these people, I am indebted to those, who number in the hundreds, with whom I have informally discussed and argued over the details of the ideas of this book. In these conversations, I was pressed and pulled in different directions to rethink ideas, which forced me to resist simple and reductive arguments and conclusions.

I reserve my special thanks for Professor Sarah Williams, who took the time within her busy schedule to offer a close reading of this book late in the piece. Sometimes it is difficult to see the glaring problems in one's own writing. On issues concerning gender and sexuality, it is easy to uphold patterns of thought and speech that reiterate the very kinds of harm this book seeks to purge. In this way I am sincerely grateful for Sarah, who pointed out structural, tonal, and content lapses. Sarah's genuine desire to see this book become as good as it can be has pressed me to work even harder towards achieving that end.

Finally, I acknowledge my wonderful wife, Katie, and our two precious daughters, Svetlana and Mimi. Each, in their own way, has cheered me on to reach the finish line. They are God's blessing to me and my delight.

This book is a genuine attempt to be prayerfully patient and rigorously responsive, not only to Butler's thought, but also to the Holy Spirit. Where impatience arises and where mishearing and misrepresentation of Butler's thought or God's Word becomes apparent, I take full responsibility, and I look forward to another time whereby I can respond by giving another account of myself.

Sofia, Bulgaria
July 2021

Abbreviations

AC   Judith Butler, *Antigone's Claim: Kinship between Life and Death*. New York: Columbia University Press, 2000.

BTM   Judith Butler, *Bodies That Matter: On the Discursive Limits of "Sex."* 1993. Reprint, London: Routledge, 2011.

ES   Judith Butler, *Excitable Speech: A Politics of the Performative*. London: Routledge, 1997.

FW   Judith Butler, *Frames of War: When Life Is Grievable?* 2009. Reprint, London: Verso, 2016.

GAO   Judith Butler, *Giving an Account of Oneself*. New York: Fordham University Press, 2005.

GT   Judith Butler, *Gender Trouble: Feminism and the Subversion of Identity*. 1990. Reprint, London: Routledge, 2007.

PL   Judith Butler, *Precarious Life: The Powers of Mourning and Violence*. 2004. Reprint, New York: Verso, 2006.

PLP   Judith Butler, *Psychic Life of Power: Theories in Subjection*. Stanford: Stanford University Press, 1997.

PTA   Judith Butler, *Notes Toward a Performative Theory of Assembly*. Cambridge: Harvard University Press, 2015.

SD	Judith Butler, *Subjects of Desire: Hegelian Reflections in Twentieth-Century France*. 1987. Reprint, Columbia University Press, 2012.
SS	Judith Butler, *Senses of the Subject*. New York: Fordham University Press, 2015.
UG	Judith Butler, *Undoing Gender*. London: Routledge, 2004.

Introduction

A Prophet

JUDITH BUTLER IS NO stranger to theology,[1] yet for all the ways her gender theory has been put to work in the academic discipline, very few theologians have, from a theological perspective, attempted to narrate how Butler's thought is operating theologically.[2] This book fills this lacuna by transposing Butler's queering gender theory into a theological register revealing a novel question for reflection: what law justifies some

---

1. For example: Alliaume, "Disturbingly Catholic"; Bodley-Dangelo, *Sexual Difference*; Coakley, *Powers and Submissions*; Cornwall, *Sex and Uncertainty*; Jantzen, "Promising Ashes"; Hornsby, "Annoying Woman"; Kamitsuka, "Sex in Heaven"; Kotsko, "Failed Divine Performative"; Loughlin, *Alien Sex*; Marchal, "Queer Approaches"; Mawson, "Subjectivity and Embodied Limits"; Murphey and Starling, eds., *Gender and Sex in the Context*; Rees, *Romance*; Riedl, *Judith Butler and Theology*; Rogers, "Bodies Demand Language"; Rudy, *Sex and the Church*; Sanlon, *Plastic People*; Starling, "Family Drama"; Stone, "Garden of Eden"; Stuart, "Sacramental Flesh"; Toh, "Enculturated or Created?"; Tonstad, *Queer Theology*; Ward, *Cities of God*; Yarhouse, *Understanding Gender Dysphoria*.

2. A notable exception is Anne Daniell, who brings together the thought of Butler and the apostle Paul, but when she broaches the question of the law in Paul, she does not make the link between Butler's "law of heterosexuality" and the productive and regulative impact of the Christian Edenic creatures of Adam and Eve. Daniell, "Spiritual Body." Anna Riedl achieves something similar to the goals of this book, but whereas she uses Butler as a *ground* for developing theology broadly conceived in terms of liberation, politics, and prophetic critique, I use Butler as a *dialogue partner* to critique an existing conservative theology of gender. Riedl, *Butler and Theology*, 111–52. Appropriating Butler's thought to construct theology must not precede what Adam Kotsko describes as "an uncompromising critique of what [Butler] calls 'theological' patterns of thought." Butler's thought is not, first, a tool to construct theology, but one that critiques theology. Kotsko, "Failed Divine Performative," 209.

and condemns others in their bodies?[3] The response I offer is *the law of Adam and Eve*, and further theological reflection does not lead to a predictable queering of man and woman but *reforms* how Adam and Eve function within Christian theology and ethics.

The basic claim of this book is that an attentive reading of Butler's theory provokes the Christian to account for the two-pronged confession that humanity no longer lives in Eden, *and* this matters for what it means to fulfill the scriptural exhortation to glorify God in our body.[4] Moreover, Butler prompts us to see that Eden is a problematic haven to which many of us return to negotiate gender trouble besetting only "some" people's lives. I argue that returning to Eden is not a righteousness orientation but a futile quest for life that doubles as a mode of self-righteousness that undermines the gospel of Jesus Christ. This calls into question theologies of gender and their ethical corollaries that rely on the notion that conforming (or being forcibly conformed) to Adam and Eve—often under the rubric of what is naturally a man and woman—is a means to life for ourselves and society.

Butler's gender theory can be interpreted as a secular attempt to justify nontraditional gender arrangements, but it can also be heard as a *call* to give an account of ourselves as people who no longer live in the beginning but dwell with others in an age in which we wait patiently and with hope for the final glorification of our bodies.[5] Butler's theory, when understood through a theological lens, provides us with the impetus to shift our gaze from the seductive bodies of Adam and Eve to the bloodied and scarred, risen body of Jesus Christ. This makes *Butler's voice strangely prophetic and redemptive.*[6]

---

3. Graham Ward claims that Butler's thought lends itself to being pressed in a theological direction because she likens performance to ritual. This is used by Ward to deepen Karl Barth's emphasis on the symbolic use of the male and female anatomy to point beyond their own divinely ordered differentiation to the differentiation between "I and Thou, Self and Others, Yahweh and Israel, and Christ and His church." The "body" in each case is not limited but finds itself in an ever-expanding symbolic field giving rise to new modes of corporeality. Ward also uses Butler theologically to reveal the way Christians come to self-understanding by practicing the liturgy and social rituals of the church. While Ward narrates Butler theologically, this is limited to extending Barth's anthropology, which means that he does not use Butler to critique Barth's apparently crude return to natural theology. Ward, *Cities of God*, 196–97.

4. 1 Cor 6:20. All Scripture quotations, unless otherwise indicated, are from the New Revised Standard Version, 1989.

5. Rom 8:23–25.

6. Butler's voice is like the nations' question of Israel in Ps 115:2: "Why should the

Yet despite this claim, Butler's gender theory and Christianity are not allies. They are better understood as strange bedfellows. Butler is an agent provocateur who rouses Christians to snap out of their idolatrous obsession with the bygone days of Edenic beauty. Without queer friends like Butler, we tend to ask dull, lifeless, and abstract questions that lead to death in life. What is a man or a woman? What is natural God-given gender? And what is good moral sexuality? Questions like these send us down the same well-worn track in ruts that operate like autopilot, keeping the cart's wheels on course, bumping over the same bumps, and predictably ending up in the same place each time, Eden, which is ironic because we cannot enter Eden. Returning to Eden to find answers to abstract questions about gender usually works, but only because lifeless questions (in the sense that they do not pertain to our lives) fail to broach the complexity of embodiment that we find outside of Eden, where we all live.[7]

This book acts upon the disquiet that many feel—that the well-worn path back to Eden cajoles our thinking about gender, sexuality, and the body by curtailing what questions can be asked, what possibilities can be discussed, and most importantly, how to make sense of non-Edenic bodies in the present. Butler's gender theory jolts the theological cart, forcing it out of the tired ruts to *wonder* afresh about bodies.

---

nations say, 'Where is their God?'" This question is not as redundant as the Psalter seems to assume, especially in light of Israel's history of idol-making. To be provoked to give an account of where one's God is can reveal the subtle installation of idols that would otherwise go unnoticed. The nations here, like Butler, function like the Old Testament prophets who discern where the people of God have strayed from God's law.

7. Carl Trueman boldly asserts that Butler's gender theory represents "a psychological approach to reality" that is "both a symptom and a cause of the many social, ethical, and political questions we now face." The former claim is patently dubious, as Butler repeatedly demonstrates and this book will reiterate, but to the latter claim, one wonders why "questions" is posed in a negative light? Trueman claims that "one does not have to have read Descartes—or Judith Butler—to think intuitively about the world in terms for which they provide a theoretical rationale," which is incontestable only if Butler's thought has nothing to add to the field of reference that grounds our intuition. I suggest that reducing Butler's theory to psychology, as seen in Trueman's thought, is a misreading that undermines the church's voice. In the short term the full force of her theory is evaded, which precipitates the longer-term situation (which has already arrived) where the church is ill-equipped to respond to the questioning of gender in a society that has been soaking in Butler's gender theory for over two decades. Carl Trueman, *Rise and Triumph*, 70–72.

The Mission of Wonder

It seems inevitable that with time knowledge replaces wonder, and with knowledge comes mastery. The desire to wonder dissipates, hampering our God-given ability to be encountered by the world, surprised by creation, and to learn something new, and perhaps true. When we lose the desire to wonder we lose the passion for the encounter and the possibility of new life; we have mastered the world in which we live.

But mastery of creation is an illusion. Scripture, particularly the Psalms and the book of Job, testify to this. Who can fathom creation? Indeed, who can fathom the body? In this book, I exercise the God-given gift of wonder to rupture the mastery of the body that too often characterizes traditional Christian views on gender. If wonder is a practice of un-mastery, then wondering about the body has the potential to animate new theological and ethical possibilities for receiving our own and others' bodies.[8]

The goal of this book, however, is not merely to induce wonder at the body. While wonder is an indispensable aspect of Christian inquiry, wonder does not necessarily lead to what is good and true about my body and my perception of it. I do not gaze innocently on the body like the naked man and woman in the garden, but more like the same people who subsequently learned to hide their bodies because they could *see* the body, ironically, with their eyes opened.[9] This ruptured capacity to see clearly reiterates the Pauline characterization of human sight that we see only in part.[10] Wonder might reveal the body in a new light, but we take such revelation as an invitation for Christian theological and ethical reflection because the body we see might not represent the body in its wonderful fullness.

In the part of the church that is characterized by more conservative views about gender, the thought of learning something new about the body is distressing. New is different, and conservative by its very definition inherently resists such notions. Unfortunately, within this cultured

---

8. Sarah Coakley coins "un-mastery" in response to John Milbank's "non-mastery." For Coakley, "un-mastery" is not merely the desire not to master, but "a transcendent undoing of manipulative human control or aggression," which I take to narrate the spiritual impulse of the operative mode of wonder that is crucial for theological reflection on creation and God. Coakley, *God, Sexuality, and the Self*, 43, 45, 46–47.

9. Gen 3:7.

10. 1 Cor 13:12.

pattern of thinking, in order to be wise one learns to shun wonder. But the fear of wonder is *not* the beginning of wisdom, and so taking up a posture that denies the call to wonder not only perverts the famous biblical proverb but might result in safeguarding what is problematic about the status quo. The posture of "un-wonder" toward the body is ultimately unwise.

When we begin to wonder about the body, we learn that the body is much more than a bunch of cells that together take on a particular shape and perform a certain function. Wonder leads to opportunities to explore scriptural claims that the body is not circumscribed by time and determined by material existence. A view of the body that is reducible to its material function, or lack thereof, is a grossly underwhelming vision of what God created in the beginning, who we are today, and what we will be in the new creation. Unlike a rock or tree stump, the human exists in relative openness to the world and radically to its divine creator. When we begin to wonder about the body as a part of, and open to, a web of complex relations in the world and with God, we begin to see that the body might not be as limited and self-explanatory as we once thought.

Understanding the complexity of the world and our lives within it requires numerous sources, a task for which the church has historically included Jesus Christ.[11] Yet Scripture does not draw Christ into the explanatory matrix as just another source to help account for creation. It makes a much stronger claim: Christ is the means and end of all creation.[12] We must avoid the fundamental error of assuming creation to be self-explanatory formed matter or comprehensible without the gospel of Jesus Christ. Creation is a theological category that renders the body in need of an explanation in relation to Jesus Christ who is its "inner logic."[13]

Christ's relation to creation cannot be limited to his *redemptive* work, but must also include his *creative* work,[14] which implies that Jesus Christ is before, after, and above all creation. Where Christ is not the presupposition of the creation *and* recreation of the body in relation to the world in time, we cannot fully account for how God conceives of glorifying the body in the beginning, now, or the eschaton. Providing a richer account of Christ's work in a theology of gender via the doctrine

11. This is especially evident in the ancient Greek church. See, for example, Behr, *Mystery of Christ*, ch. 3.
12. Col 1:16.
13. Rae, "Jesus Christ, the Order of Creation," 29.
14. John 1:3; 1 Cor 8:6; Heb 1:2–3.

of the *imago Dei* disrupts an overly static or telic rendering of gender as well as an overly labile or fluid view and so better positions us to think about what Christian living as men and women might look like in the present.[15] This book therefore is concerned ultimately with the task of what Stanley Hauerwas calls "learn[ing] to be God's creatures," a task that takes seriously our status as learners within a created and also a redemptive environment—as people who have *arrived* and are *arriving* by faith in Christ by the power of the Spirit.[16]

The desire to wonder about the body is not to achieve right understanding, as if this is what God desires of us. The problem with a wrong understanding of the body is not error but idolatry and rejecting as well as holding back the hope of life that God offers to everyone through Jesus Christ alone. The pursuit of truth about the body and gender is not to get our thinking right in order to correct others, but to orient ourselves rightly toward God and then others in the world as we find our true life in Christ. This book then is not apologetic, in the sense of seeking to defend a particular position on gender, but missional, which Brian Brock describes as "engaging the lords of this age and in hopes of breaking their hold on ourselves and our neighbors."[17] The lord of lords of this age is no doubt *my* desire unmoored from *my* Creator, which makes rooting out idolatrous desire very difficult, particularly where I assume my desire as being one with God's. This book is therefore not about them—the transgressive other and how we might better theologically narrate them into or out of God's plan to save them from their bodies of death—but me and you, the ones who are prone to justifying embodied life by gazing at the static images of Adam and Eve rather than the perfect living image of God, Jesus Christ.

Finally, wondering about the body and gender is provoked by a range of questions that for most people are hypothetical. For others, however, questions about gender concern life and death for themselves, one's child, or friends. How should we respond to people around us who do not fit within a traditional Christian understanding of gender? Medical professionals are facing questions about how to navigate complex questions about a person's right to access various forms of medical treatment

---

15. "A telic narrative is one in which key truth claims are locked into the beginning, such that no recourse to a later event is required to establish these truths as axiomatic." Rae, "Jesus Christ, the Order of Creation," 166.

16. Hauerwas, *Peaceable Kingdom*, 27.

17. Brock, "Jesus Christ the Divine Animal," 74.

for gender reassignment, including forms of professional counselling, medication, and surgery. Legislators are required to negotiate the quickly changing landscape of what society values regarding gender. Local churches are facing pressure to adapt buildings, constitutions, theology, and sacraments like marriage to welcome people who do not or cannot "fit" within the established church parameters. Private Christian schools and public government schools are facing similar questions, but face the added complexity of equal opportunity employment legislation, unisex school populations, and uniforms that are traditionally linked to one gender or the other. These questions merely scratch the surface of the number and complexity of issues on this topic. Despite the need to address these pressing questions, this is not the function of this book. I seek, rather, to guide us to see why these questions are questions at all. Being caught off guard induces an impulsive response—something akin to activism—but we must compose ourselves and develop a posture that should have been ours all along. We must redirect the sense of urgency that drives us to speak in haste and at a volume that resembles a loud clanging cymbal toward forming a posture that is capable of engagement. In other words, we must engage the basic principle of communication of careful listening before careful speaking. Speaking before listening is mere activism and adding the descriptor "Christian" is futile. This book is therefore a small, first step in this direction. Listening to the voice of Judith Butler and reflecting theologically on it through God's voice in Scripture seeks to equip confessing Christians with the tools needed to listen further and more carefully to the world and God so that they can take up the pressing questions in a manner befitting a learned disciple of Jesus Christ.

Provoking Fear

Butler's thought provokes wonder, but also fear, particularly fear of where one's theological reflection might lead. This begs the question: what is in a question? What characterizes the questioning of gender that by even posing the question one flirts with danger? Why does asking questions about the body generate such widespread fear that the inquirer will not emerge clean?[18] Thinking more broadly, what is being assumed about the risk of

---

18. This was evident when I was working on my doctoral thesis when people expressed nervousness that my research topic would lead me to lose my salvation or at

making an inquiry into the body and gender that would not be risked asking a whole range of doctrinal or moral questions related to race, disability, war, or economics? Perhaps Geoffrey Rees's critique has merit when he suggests that sex and gender have been imbued, not merely with normative, but biblically indefensible redemptive significance.[19]

Fear also emerges in response to voiced (and the internalized) regulation of questioning the body by those who have mastered it. This regulation leads to an assumed view that even posing the question—wondering/wandering—crosses a fatal boundary that separates what is clean from unclean, the inside from the outside. Metaphorically speaking, questioning the body and gender is to peer over the fence to see what is on the other side, with the added complication that even peering is imperiling because of what lies there. When we manage to overcome the tremendous weight of the guard's presence, the panoptic glare, the anxious eye of those who, or that which, regulate theology and its ethical implications, we see that engaging Butler's thought mobilizes stunted and superficial thinking about the body, and the complexities of gender. We do not need to fear where discerning and diligent Christian inquiry about gender might lead us, and we do not need to fear those who seek to regulate what inquiry we can or cannot pursue.

Finally, some fear reading Butler because they worry that it might render a conservative position vulnerable to views that are hostile to Christianity and its foundational claims. This fear, however, is misplaced. Certainly, Stanley Hauerwas perceptibly observes that Christian reflection on sexual ethics (to which we can add the topic of gender) is in a mess because it has been directed by presuppositions that are antithetical to Christianity and its claims.[20] This does not in fact lead us away from Butler but rather provides a basis for engagement with her. While Butler's claims do not ultimately mesh with a conservative viewpoint on gender, the presuppositions that ground her queer theory are rooted in the thought of many continental philosophers whose work is formed often within a Jewish or Christian frame of reference. Thus, her presuppositions are not antithetical but enable and encourage engagement. Moreover, as it will be shown, Butler is heavily reliant on the theological thought of the seventeenth-century thinker Baruch Spinoza, who she confesses is at the

---

least my conservative and reformed theological convictions.

19. Rees, *Romance*. I explore Rees's claim in depth in chapter 4.
20. Hauerwas, *After Christendom?*, 26.

core of her work.²¹ For these reasons I reject the view that queer theory in general, and Butler in particular, represent incommensurable dialogue partners for conservative Christian theologians.²² Butler's theory lends itself to Christian reflection on gender because she operates within the architecture of thinkers who are broadly shaped by Christian and Jewish worldviews.

The Contextual Landscape

Butler's queer theory emerges from the broad discipline of philosophy, and more specifically, comparative literature and critical theory. In her early work, she questions the assumed foundations of 1970s and 1980s identity-driven feminist theory and traditional concepts of gender and sexuality. Butler develops a theory in which gender is performative, which means that gender is not what one *is* by virtue of one's morphology or chromosomal makeup, but something one has *become* and is *becoming* by repeatedly acting out what they have come to understand is the meaning of their given gender. This is not an identity theory to be believed and implemented to achieve a particular social vision for the future, but is a way of (re-)reading history to show how language, and our participation as the vehicles that transport and implement that language, determines what is gender in history and now. We can see from this snapshot of Butler's thought that time is an important element in her theory, as is the communication of ideas and the notion of how past immaterial ideas continually arrive in the present in material form. Butler helps us to see that the coalface for thinking about gender in this moment is where time, culture, and matter intersect. This flags the central point for theological reflection of whether gender is a crass biological reality (essential) or a form of immaterial materiality that is ineradicably bound to sociality in time (constructed). I argue that both accounts are theologically inadequate.

---

21. This observation does not appeal to her claim that she is Jewish (Butler, "Response," 394).

22. MacIntyre, *After Virtue*. Anna Reidl takes up Butler theologically but explicitly avoids "[Butler's] roots in gender theory" because it might "prevent a fruitful dialogue between Butler and theology." I suggest the possibility of unfruitfulness needs to be explored by rehearsing dialogue with Butler theologically before deferring to the more conversational parts of her corpus. Reidl, *Butler and Theology*, ix.

A cross-disciplinary approach is used by Butler to construct this complex theory. She draws the reader into deep personal and cultural reflection, but not *via* personal and cultural reflection *per se*, because that would only reveal the status quo. The function of ancient mythology, modern documentary films, novels, religion, law, her own life, and the lives of others, as well as classic texts from the disciplines of philosophy, feminism, linguistics, and critical theory, draws the reader to reflect upon their self and society through other lenses. Butler's thought reveals me to myself through the refracted light that is shed by the diverse sources and forms of inquiry through which Butler herself wonders about herself as sexual and gendered. The result is not a critical theory of gender but a reformed conception of gender.

My theological engagement with Butler approximates her cross-disciplinary approach. I draw upon the genres of biography, autobiography, and poetry, as well as the disciplines of philosophy, Christian ethics, systematic theology, and biblical studies. The result is not a classical biblical study on the theme of gender, nor a pure theology or ethics of gender, but *a cross-disciplined theology of gender*. This means that reforming a theology of gender is not the goal of this book but a by-product of serious theological interaction with Butler.

The Conversation

Both in terms of content and method, reflecting theologically on Butler's thought requires an intimate knowledge of the theory I ascribe to her. An interaction with Butler that takes the shape of a conversation takes into account both concerns. A conversation does not allow a one-way critique *or* blind acceptance of her queer theory, but draws our two viewpoints together to confront and challenge each other to consider the other's perspective.[23]

---

23. An example of conservative theological engagement without conversation is Sanlon, *Plastic People*. While I am sympathetic to many of the broad conclusions Sanlon makes, his account of Butler is inadequate because he construes her thought as an identity politics rather than a queer politics, which enables a "describe and critique" approach. Despite my strong reservation of Deryn Guest's claim that listening *requires* change, he observes: "As much as Sanlon gives the impression of taking a considered, listening approach, he never allows this to alter his central affirmation that trans bodies run counter to God's template for humanity." Guest, "Troubling the Waters," 36–37. Annika Thiem also treats Butler's thought dialogically. She claims that the force of Butler's work is felt when it is taken up in dialogue. Thiem, *Unbecoming Subjects*, 8.

The decision to choose dialogue as the mode of engagement with Butler is to safeguard the hermeneutical principle that interpretation does not happen in the realm of the abstract, but via encounter. In this moment of conversation, a traditional Christian view becomes vulnerable to a queer theorist's thought, but in so doing, Butler's thought becomes vulnerable to a considered Christian view. I will demonstrate that this methodological move of encounter and vulnerability is not a rhetorical flourish, but a genuine attempt to account theologically for one of the most impactful thought systems of recent times.[24]

The dialogical method this book employs also provides a distinct vantage point for those who have conservative convictions on gender and sexuality issues and want to begin interacting with Butler's and queer theoretical thought. It is difficult to pick up Butler's *Gender Trouble* or *Bodies That Matter*, for example, and begin reading. By reading Butler in a mode of generous conversation, as this book models, the reader is able to gradually—as gradually as one can—acclimatize to her thought structure and writing style, gaining the tools not only to comprehend Butler's thought, but also to interpret it theologically. This book therefore fills a desperate need in the growing area of gender studies in more conservative Christian higher education institutions that realize the need to confront thinkers like Butler but lack the academic tools to do so.

Another consequence of using conversation to structure engagement with Butler is to position this book where Butler's thought is winning over minds and hearts in society and the church. "Judith Butler rules" is how Ellen Armour begins her overview of Butler's impact on the present. She invokes Copernicus's revolutionary developments of human understanding to help us grasp Butler's impact.[25] Whether this overstates the case does not diminish the remarkable reach Butler's thought has had and is having on people in all parts of society. This book seeks to speak into this context, saturated as it is by Butler's ideas, by absorbing the challenges her thought presents. In other words, my desire is not to rid society and the church of her thought or influence. Not only is that impossible, given the reach and sedimentation of her thought, but it is also a problematic methodological decision to refuse to hear and take

---

24. For an argument for why sociology is important for the task of Christian theology, see Coakley, *God, Sexuality and the Self*, ch. 2. While it has not been my intention to take up Coakley's *Théologie totale*, this book demonstrates many of its hallmarks.

25. Armour, "Annoying Woman," 71.

seriously the reasons why Butler's thought has been so persuasive in the last thirty years.

Overview

The conversation with Butler focuses on three themes: *subjectivity* (chapters 1 and 2), which feeds into a discussion about *violence* (chapters 3 and 4), leading to a final interaction about *life* (chapters 5 and 6). The three themes amount to one interactive dialogue. Each discussion comprises two chapters: the first chapter explicates Butler's thought, which is then brought into dialogue with theological interlocutors in the following chapter. While the three discussions build on the previous discussion/s, they do not move on, but "circle" back to draw out the complexity and nuance that could not be realized at first.[26] The decision to proceed in this manner reflects my view that a chronological account of Butler's thought results in it becoming static or frozen in time and unable to function as a corpus that is "alive." A dialogue that has the expressed intention of circling back on itself can resist the desire to have everything "sorted out" before moving on. It is inevitable, therefore, that there will be some loose threads left to "dangle" in the opening chapters, but these will come back into the discussion in later chapters once more layers have been put down. For this reason, there is no chapter that should be read in isolation from the others because they are an integrated whole. Some readers who are versed in Butlerian scholarship may become frustrated with the way the argument builds, but this strategy is necessary to ensure all the pieces are in place before I engage theologically with Butler. I realize that this places a heavy burden on the reader, but as any reader of Butler understands, there are no shortcuts when it comes to comprehending or responding to her thought.[27]

Reflecting theologically on Butler's thought requires taking seriously the aforementioned themes as questions rather than statements. In chapter 2, I respond to Butler's account of subjectivity and desire (chapter

---

26. Campbell and Harbord describe her thought as "repetitive and interrogative, repeatedly circling back and moving over ground once again.... In such a way her text enacts a repetition of dominant theories." Campbell and Harbord, "Playing It Again," 232.

27. Honeysett, who is an evangelical Christian author, actively discourages his readers from reading the essay he focuses on "unless you have a specific interest in this area" because it "is quite complicated." Honeysett, *Meltdown*, 63.

1) and show that it has structural significance for thinking about a Christian account of gender. Man and woman are not static categories but modes of intersubjective being, which is a realization that sensitizes us to the role of the other for perceiving ourselves as gendered. In chapter 4, I contemplate theologically Butler's conception of violence (chapter 3). I suggest that Christian engagement with the body and notions of gender can heed Butler's critique of violence, as I seek to show by offering my own critique of violence by framing Adam and Eve as an idealized expression of gender, which, by posing as a law of normal or natural gender, are used to produce unjust forms of hierarchy and exclusion. I coin the *law of Adam and Eve* to constrain present usage of the prelapsarian couple in discussions on gender.

By reflecting on Adam and Eve inside *and* outside of Eden, we see that time and space impact more fully on a Christian concept of gender.[28] If humanity no longer exists in Eden, then Adam and Eve are a memory, functioning as an ideal standard on the horizon of history that demonstrate that I am not the man God created in the beginning. Furthermore, this righteous law that Adam and Eve embody teaches me that no amount of enacting what they *were* can make me become the person that God desires. The strong claim I am making in chapter 4 is that the Edenic *images* of the *created* bodies of Adam and Eve do not save me or society. Where I find myself worshiping these created images by conforming myself to their perfect bodies to become like them, I have fallen into a futile life within a regime of (body-)works-based righteousness.

The final chapter responds to Butler's nervous engagement with the question: How then should I live? (chapter 5). I take Butler's claim seriously that the possibility of embodied life is not in my own hands, but the hands of the other, which, rather than propound the modern Western view that sovereign agency is mine to grasp and exploit to further my own desires and ends, renders each person finite and vulnerable in the face of the other who holds the power to give life. A theological reflection on this aspect of Butler's theory reveals that embodied life is not seized but a gift that is given by the other and received. Butler's account of

---

28. This point is building upon Parsons's observation and use of Butler's distrust in the idea of the term "nature" as a static given in matters of gender. What God creates in the beginning is different to what one experiences day to day in the postlapsarian era. This does not undermine an ethics of gender, which according to Parsons characterizes Butler's response, but in my view ought to chasten it. Parsons, *Ethics of Gender*, 162–63.

embodied life recognizes one's need for life and so represents a desperate search for life apart from the originary law and the self. This, we come to see, is a secular counterpart to the apostle Paul's cry: "Wretched man that I am! Who will rescue me from this body of death?"[29] But where Butler turns to people with bodies of death for salvation from her own body of death—a case of the dead leading the dead—Paul immediately turns to the one who defeated death: "Thanks be to Jesus Christ our Lord!"[30]

Embodied life that is gendered, therefore, is indexed not to one's ability to approximate the desires and bodies of Adam or Eve, nor by presently living into a future eschatological "angelic" reality or one speculatively imagined. A life that honors God with our bodies is one that is indexed to the life of Christ that is worked into our bodies by the Spirit of God. This union with Christ by the Spirit is risky because we learn to desire Christ's desire, which may conflict with our own desires. The final chapter, therefore, indirectly explores the psalmic exhortation to "delight in the law"[31] whereby the law in which we learn to delight is not Torah, the law of Adam and Eve, or the law of sin or desire, but the law of Spirit.[32]

In sum, my engagement with Butler does not result in the deconstruction of gender, that is, the annihilation or blurring of the concepts of man and woman. The final account of gender I offer continues to uphold the historic Christian confession that in the beginning God created the world, including the man and woman, but I set this confession in time, and importantly, in its place within redemptive history so that it cannot continue to underwrite unethical modes of relating to oneself, others, and God. Learning that our vocation is to glorify God in our bodies as God's creatures is a risky and faith-filled exercise that is simultaneously life-threatening and life-giving.

---

29. Rom 7:24.
30. Rom 7:25a.
31. Ps 1:2.
32. Rom 8:3.

Chapter 1

Re-forming the Subject as Desire

Introduction

GENDER REFORM WAS NECESSARY because the sexual revolution failed to deliver on the promise to secure sexual freedom for all. The political and cultural shifts that occurred between the early 1960s and the mid-1980s may have been dramatic, but not dramatic enough to recognize Butler's own proscribed sexuality as legitimate.[1] In response Butler did not develop a new vision of sexuality that included her own sexuality for society to pursue. Instead, she ventured into the historic past to find the foundation that shaped how society thought about sex. What she learned and came to theorize is *how* the beginning produces and regulates how sex and gender are thought about and experienced in the present.

The beginning for Butler is not a mythical location or event, but something real and captivating. The beginning is the location where a powerful force not only forms bodies, but continually manifests in people's lives even after they have departed the beginning. She explains that as people grow up, they always have a connection to the past, as they conform their selves to the *call* of the original formative moment. Gender and sexuality in Butler's thought, therefore, do not describe what someone is, but describe the beginning form to which someone is always in the process of becoming. If the form in the beginning is a heterosexual couple, then gender and sexuality in the present will reflect that original

---

1. Butler, *GT*, xx–xxi.

heterosexual form.² More poignantly, from Butler's point of view, the original heterosexual form will continue to exert itself in the present to conform people where they fail to live up to their original formation in the beginning.

The fundamental problem that Butler diagnoses is not the causal relation between the beginning and the present,³ but the unquestioned privilege of the heterosexual couple, which Butler calls the "heterosexual matrix," that assumes to reside in the beginning. With this heterosexual foundation determining what is recognizably legitimate in the present, Butler was critical of feminist efforts because they were operating from a foundation that contradicted their effort and goals. In other words, the legitimate woman Butler was fighting for was not the woman in the heterosexual matrix in the beginning who desired a man.⁴ If Butler was ever going to have her own sexuality recognized, then the beginning needed to be reformed such that her desire was recognized by it.

The kind of reform Butler theorizes and enacts does not amount to an installation of a homosexual couple in the beginning. Her desire is much more radical: to change society's understanding about the beginning so that the beginning is *always open to reform*. Butler desires to depart from the traditional concept of the beginning, which means departing from the beginning as an immoveable, static, or incontestable truth.

While Butler's gender theory is a departure from more traditional forms of feminism, she maintains the distinctive feminist strategy of social engagement by consciousness raising. Recognizing new modes of gender and sexuality as legitimate requires society to be made aware, first, of how the beginning operates in the present; and second, that the content of the image that populates the beginning is contestable. Butler does not theorize in order to eradicate the beginning but to reform it so that new forms of being gendered and sexual in the present are possible: "There is a certain departure from the human that takes place in order to start the process of remaking the human."⁵

If, as Butler believes, a person is not a particular sex and therefore gender by nature, but is constantly receiving and becoming what it was

---

2. This is a simplification of Butler's view because, as we will soon see, the originary form is in fact a prohibition, which is subsequently masked by the obedient subject.

3. Butler, *PLP*, 7.

4. Butler, *GT*, ch. 1.

5. Butler, *UG*, 3–4.

created to be in the beginning, the question of how this original and subsequent formation happens is crucial. Where does meaning come from that formed *and* is forming who I am? How does this meaning come to me? And finally, what human faculty allows the transfer of meaning to come to me and form me in this way? Butler answers these questions by theorizing the body and mind as an inextricable unity with society, which is another way of saying "an account of subjection . . . must be traced in the turns of psychic life."[6] Butler begins to develop this subject of her gender theory by drawing together several powerful theories.[7] First she draws on the twentieth-century French postmodern philosopher Michel Foucault (1926–84), who theorized subjectivity as a production of power. The second philosopher Butler uses to structure her subject is the German idealist Georg Hegel (1770–1831). Of use to Butler is Hegel's idea of progress as a dialectical movement described most memorably in his master-slave dialectic in *Phenomenology of the Spirit*. The final theoretical contributor to Butler's subject is Sigmund Freud (1856–1939), who is the father of psychoanalysis and the pioneer of the study of sexuality. In Freud, Butler finds an origin myth of the human that becomes the foundation from which her subject emerges in time.

Butler does not take up these theories in their usual forms, but by way of critique augments them for her own purposes. Foucault's theory of power lacks agency, Hegel's dialectic eventually leads to synthesis, and Freud harbors heterosexual bias. By purging the theories of these perceived shortcomings, Butler develops a complex notion of subjectivity that is grounded in time, organized around an originary prohibition, characterized by desire, and somewhat unknown to the self. More broadly speaking, Butler situates a person in the present time but with an inextricable link to the beginning, that manifests a desire for completion, while not knowing what was lost that needs to be replaced to realize one's completion. This person is not a sovereign object who knows who they are, but a floundering subject who is groping about for his existential bearings.

---

6. Butler, *PLP*, 18. Lloyd, *Judith Butler*, 78. Chambers is one Butlerian scholar who focuses on this aspect of her theory. See Chambers, "Subjectification," 197.

7. Butler integrates many more theories into her gender theory than these, which will be the looked at in chapters 3 and 5.

A Power Operation

Forming Power

Butler seeks to account for deeply ingrained social beliefs about sexuality and gender by revealing that what appears to be natural and normal (i.e., heterosexuality) is merely a human idea that has solidified into incontestable truth over time. Butler seeks to unmask the naturalizing power of the heterosexual matrix by thinking about the body as a site of cultural struggle. This Foucauldian approach treats the body like a historical artefact, an effect of time, that is open for being interpreted like any other aspect of history. While Butler's genealogy of the body is not strictly a historical inquiry, she begins with the assumption that the person does not have a body that harbors essential truth but rather derives its meaning from not only being in the world, but being a part of it. Butler's genealogical approach is not concerned with history like Foucault, but with theorizing the body in time to observe what effect this has on what is recognizable as legitimate gender and sexuality.[8]

The body does not possess meaning but comes to embody meaning as the self finds itself formed by external factors. Butler derives the idea from Foucault that people emerge out of a complex arrangement of power, which in turn leads Butler to rename the person a "subject" because they live in subjection. "Subjection," Butler states, "signifies the process of becoming subordinated by power as well as the process of becoming a subject."[9] As power forms a person, the person becomes attached or dependent on that force for their form. Becoming formed is not a one-off event, but a continual process of conforming with one's original formation.

Foucault's notion of productive power is inadequate, according to Butler, because it is overly materialistic. Foucault was focused on external forms of technology that arranged material bodies in society (bio-power)[10]—think of the guard's gaze in the panopticon or the priest's adjudication of sin in the confessional booth.[11] Butler, on the other hand, was more concerned with *how* we come to understand our gendered and sexual selves by means of a power operation that happens inside us.

---

8. Butler, *SD*, 236–37.
9. Butler, *PLP*, 2.
10. Foucault, *Security, Territory, Population*, 1; *History of Sexuality*, 139.
11. Foucault, *History of Sexuality*, 140–45; 95–96.

Foucault viewed forms of power as providing the conditions for existence and considered those conditions to be discursive (knowledge or ideas that constitute), but the problem this posed for Butler was that by neglecting the domain of the psyche (or for ease of explanation, the mind),[12] he was neglecting the very means by which the subject is constructed and therefore potentially deconstructed and reconstructed.[13] Butler therefore reforms his view to be an *internal* operation, which is not only a theoretical shift but also a political shift from bio-politics to psyche-politics. This relocation underground does not forfeit power's capacity to produce subjects, but inextricably links the psyche with one's material body. The body and mind in Butler's thought are therefore a functional unity. The question is: "If submission is a condition of subjection, it makes sense to ask: what is the psychic form that power takes?"[14]

Butler's critique of Foucault's materially anchored theory of power focuses on his theorization of the "soul" in *Discipline and Punish*. Foucault theorizes that the body is the locus of power and that through processes of obedience (training, confession, repetition, drill, etc.), the body is *inscribed* with norms or behaviors.[15] The example Foucault operates with is the impact of surveillance on the subjectivity of the incarcerated criminal. He explores how the experience of imprisonment is not merely physical, but by virtue of the prison's discipline of the body, the prison is internalized, thereby disciplining the soul. The result is that the person is doubly imprisoned. The body is imprisoned, first by the cage, then by the self as the self is subjectified by the disciplining cage. Through processes of drill, a person becomes a principle of their own subjection,[16] or as Foucault says, "the soul is the prison of the body."[17]

But according to Butler, this view of the imprisoned body neglects the question: *which soul* imprisons the body? This is a methodological maneuver to introduce psychoanalysis as a means of exposing and rooting out the oppressive "soul" at the originary or foundational moment.

---

12. The psyche is not the mind in Butler's theory, but for now it is a useful term to use for the benefit of those who have yet come to grips with Butler's terminology.

13. Butler explores this in detail in *PLP*, 83–106. For an earlier brief treatment, see Butler, *BTM*, 33–37.

14. Butler, *PLP*, 2.

15. Butler critiques Foucault's idea of the body as a canvas or site that is inscribed with meaning. Butler, "Foucault and the Paradox."

16. Foucault, *Discipline and Punish*, 135–36.

17. Foucault, *Discipline and Punish*, 30.

By asking, "Which soul?" Butler makes the claim that, despite Foucault's aversion to psychoanalysis, he cannot achieve what he desires without it, that is, to offer a form of resistance to ubiquitous power operations on the body.[18] The question "Which soul?" is a rhetorical gesture containing the force of the dual claim that the soul preexists in an ek-static relation to the body, and that the soul's contents are not essential to the body.[19] The soul is therefore an ideal that exists outside the self, demanding obedience and conformity, which identifies the body as not inherently whole or coherent but fundamentally in lack. Butler states: "The soul is precisely what the body lacks; hence, the body presents itself as signifying lack."[20] While lacking the nuance of her later reading in *Psychic Life of Power*, this early description of Foucault's soul in *Gender Trouble* provides Butler with a form of subjectivity that is inessential. If the body is subjected by that which is not essential but other, then the question "Which soul?" might appear wholly appropriate.

An example will make Butler's argument more perspicuous. Think briefly of the equestrian sport of dressage in which a horse that is disciplined or drilled performs certain "unnatural" feats in concert with the rider.[21] Now let us apply the Foucauldian terms to the horse and rider: the horse's body is imprisoned by the soul in that the horse's body, having been disciplined (the definition of dressage) by the soul, responds to the rider in ways that are imperceptible to an onlooker. To apply Butler's critique: whose soul imprisons the horse's body that it should behave in that particular manner? In the context of the arena in which the horse performs, the horse is imprisoned by the rider's "soul." The rider has drilled the horse to know the rider's mind and to behave accordingly. The horse's behavior—the "unnatural" feats—are produced by an internalized exterior mind. Of course, if the soul that imprisons the horse's body is the rider's, then the soul's contents (or the content's author) is substitutable.

Under the weight of this critique, Foucault's soul is a placeholder for the synonymous Butlerian internalized and productive notions of the "originating principle"[22] or originary moment: frame of reference, horizon of knowledge, matrix, conditions, and the form of power. Butler

18. Butler, *PLP*, 87.
19. Butler, *PLP*, 86.
20. Butler, *GT*, 184.
21. This example was helpfully raised and discussed in a political theory seminar lead by Dr. Christopher Brittain at the University of Aberdeen.
22. Butler, *BTM*, 7.

seeks to locate and re-narrate or *re-form* the originary moment to release one from the "violence" that characterizes subjectivity: having to perform "unnatural" feats by order of that particular "soul."

The prisoner, like the horse in the arena, is a subject by virtue of an internalized relation with the external other. Stated otherwise, Foucault's soul figuratively represents the internalized exterior producer and regulator of subjectivity. As in the case of the horse, subjectivity is imposed from outside the body, but is actually incorporated in the form of the body. But if the question "Whose soul?" can be posed, then it becomes clear that the exterior terms used to describe the body are also vulnerable to questioning. Butler states the implications for gender:

> The redescription of intrapsychic processes in terms of the surface politics of the body implies a corollary redescription of gender as the disciplinary production of the figures of fantasy through the play of presence and absence on the body's surface, the construction of the gendered body through a series of exclusions and denials, signifying absences.[23]

But this redescription of gender and thus the terms that narrate the body is dependent on first having the intrapsychic processes re-described. Butler achieves this by introducing that which is vital for her overall project and central to her idea of performativity, namely, slippage or excess, as well as denial.

In Butler's reading of Foucault's account of the soul, there is no slippage between the soul and body because the body is imprisoned in the soul. The claim Butler is making in this assessment is that Foucault has synonymously linked the soul and the unconscious. Butler, however, argues that Foucault has misunderstood the difference between the unconscious and soul, and counterposes the soul as psyche. While she grants that the psyche includes the unconscious, "the psyche is precisely what *exceeds* the imprisoning effects of the discursive demand to inhabit a coherent identity, to become a coherent subject."[24] To return to the example, the horse leaves the arena to trot and gallop in ways that do not conform to the imprisoned "dressaged" soul. But even within the arena, there is not a one-to-one correspondence or self-same link between the "idea" of the rider and the horse's behavior, and what the horse does or does not want to perform at any given moment. Indeed, the task that confronts the

---

23. Butler, *GT*, 184.
24. Butler, *PLP*, 86 (emphasis mine).

horse is to *pass* as entirely subjectified by the rider. The competition horse is judged according to the degree that it can "be" the rider's soul.

The psychoanalytic critique Butler presents is that the same can be said of Foucault's prisoner. There is slippage between the *soul* (or the external ideal), what one *attempts to do*, and what one *actually does*. Here, the Freudian psychic constitution to which Butler subscribes has been outlined: "In the psyche, the subject's ideal corresponds to the ego-ideal, which the super-ego is said to consult, as it were, to measure the ego."[25] For Butler, the psyche is not the wholly passive or disciplined aspect of one's inner reality, but that which can "resist the regularization that Foucault ascribes to normalizing discourse."[26]

According to Butler, Foucault's theory of power is psychically deficient. The problematic result of Foucault's theory is that the subjectification that occurs by an external power is a unilateral activity within which there is no possibility of agency. If the horse is pure incorporated soul, then it cannot understand existence other than from within the body as disciplined—and it cannot do otherwise than act as one disciplined. There is no agency, and no prospect of agency. The same would be true of the human subject. Even though the theory conceives of power as a producer of subjectivity, the subject does not have the capacity to harness or co-opt the subjectivizing power to reproduce another form of subjectivity. Butler rejects this aspect of Foucault's theory because it is a unilateral operation and does not allow for possible modes of subversive resistance. For Butler resistance does not simply mean to slow down or push back, but to undermine the existing subject through subversive deployment of different terms that structure subjectivity.[27]

While Butler rejects Foucault's theory of the subject, his notion of productive power is useful because it provides her with the tools necessary to conceive of gender as produced by external power operations. The problem is that power in Foucault's thinking does not possess the capacity to be harnessed for re-production. To realize agency for purposes of re-subjectification, Butler counterposes a psychoanalytic rendering of soul as psyche, whereby "the psyche (or the psychic)" is not only "one name for this stubborn tie that binds the subject to the power of domination"

---

25. Butler, *PLP*, 86.

26. Butler, *PLP*, 86.

27. Butler contests the use of "resistance" in favor of "subversion." See Butler, in Armour and St. Ville, *Bodily Citations*, 284–85.

but also names that which exceeds the power of domination.[28] The inner working of Butler's psychic-inflected Foucauldian notion of productive power requires explanation. For this, we turn to Butler's revised use of Hegel's notion of desire and recognition.

Desiring the Other

Desire Is Basic

Understanding the profundity of desire in the work of Butler is made easier with the use of a metaphor. The problem of desire is like a loose thread in a knitted garment. The loose thread jeopardizes the integrity of the whole garment, threatening to cause its unraveling even on the least invasive investigation. The thread cannot be left dangling, but any attempt to repair it seems destined for a wrong move, marking the beginning of its unraveling. Likewise, desire is a precarious problem one cannot let be, yet "philosophers cannot obliterate desire, they must formulate strategies to silence or control it."[29] This is problematic for Butler because desire cannot be silenced or controlled. Rather, it should be embraced as representing the ongoing split within the self from which there is no offer of hope for respite. This view leads to the threatening problem of desire being reframed into a question of desire that reveals potential.

Accordingly, Butler argues that the theme of desire must be pursued. If the subject is split or incoherent because of desire—not satisfied and looking for wholeness—then desire poses a real threat to the surefootedness of systems that deem the subject as stable. Butler does not mention Christianity, but one may assume that she includes the Christian tradition when she asserts that philosophical thinking has long presented itself as "theoretical purity," and "not needing the world it seeks to know."[30] Such thinkers, whether philosophical or theological, remained outside the world looking in, unfettered by their own particularity. But, Butler explains, desire undermines their pretentious and deluded self-extraction from the world. The desire to know, ironically, demands contemplation

---

28. Chambers, "Subjectification," 197.
29. Butler, *SD*, 2.
30. Butler, *SD*, 1.

about desire or, as Butler concludes of such thinkers, that they "must, in spite of themselves, desire to do something about desire."[31]

Desire not only problematizes the possibility of a complete or coherent subject: it proves problematic for even engaging in the task of "doing something about desire." Picking up the metaphor to elaborate further, the loose thread of desire is not something to be feared because it threatens to unravel the subject if pulled. Rather desire reveals the fictive nature of the subject that claims to be a unified whole that must not be undone. By pulling the loose thread one might unravel the woolen garment, but this reveals that the garment is *formed* and so can be *reform*ed. The garment comprises thread and, having been unraveled, is ready to be knitted (or not) into something else if one wills. While this metaphor is grossly inadequate, it is instructive in communicating the basic view that for Butler, desire is not necessarily a problem to be feared, but a question to be explored because of its potential to birth new forms of life. Butler's inquiry into the theme of desire reveals a "new" incoherent subject within the fictive "threads" that have, in the past, been mythically posited as a coherent unity.

As a basic characteristic of the subject, Butler views desire in a twofold manner. One desires things, but this *mundane* fact of desire leads to a second more fundamental or *originary* revelation that the self is a desirous being and so permanently in need. This twofold view of desire is evident when Butler states: "Desire is *intentional* in that it is always a desire *of* or *for* a given object or Other, but it is also *reflexive* in the sense that desire is a modality in which the subject is both discovered and enhanced."[32] There are parts to this complex statement that this chapter will treat in due course, but for now, one seeks to reinforce that in Butler's thought desire is characteristic of the person in two ways. Firstly, their desire is "*of* or *for*" something, and so is characterized as being *in* lack: I am thirsty, and my desire is for water, therefore I lack water. Desire indicates one's corporeal appetite. Secondly, they desire, and so they are reflexively discovered *as* lack: I am thirsty, and my desire is for water, therefore I understand that I am not essentially quenched. I am *in* lack; therefore, I am essentially characterized *as* lack or lacking. Thinking about desire reveals things about ourselves. It structures the subject and

---

31. Butler, *SD*, 2.
32. Butler, *SD*, 25.

its relation to other subjects. A person is therefore one who needs the world for life and one who is always striving for life.[33]

Rather than categorizing desire in Butler's thought as Graham Ward does as an internal nature and external structure,[34] from hereon I will take up Butler's terminology and refer to this dual mode of desire as *mundane desire* and *originary desire*.[35] In broadening the scope to more complex forms of desire, like the desire for sex, love, or societal recognition, one does not merely lack those things at the mundane level. One's desire for them teaches the desiring subject that he or she exists *as* lacking those things, which is to say that one *is* essentially not whole, incomplete, or *incoherent* without them. Butler's subject is fundamentally characterized by *desire-induced incoherence*.

The Utility of the Danger of Desire

According to Butler, systems of thought like philosophy and theology attach "danger" to the theme of desire. But in her estimation, the danger of desire is what gives desire the potential to give life. For some, desire is dangerous because "of its propensity to blur clear vision and foster philosophical myopia, encouraging one to see only what one *wants*, and not what *is*."[36] For Butler, however, the very capacity to challenge what *is* gives desire potential utility.

This rendering of desire as potentially dangerous is similar to the way desire is construed in the Christian primeval creation account and the traditions that followed. In the book of Genesis, we read that fruit from a particular tree is desirous to the eye, but forbidden by God to be eaten.[37] In Augustine's *Confessions*, an autobiographical account relates a childhood event in which he also desired forbidden fruit, which he subsequently took. When he reflects on taking the fruit, he observes that sin enters when "immoderate desire" takes hold and "we thereby turn away from the better and higher: from you yourself, O Lord our God, and your

---

33. This will be explored in depth in chapter 5 when we investigate Butler's dependence on Spinoza's notion of *conatus*.
34. Ward, *Cities of God*, 121.
35. Butler, *GT*, xxi; *UG*, 136.
36. Butler, *SD*, 3.
37. Gen 2:17 and 3:6.

truth and your law."[38] In the originary and fourth-century gardens, the desire to take the fruit posed a threat to the respective commands that forbade their consumption. In these accounts, we see desire "speak" to the prelapsarian man and woman, and the postlapsarian man so they see only what they *wanted*, rather than believing and obeying the command, which in the first garden was God's command, and in the second, the common law—what *is*. Butler observes that desire has proven troublesome because it not only opens up possibilities for happiness and gratification, but reveals that such possibilities are *wanted*, which, most problematically, challenges and undermines what *is*.

But what constitutes this notion of *is* that Butler believes desire can usefully question and potentially undermine? To recall the previous accounts involving fruit as metaphorical examples, Butler seeks to bring into question and undermine both the rule (don't eat the fruit) and that which institutes and polices the rule (God and the judicial system). With regard to gender, the *is* that Butler seeks to question and undermine includes gender ideals or norms, and the justification of how these are established and enforced.[39] These very specific notions of truth and authority take on a more generic representation within Butler's early doctoral work on desire, in which she describes *is* as "knowledge of philosophical truth."[40] This philosophical knowledge is "practical knowledge,"[41] an ethic pertaining to the truth. The *is* under interrogation is knowledge that orders a true moral gendered and sexual life.

According to Butler, however, the problem with true philosophical knowledge—what *is*—is that it is characterized by slippage, which belies the truthfulness of *is* as ultimate truth. If "knowledge of philosophical truth" inadequately describes what actually is (experienced), then *is* stands as an inadequate account of truth that orders a true moral life. Butler states: "When knowledge of philosophical truth becomes a function of living a philosophical life, as is the case in moral philosophy traditionally, the question is necessarily raised, does ought imply can?"[42] This is a critique of the *is/ought* fallacy whereby *is* is brought into question by the observation of the impossibility of *ought* for some. This recognizes

---

38. Augustine, *Confessions*, 2.5.10.
39. Butler, *GT*, xxi–xxii.
40. Butler, *SD*, 3.
41. Butler, *SD*, 3.
42. Butler, *SD*, 3.

the existence of people who cannot enact what apparently *is*. Butler aims to redeem the subject from the originary conditions that are impossible for some to enact at the mundane level, which consequently become the grounds for the charge of transgression and a response involving discipline.

But having critiqued philosophy's problematic preoccupation with abstract knowledge, Butler also observes moments where philosophy has shown the potential to engage in the task of ethics concerning non-abstract human existence. She recalls Spinoza's *Ethics*, and Kant's *Critique of Practical Reason* as examples of philosophy where each "interrogates its own possibilities as *engaged* or practical knowledge."[43] We learn here that Butler demands those engaged in philosophy (or theology) to reject abstract truth-telling and the regulating of existence according to such truths, and instead embrace the rationalization of the "messiness" of the incoherent life of desire. "Good" philosophy and theology are not concerned with treating incoherence as a sickness that only some have, and that must be overcome, but in establishing desire as the human reality, the very substance of human subjectivity, and how humans intra- and inter-relate. When philosophy and theology are concerned with knowledge that engages real human experience, they tend "to ask after the philosophical potential of desire."[44] This is the nub of Butler's theoretical project about gender.

Butler is aware that rethinking the Hegelian subject of desire as an incoherent self breaks with the Western tradition on this point. She regards the rendering of desire in the philosophies of Plato, Aristotle, Kant, and Spinoza as being "a necessary psychological premise,"[45] in the "pursuit of integrity,"[46] and notionally sufficient in their own contexts. But their premises are now not merely unnecessary, but incomprehensible, and as such, an imposition and repressive. In response, Butler explicitly formulates the view that the eradication of desire through satisfaction is deeply problematic for thinking about the moral life:

> Without a discrete subject with internally consistent desires, the moral life remains indefinite; if the subject is ambiguous, difficult to locate and properly name, then to whom shall we ascribe

43. Butler, *SD*, 3.
44. Butler, *SD*, 3.
45. Butler, *SD*, 4.
46. Butler, *SD*, 4.

this life? And if desires are random or, at best, self-contradictory, then the moral life is either impossible or, when possible, based on repression rather than true autonomy.[47]

One sees at this early stage in Butler's thought an allusion to a particular ethic not merely characterized, but wholly constituted by the "indefinite" by virtue of the subject's ambiguity or incoherence. One does not achieve a moral life by overcoming the problem of desire, but despite it. Autonomy is not, therefore, the reason Butler reworks Hegel's subject of desire. The exercise of true autonomy in Butler's thought, which will be taken up in chapter 5, must afford a particular moral agency that offers individuals the capacity to give an account of their own *incoherence*.[48]

It becomes evident then that this vision of autonomy amounts to the repudiation of "the necessity of external authority," like the voices that speak in the gardens.[49] Butler rejects the Kantian view that one submits to the rule one gives to one's self, as well as the classical view in which one acts out of a desire for the good.[50] Even though morality is broadly conceived in these views as essentially self-government, according to Butler, the self-government invoked in these accounts is problematically ordered toward a particular end according to a particular "soul."[51] It is the notion of a particular end that creates difficulty for the kind of autonomy Butler seeks. When one desires something because it is ordered toward a specified end, "a moral agent acts against its desires, it acts from contradiction, opposing desire to reason, undermining the possibility of moral autonomy as a function of a thoroughly integrated moral subject."[52] For Butler, it is simply not the case that desire is imbued with "a nascent

---

47. Butler, SD, 4.

48. At this early stage of her thought, Butler is critical of post-structuralism. For this reason, the notion and possibility of autonomy while still evident and possible will become increasingly fraught as she comes to terms with the implications of her theory of the subject. For a brief overview of Butler's relation to post-structuralism and structuralism, see Lloyd, *Judith Butler*, 10–13.

49. Butler, SD, 4.

50. See also Butler's account of the problematic notion of ethics as "transference" in Butler, GAO, 64.

51. Butler demonstrates where she departs from Kant and Foucault in this way in Butler, "What Is Critique?"

52. Butler, SD, 4.

essence of reason," which puts her subject in perpetual risk of "homelessness" and "fragmentation."[53]

This claim has much broader and radical implications than merely stripping a concept of desire of a metaphysically geared telos. This is the conceptual moment where Butler finds desire's generative capacity to undo what *is*. If what is moral is irreducibly concerned with desire, then morality is at root concerned with the conditioning structures that give rise to the possibility of coherent moral subjectivity. Crucially, and theologically speaking, Butler's theory is seen at this point to be protological (concerned with the beginning) rather than eschatological (the end). Butler summarizes this apparent assumptive systematization thus:

> Moral psychology thus has assumed a moral ontology, a theory about what a being must be like in order to be capable of moral deliberation and action, in order to lead a moral life and be a moral personality. And it has also assumed a more general ontological scheme in which not only the "unity" or "internal integrity" of the moral subject is conditioned, but the unity and integrity of any being.[54]

By observing the originary (or protological) condition from which mundane desire emerged, Butler locates where the deception of moral unity or coherent subjectivity is grounded, and therefore, that which must be questioned and undermined. The generative potential of desire exists where mundane desire to be *or* to act exceeds or transgresses the originary conditions of subjectivity that define what *is*. This is the point of intersection between Butler's consideration of desire and Hegel's subject.

Theorizing Slaves of Desire

Butler theorizes her subject as desire for recognition. In *Subjects of Desire*, she takes up Hegel's slave and master metaphor to explore a notion of desire and its relation to the ontological structure of alterity that conditions subjectivity. In her autobiographical account of her own intellectual formation in *Undoing Gender*, Butler notes the significance of Hegel in forming her own position.[55] This significance is located in large part within *Subjects of Desire*, which Butler confirms in the preface to the

---

53. Butler, *SD*, 4–5.
54. Butler, *SD*, 5.
55. Butler, *UG*, 236.

paperback edition of *Undoing Gender*: "In a sense, all of my work remains within the orbit of a certain set of Hegelian questions: What is the relation between desire and recognition, and how is it that the constitution of the subject entails a radical and constitutive relation to alterity?"[56] The basic premise on which Butler grounds her notion of subjectivity is that "desire is always a desire for recognition."[57] Note that in this pithy statement Butler uses desire in two ways: the first refers to mundane desire, whereas the second to originary desire, which she reframes sociologically. I lack recognition, but only because I am not recognizable. What I desire, therefore, is the other person's desire for me or my desires. The originary terms by which I am recognized are found external to me, which renders subjectivity ek-static, meaning that subjectivity is now intersubjective because the terms of my subjectivity exist in the mind of those not me, a dynamic analogous to the relationship between the dressage horse and rider.[58]

Another metaphor is useful to elucidate the role of originary desire for thinking about mundane desire, and for when Butler inverts traditional notions of recognition by theorizing the link between mundane desire and originary desire. Think for a moment about the shape of a gingerbread-man biscuit. The shape of the cooked biscuit points backward in time and describes the conditions that formed it, namely, a particular gingerbread-man-shaped biscuit cutter. The quality of biscuit that emerges from the oven is determined by how it tastes, but also to what extent it represents the form that conditioned its shape in the first place. Likewise, mundane desire gives voice to that which shaped it. By probing the conditions that frame one's mundane desire, the individual's subjectivity is further detailed. The form or originary conditions could comprise static terms resulting in what is right mundane desire—a particularly formed and rightly ordered man or woman. Alternatively, Butler suggests, because human desire for recognition exists that does not reflect the static forms or conditions, an originary form must be installed that is pliable and malleable, and can accommodate fluctuating or changing mundane desires, that which exceeds the existing form.

Returning to the biscuit metaphor, when a misshapen gingerbread man comes out of the oven, instead of forcing the form over it to make

---

56. Butler, *SD*, xx.
57. Butler, *UG*, 2.
58. Butler, *UG*, 2.

it look "right"—as the form dictates, the misshapen biscuit informs the baker that the original form needs now to accommodate this "new" man. The metaphor begins to break down dramatically at this point, but it is evident that a static originary form, as seen in many Christian creation accounts, does not and cannot accommodate the breadth of human mundane desire for recognition. So where "new" desire emerges, there needs to be a feedback loop in place—from the mundane (the present) to the originary (the beginning)—to prompt an adjustment of the terms that structure the originary conditioning frame.

Butler's concern is not assimilation or inclusion but originary re-form. In this regard, Butler states: "What is important, of course, is to keep the 'redefining the norm' from being 'an assimilation to the norm.'"[59] Butler is clearest in *Excitable Speech* when she states that "there is no opposition to the lines drawn by foreclosure except through the redrawing of those very lines."[60] By re-forming the terms that constitute the originary structure (redrawing the lines), "new" desires in the mundane are validated or recognized. Desire is therefore a language that communicates originary knowledge, and Hegel's thought provides Butler with the basic framework regarding forms or conditions of knowledge: "The conditions that give rise to desire, the metaphysics of internal relations, are at the same time what desire seeks to articulate, render explicit, so that desire is a tacit pursuit of metaphysical knowledge, the human way that such knowledge 'speaks.'"[61]

Internal relations constitute the conditions for desire's emergence, which in Hegel's thought are metaphysical, given laws by which one is recognized or known by the self and others. The emergence of desire and the voice of desire are indistinguishable and result in coherence, unless Hegel can be read differently, which Butler does: "Reading Hegel in a Nietzschean fashion, we can take the *Phenomenology* as a study of desire and deception, the systematic pursuit and misidentification of the Absolute, a constant process of inversion which never reaches ultimate closure."[62] For Butler, the desire to know one's self by tracing one's desires back to the originary conditions will never be realized unless one begins the quest

---

59. Butler in Breen and Blumenfeld, *Butler Matters*, 59.
60. Butler, *ES*, 140.
61. Butler, *SD*, 25.
62. Butler, *SD*, 23.

with an understanding of the deception of coherence. By acknowledging this deception, claims of coherence can be appropriately redressed.

The Hegelian subject of desire is therefore ultimately flawed because it embraces coherence or synthesis as true, but this does not undermine the basic utility of the ek-static subject. Butler describes the Hegelian subject of desire like the automobile of Mr. Magoo, which careens through the neighbor's chicken coop only to land on all four wheels all set to embark on the next adventure.[63] This Hegelian subject exists in a perpetual cycle of identity failure, yet it never loses the impetus to move forward to try again to know itself with certainty. Thus, for Butler, the desire to live drives the subject even though to know and be known is ultimately an impossibility.

In *The Phenomenology of the Spirit*, Hegel uses the relationship between a slave and master to speak about intersubjective recognition or ek-static subjectivity, which Butler reads as not resulting in synthesis.[64] Who the slave and master represent in Hegel's thought is not immediately clear. This leaves the door open for diverse readings of the metaphor. In Geoff Boucher's book *The Charmed Circle of Ideology*, he asserts that for Butler, the master represents heterosexuality and the slave represents homosexuality.[65] Certainly, Butler's inquiry in *Gender Trouble* is concerned with a hetero-/homosexuality binary, but her early critique of Freud's psychoanalysis reveals that her contention is not with heteronormativity as an exclusionary conditioning matrix that only works against gays and lesbians, but also as it works against other forms of sexuality and gender-diverse individuals. For this reason, I suggest the master is more likely to personify gender and sexuality norms, a set of abstract ideals, perhaps reflective of the image of Adam and Eve in the primeval creation account. The slave, then, represents those who cannot *pass* as the idealized gender norms—Adam (Man) or Eve (Woman)—and so live under the adjudicating glare of the idealized masters.

The master and slave dialectic begins when two self-consciousnesses, on encountering the other, realize that they are not the other. They recognize themselves in relation to the other—I am not you. While they might like to coexist in harmony, this is not possible because they do not want to conceive of their self in relation to the other, but as free and

---

63. Butler, SD, 21.
64. Hegel, *Phenomelonology*, 111–18.
65. Boucher, *Charmed Circle*, 144.

autonomous. A potentially deadly situation emerges with the realization that both cannot be free and autonomous, necessitating their disavowal (or annihilation) of the other. After a struggle, one self-consciousness submits to the other, not because of a preference to live in subjugation, but because of the fear of death. This decision to submit precipitates an unequal yoking that takes the metaphorical form of master and slave. By becoming yoked in this way, they preserve each other within their respective social roles, which means the reality of who they are is understood in relation to the other; the respective subjectivities of the slave and the master are not self-referential (being for the self) as they were before the subjectification. Now each knows their self in inextricable relationship to the other (being for the other), not in mutual recognition, but in mutual dependence. Over time, the final structuring of master and slave see the two self-consciousnesses duped into thinking their entire existences are, respectively, their own.

As Lloyd notes, the principal reason Butler returns to this Hegelian metaphor is to draw out a notion of subjectivity that is a normalized social reality.[66] With regard to gender, one must cite or produce the norms that mediate what it means to be a man or woman so that one can be seen as man or woman in the eyes of the other. One can trace this notion of citation or production back to the metaphor where the slave and master are linked by an operation of production and consumption. If we refer to the master as the ideal of man and woman, then every person is a slave that must produce "boy-ness" or "girl-ness," "manliness" or "womanliness," which serves to "feed" and perpetuate the truthfulness of the ideal in one's life and society. One is recognized as a boy or girl, or man or woman, by virtue of *producing* and exhibiting what the ideal demands. Hegel's metaphor is useful for Butler because it demonstrates that identification is predicated on the concealed originary relationship and the subsequent notion of mundane recognition in relation to the other by producing that which it desires for its own recognition for life.

Moreover, the metaphor is crucial for Butler's purposes for identifying a notion of subjectivity as recognition that naturalizes or normalizes and so conceals a violent hierarchically ordered set of social relations. Here the dialectical structure of the metaphor becomes central to Butler's interpretation: the master/slave binary is a paradigm for understanding the differential allocation of life. While some thought systems seek

---

66. Lloyd, *Judith Butler*, 17.

to formalize binary existence as necessary for coherent identity, Butler, in accordance with her Nietzschean reading of Hegel, merely observes this as "the dramatic integrity of a comedy of errors."[67] Intersubjective relationality does not end in a synthesis of mutual recognition, akin to Alexandre Kojève's utopic democratic Marxism.[68] Rather, its end is a form of dystopia. In the end, where Hegel dissolves the agonism inherent within the dialectic, Butler seeks to keep it alive. Desire teaches the subject that what comprises life is not recognition, demanding a society characterized by mutual recognition, but a desire to survive at the cost of the other. This brings the focus back to the original concealed or invisible life-and-death struggle of the dialectic as characteristic of life itself.

On the other hand, static subjects like the controlling image of the man and woman are constituted by satiated desire, thus signifying "death in life." Butler invokes Derrida to make the claim that those "who accept the metaphysical promise of desire . . . remain entranced by an *image of finality* and self-identity which is itself a kind of death."[69] She poses the rhetorical question: "Is Hegelianism in its metaphysical mode a death-bent enterprise?"[70] Butler repudiates the possibility of synthesis that Hegel offers, but takes the dialectical mechanism that propels the subject forward by installing his account of desire as a perpetual struggle for recognition, which is concealed in normalized socially dependent, hierarchical relations.

Recognizing Gender

To enliven or throw into motion the originary scene, Butler reconditions its terms (or the form—think of the biscuit cutter) to respond to, or to accommodate, the emergence of mundane desires. Butler achieves this, not by eradicating norms, but by subjecting existing norms to an ek-static reconditioning. This means Butler does not oppose gender norms, but opposes particular "hard" forms of norms, which condition the subject at the originary site that foreclose certain forms of mundane desire in the present.

---

67. Butler, SD, 23.

68. For Butler's explication and critique of Kojève's disembodied utopia, see Butler, SD, 63–79.

69. Butler, SD, 15 (emphasis mine).

70. Butler, SD, 15.

In the introduction to *Undoing Gender*, Butler poses the question: "What does gender want?"[71] One must regard this peculiar question as a statement: if gender *wants* something, then gender is *in* want by virtue of its desire *for* something. Thus, gender is characterized by lack and so is essentially incoherent. What does gender want that it does not have? Gender wants recognition. For example, if one wants to be recognized as a man, what does that involve? Firstly, it desires *others* by whom one is recognized as a man. Secondly, it involves *norms* by which one can be recognized as a man. These two aspects of recognition reveal that it is dependent on that which is external to me: others and norms.

According to this reading, those whose task it is to recognize me as a man do not recognize me according to my desire, but according to the originary conditions that frame their own ideas of what determines a man. The others only recognize me as a man (as I desire to be) insofar as what I deem to be a man coincides with what they deem to be a man. Gender wants to be recognized, but my own frame of reference does not determine whether those whose task it is to recognize me do so in a way that reflects my desire. Extending this framework of recognition across the breadth of a community or society implicates everybody in the process of recognizing everybody else. Butler's question "What does gender want?" illustrates that one's desire to be recognized as particularly gendered is *contingent* on those outside oneself and the historical terms they use to identify this or that.

By posing the question above, Butler is at her rhetorical best when she personifies gender and ascribes to it a desire *for* something. Instead of asking the question "What is a man?" or "What do you want as a man?" Butler relocates me within the discussion by stripping me of the capacity to assume an identity as a man by re-narrating my subject as a sociological phenomenon that desires recognition. This reinforces Butler's aim to render each person incoherent and dependent, and therefore vulnerable: "the viability of our individual personhood is fundamentally dependent on these social norms."[72] Butler continues, "If part of what desire wants is to gain recognition, then gender, insofar as it is animated by desire, will want recognition as well."[73] The claim is that one cannot be gendered

---

71. Butler, *UG*, 2.
72. Butler, *UG*, 2.
73. Butler, *UG*, 2.

without being recognized, and one cannot be recognized without others *and* (their) norms.

The problem, Butler observes, is that social norms do not allow some people to be recognized as gendered (or sexual) in the way they desire to be recognized. This is also a poignant claim that recognition is differentially allocated based on whether or not one cites or produces the norms that social recognition demands. Here Butler seeks to demonstrate that gender is a social reality and, in a sense, "democratized." Society decides what it will recognize as gender, which means that Butler's thought does not lend itself to the claim that a person chooses what gender they will be on any given day, because such autonomy does not exist. The limits of the metaphor of the horse and rider are revealed, which further reveals the limits of Foucault's thinking. The horse, if it had a will like a human, could at any moment reject the rider's instructions and gallop out of the arena. Gender, for Butler, is produced from outside us in the beginning *and* in the present moment. One's subjectivity as man or woman is so deeply ingrained from the very beginning that one knows nothing else in the present.

While individuals are stripped of the possibility of waking up in the morning and choosing their gender, at a societal level all forms of gender are said to be *possibly* valid, good, and normal. Here mundane desire is unleashed, which is to say that it is not leashed or anchored to eternal or transcendent ideas of what gender is. This is the promise of democracy and inclusion that Butler hopes to achieve through her work of immanent critique.[74] Butler imagines and theorizes a society in which inanimate ideals that *master* the subject do not rule and allocate life and death with "cold righteousness."[75] By reconditioning the subject at the originary scene, Butler can be read as achieving her goal to depart the human so that it can be perpetually remade to accommodate slippage, which is understood as the emergence of mundane desire for recognition. By virtue of the human's ontological re-forming or reconditioning, essential gendered and sexual limits are abolished, and desire's possibility is revealed. Butler does not deliver each person into his or her own hands, but into the hands of others. Such "deliverance" means that Butler does not desire to remake the human into a particular thing, but to render it capable of being perpetually remade by society according to its desires.

---

74. Butler, *GT*, vii.
75. A phrase and concept Butler uses in Butler, *FW*, xxiv and xxvii.

Configuring the Originary Scene with Freud

So far, I have described Butler's subject as characterized by desire-induced incoherence with the term "lack." But while lack might describe my essential and basic desire for recognition, it does not accurately represent how Butler configures the *emergence* of my desire or why, for example, I desire women and not men. This aspect of Butler's thinking about the subject adds another complex layer of contingency, which undermines any appeal to this desire or that desire as inherently natural and normal.

Butler theorizes the contingency of desire by taking into account the impact of originary prohibition on mundane desire. In simple language, I desire women in the present because I was not allowed to desire men in the beginning. That is, where prohibition is a condition of the originary moment, we learn that we are not only characterized by lack, but also by loss. Lack does not account for the *loss* suffered by virtue of the prohibition. Again, Butler is not merely describing what the mundane subject is or is not, but is explaining the subject's psychic structure that ought to be considered when thinking about not only what is good mundane desire, but why I desire women, and why my friends Steve or David desire men. According to Butler's narration of the originary scene, our respective desires are not natural, but are formed in response to prohibited desire. In short, my desire for women, and Steve and David's desire for men, are effects of an originary law—we are always in a state of becoming because we are "running" from who we *really* are: who we were not allowed to be in the beginning.

Butler's narration of the originary scene relies on Freud's notion of attachment and melancholy, which, though harboring a problematic heteronormative bias, provides the basic psychic framework. Butler brings these together when she states:

> What critical strategies and sources of subversion appear as the consequence of the psychoanalytic accounts considered so far? The recourse to the unconscious as a source of subversion makes sense, it seems, only if the paternal law is understood as a rigid and universal determinism which makes of "identity" a fixed and phantasmic affair. Even if we accept the phantasmic content of identity, there is no reason to assume that the law which fixes the terms of that fantasy is impervious to historical variability and possibility.[76]

---

76. Butler, *GT*, 90.

By the time Butler had written *Bodies That Matter*, her thinking about the utility of psychoanalysis was much clearer: "Gender is neither a purely psychic truth, conceived as 'internal' and 'hidden,' nor is it reducible to a surface appearance; on the contrary, its undecidability is to be traced as the play *between* psyche and appearance."[77] Butler appeals to Freud's notion of melancholia because in it she finds a psychic rationalization for "how gender *appears* and what gender *signifies*."[78] Butler develops this line of thought in *Psychic Life of Power*. The exact point of inquiry is stated succinctly: "Is there a way in which *gender* identifications or, rather, those identifications that become central to the formation of gender, are produced through melancholic identification?"[79] By answering in the affirmative, Butler is posing the view that gender is not who one *is*, but is an effect of disavowed or disowned originary desire. Gender is a mode of becoming what one is not, which means that being a man or woman does not reflect coherence, but essential incoherence.

Butler uses the logic in Freud's Oedipus mechanism to set up her originary conditions of desire *and* attachment to identify how gender is formed in response to prohibition. For example, Freud's logic is that a girl desires to have her father but cannot because her mother already has him. This originary sexual prohibition is incorporated into her character as melancholic identification. Normal and good sexuality for a girl is to desire a man not her father. Butler does not draw on this logic to make claims about what is normal or good sexuality, but to observe how normal and good sexuality is produced though a prohibition of an object of desire and the subsequent incorporation of that loss into one's character. The girl's good mundane desire for a man not her father reveals that the girl's mundane desire is an effect of an originary loss and lack and thus her incoherence.

But why does Freud assume the girl desires the father in the beginning? This question demonstrates Butler's dependence on Jacques Derrida's critical or deconstructive approach to reading—double reading.[80] The first reading is concerned with the author's intentions, and the second with what was "said" but not intended. For Butler, the question of why the girl desires the father reveals that Freud's mechanism has a

---

77. Butler, *BTM*, 178.
78. Butler, *BTM*, 179.
79. Butler, *PLP*, 134–35.
80. Derrida, *Of Grammatology*, 157–64.

tacit bias, which Butler reads as precisely enacting the logic the theory is describing. The girl desires the father because she is first not allowed to desire her mother, which means that the incest taboo is founded on a more basic homosexual taboo. What is normal and good sexuality is produced in the girl by a law that denies not only the object of desire (the father) but also a prior orientation or aim of desire (for one like her mother). Thus, according to Butler's critique of Freud's thinking, normal and good mundane sexuality is produced by the melancholic incorporation of the denial of her original desire for a woman (aim), and her father (object). Thus, good and normal sexuality for the girl is an effect of two prohibitions: a desire for not women (the homosexual taboo) and not her father (the incest taboo).

Butler extends this logic of the emergence of desire to develop a radical possibility about gender: that gender is produced by being trained away from certain sexual possibilities in the originary scene. The presupposition is stated: "Consider that gender is acquired at least in part through the repudiation of homosexual attachments."[81] If our idea of good and normal sexuality is an effect of incorporated denied originary desires, then Butler suggests gender too ought to be considered according to the same logic. Whereas a traditional account of sexuality is usually conceived as an expression of gender, Butler's deployment of the Freudian notion of attachment and melancholia holds that gender is an effect of denied sexuality: a man is someone who does not desire men but desires a woman (not his mother) because he repudiated homosexual desire and incestuous desire in the beginning; in his infancy. This inverts the traditional arrangement of sex and gender, which Butler summarizes: "Gender itself is here understood to be composed of precisely what remains inarticulateable in sexuality."[82] Being a man, for example, is fundamentally linked to the prohibited orientation of desire for the man at the originary scene, which also means repudiating identification with the woman. This creates an uneasy situation where to be a man one must desire a woman, except for the part of woman that desires a man. Butler narrates that he must "repudiate femininity as a precondition" for his own gendered existence.[83] This is not a one-time repudiation at the originary scene, but a perpetual mode of becoming gendered—a

---

81. Butler, *PLP*, 136.
82. Butler, *PLP*, 140.
83. Butler, *PLP*, 137.

continuous conforming of oneself to the originary prohibitions, which amounts to continuously running from what he originally desired. According to Butler's Freudian logic, I am not a man but am constantly becoming a man by desiring a woman, though not identifying with that part of the woman (femininity) that desires men.

For Butler then, gender is not an essential and positive form of subjectivity, but a contingent and negative mode of being—a mode of consistently enacting or responding rightly to the originary law. Butler thus concludes: "The 'truest' lesbian melancholic is the strictly straight woman, and the 'truest' gay male melancholic is the strictly straight man."[84] "Gender" is not a word that describes what someone always was, but, according to Butler's Freudian logic, "might be understood in part as the 'acting out' of unresolved grief."[85] In other words, for Butler, disorder does not describe the person who desires people of the same sex, but describes us *all* because we have all lost—via prohibition, rather than "separation, death, or the breaking of an emotional tie"—the one we originally loved and now cannot have.[86] According to this thinking, and against a common argument about the etiology of same-sex desire, historic loss-induced trauma does not only induce same-sex desire but also opposite-sex desire. Butler is arguing that when we continue to live as if there has been no loss, we will continue to act out of a place of unresolved grief. Melancholy, in Butler's gender theory, describes a state of being or one's character that is the result of one's loss-induced desire that if not acknowledged will continue to problematically impact how we think and relate to ourselves and the others.

A Literal Origin Story

It is important for our subsequent theological interaction that we acknowledge Butler's originary scene as a literal "creation" event. It might seem that Butler resists a literal originary scene when she states that "the subject is understood as a kind of necessary fiction,"[87] but we ought to be careful to distinguish what Butler is delineating in this moment. What is fiction, returning to the dressage horse metaphor, is the life of the horse

---

84. Butler, *PLP*, 146–47.
85. Butler, *PLP*, 146.
86. Butler, *GT*, 87.
87. Butler, *PLP*, 67.

in the ring that performs unnatural feats. The horse has internalized the external mind of the rider. In this sense, the subjectivity of the horse is a fiction, that is, not essential to the horse. The question "Which soul?" demands that subjectivity be understood as a paradoxical fictive reality.

The aspect of Butler's originary scene—the early moments of infantile development—that demands to be taken literally concerns the *condition* that permits the incorporation of an external soul.[88] Passionate attachment to subjection or the desire for recognition is what structures human beings, which is another way of saying that an *ontology of desire* is central to Butler's thematization of gender.[89] Butler's claim that "the subject . . . is a necessary fiction" is predicated on her earlier comment that "there is no formation of the subject without a passionate attachment to subjection."[90] This *revelation* of what is in the beginning opens up the possibility for a genealogical pursuit for the origin to find out what other terms populate human subjectivity in the beginning. Butler, however, denies such a possibility by figuring the beginning as always beyond one's reach to know its contents. Furthermore, if the origin is a literal historical yet inaccessible location, Butler simultaneously installs, even if inadvertently, self-unknowing as another essential human trait.

This is obviously the case when one reflects on one's earliest memories. I cannot remember the events that shaped my life or the direction and goal of my desires. Even those who were there, like my mother and father, might remember important events in my life, but they could not see how these things shaped the development of my understanding of them, others, the world, and my desires for that which is not me. Butler's point is that this unknowable past reveals to me that there is much about myself that I do not and cannot know, including my/our genesis.

Butler conceives of gender according to a concept of subjectivity that is simultaneously understood in terms of a paradoxical fictive reality installed from the outside, but conceived within a literal and essential or internal originary grammar (a nonfiction or ontological structuring concept) of passionate attachment, which induces unknowing and thus a desire to know the self—desire-induced incoherence.

When the fictive and non-fictive aspects of Butler's gender theory are placed in their appropriate relation, Butler's repudiation of the

---

88. Butler, *GT*, 89.
89. Butler, *PLP*, 67; Butler, *SD*, 24–42.
90. Butler, *PLP*, 67.

polarized debate of gender as a constructed or essential reality confronts those who hold dogmatically to either position.[91] Butler's enterprise of deconstruction, in contrast to those who she insists miss the point of deconstruction, is not to render everything subject to discursive formation, thus safeguarding her own ontology of desire and unknowing.[92] Butler's hybrid fictive/non-fictive subjectivity of desire provides not only the mechanism for mundane desires to be installed as the originary condition, but also the human condition that enables Butler to figure the constitutive force of prohibition that occurs at the originary scene.

While there is much in this account that should grate against a confessional Christian perspective, the notion of refusing to acknowledge one's originary loss and its impact on the formation of mundane desire is provocative.

Conclusion

Butler's desire is to challenge received and traditional notions of gender, proposing instead that we see gender as instances of fiction-making that have their origin in the lost and inaccessible past. Her subject of desire is a way of thinking about one's ontological makeup as constituted by mundane and originary desire which is qualified by delineating between being *in* lack and being *as* lack. Butler's subject is framed by the conceptual priority of originary desire, which receives its operating terms from mundane or temporal desire. This ontology of desire was fleshed out in terms of her readings of Foucault's conceptualization of productive power, Hegel's notion of intersubjectivity, and Freud's melancholic (passionate) originary attachment. The result is that, for Butler, gender is not something that someone is *essentially*, but something that someone is *always becoming*. This mode of gender existence is a reform of a traditional notion of gender. It sees gender as resulting from submission to an external prohibition that resides in the originary scene. That prohibition continues to "speak" authoritatively now and one must hear and perform it to be recognized as a good man or woman.

As our attention moves to reflecting theologically on Butler's thought, three points can be delineated. First, we are provoked to think about the relationship between the beginning and the present. How

---

91. Butler, *BTM*, xvii.
92. Butler, *BTM*, xvii.

do the Edenic originary creatures of Adam and Eve relate to present mundane experiences of gender and sexuality? Second, Butler raises the question of whether prohibition in the beginning conditions how humanity subsequently experiences embodiment. What is the origin of the originary terms? And where the beginning does not reflect the present, are we theologically justified to access the beginning to change what dwells there to better reflect and therefore justify as good what is presently deemed transgressive? Do we need to depart the beginning to better account for non-Edenic embodied existence? Finally, we are confronted with the possibility that what was in the beginning arrives in the present through a process of interiorization, that is, the idea that what gender is and which gender we are is an external idea we incorporate into our subconscious and act out. This last point is taken up in the following chapter and worked out more fully in the following theologically reflective chapters.

The extent to which we take up these questions is determined largely by how candid we are with ourselves. Pointing toward Butler's own ethical turn, which is explored in chapter 5, it seems pertinent to invoke a measure of epistemic humility. This does not amount to doubting our existence. Karl Barth warns that "we are forbidden to doubt existence and ourselves" because in doubting ourselves we doubt the existence of God.[93] But this faith conviction does not permit one to avoid questions concerning human existence, particularly, the question: what do we exist as? And furthermore, how do we understand this existence in relation to others and God?

---

93. Barth, *Church Dogmatics*, III.1, 346.

Chapter 2

Departing Adam and Eve

Introduction

BUTLER THEORIZES GENDER REFORM by formulating a certain departure from the human. On first hearing, this might appear to pose a serious threat to a theological concept of gender. Indeed, a wholesale departure from the human would be cause for concern, but Butler does not offer such a thing. She seeks to remake the human by virtue of a "certain departure from the human."[1] That she desires a *certain* departure is significant because it draws attention to the discontinuity *and* continuity between what is understood to be human in the beginning, and what we experience as humans in the present, a distinction to which a Christian theology of gender should already be sensitized. Butler's desire-induced incoherent subject is not an autonomous agent who is set free from the shackles of the originary human to become whatever they desire in the present mundane moment.[2] On the contrary, I have no way of evading the conditions that characterize not only the time into which I was born and now live, but also the time that goes before me. This means that Butler's gender reform is not predicated on the wholesale erasure of an originary human, nor setting free the mundane from the originary human, but a

---

1. Butler, *UG*, 3–4.

2. The question of agency in Butler is not entirely settled, which will be taken up further in chapter 5.

theorization of the interplay between the past and present to invigorate previously unthought possibilities for mundane human life.

Butler's impulse to reform the human at the originary moment is not absurd because it demonstrates a desire to give voice to and narrate more accurately the mundane experiences that do not fall within a traditional binary conception of gender. A careful reflection on this claim about Butler's desire is not an affirmation of anything particular as good, but an observation of the urgent need for some Christian views of gender to account for gendered existence that is experienced as nonbinary. Indeed, what is lacking in much conservative Christian discourse on gender is a thorough integration of a Christian truth that is foundational to Christian moral claims about what it means to live a good life now, namely, a certain departure from the human in the beginning. In other words, Butler prompts Christian reflection on the human subject that is inescapably characterized by time and the world. She invites self-reflection to come to terms with what it means to see myself in the world and subject to the world. The following engagement with Oliver O'Donovan, Ken Stone, Augustine of Hippo, and W. H. Auden addresses the need for a theological conception of gender that is intersubjective and time-bound, without undermining the role of a foundational originary moment, despite our departure from it.

I draw upon each interlocutor differently. My interaction with O'Donovan's thought in *Finding and Seeking* occasions an opportunity to explore his engagement with desire and subjectivity from a foundationalist theological viewpoint. This exploration is especially pertinent for our purposes as O'Donovan is explicitly critiquing constructivist theorists like Butler. By actively seeking to safeguard objectivity, O'Donovan undermines his own attempt to integrate subjectivity into his foundationalist perspective. Noting the pitfalls in O'Donovan's account, the course forward is plotted. Ken Stone, like Butler, seeks to (re)narrate the foundational creation account to be malleable and not binding. This provides an opportunity to explore whether traditional readings of the creation accounts, when thoroughly integrated with time, addresses what presses Stone into making his account in the first place. My subsequent interactions with Augustine of Hippo and W. H. Auden observe the departure of humanity from the beginning in order to help us conceive theologically what it means to have departed the originary scene, without becoming disoriented.

At the end of the chapter no answer is offered to the question of how to escape the body of death that characterizes a humanity that has departed the beginning. The following chapters will be used to think about the implications of dwelling outside of Eden, particularly, how we continue to relate to Adam and Eve as a lost and irretrievable ideal.

Seeing in the World

The Call of Wisdom

The drive behind Butler's desire to depart the human is like the question of the ancient sage "Does not wisdom call?"[3] which, as Oliver O'Donovan argues, demands "a response to the goodness of God's world."[4] As one who has received the call of faith, who would dare not heed the call of wisdom? But more pressing is the question, who would dare to respond to wisdom's call without taking into account the context in which wisdom calls? Wisdom is required precisely because of the context in which we live. O'Donovan notes that knowledge of the world can be deceptive and consequently blind us to aspects of the world we should know. This kind of epistemic humility is surely in view when the apostle Paul states, "For now we see in a mirror, dimly, but then we will see face to face. Now I know only in part."[5] The apostle reflects on a certain departure from the human that sees clearly by taking into account the world in which the human lives and for which wisdom is necessary. By seeing myself in the world as one whose sight is always conditioned by the world, my confidence to speak about myself and others is not obliterated, but chastened in favor of the terms of faith and hope. The temptation for the Christian thinker, however, is to push faith and hope to the margins by "constructing" a human subject that sees with perspicuity. Like Butler, I suggest the appropriate response is to depart this confident and clear-sighted constructed human subject.

O'Donovan rejects two modern rival constructivist myths used to generate overconfident vantage points to know myself (I) and ourself (We). The first is the "individual constructed society" and the second is

---

3. Prov 8:1.
4. O'Donovan, *Finding*, 48.
5. 1 Cor 13:12.

the "society constructed individual."⁶ O'Donovan and Butler come into critical dialogue because Butler's theory of the subject and gender fits into the second category, though not neatly, as I will demonstrate. O'Donovan is principally concerned with how these myths relegate the "agent-self" to a presupposition in an attempt to circumvent the problem of "locating freedom."⁷ That is, in the explanations of how one is and acts in the world, the myths do not take into account being in the world in time.

O'Donovan begins his critique of social constructivism by observing the deceptive nature of the self. No agent-self is possible in itself because society is seen "as an 'organism' out of which agency and selfhood is spun."⁸ As a product, one's agency is reduced to function, which means that the human task of thinking loses the God-given potency for discerning responsible action. Thinking and acting are severed: "The supposed social rationality of thought never meets up with its intentional content; *the way the mind frames the world is treated as an irrelevance*. But that means freedom has no place in action."⁹ O'Donovan argues that there is no account of rational agency or responsibility in social constructivist positions, which leads to a hefty critical observation: "The 'I' appears as a *deus ex machina* lowered onto the stage of the social self precisely to supply what it lacked, which is to say freedom."¹⁰ Such theorists, O'Donovan concludes, have taken the easy theoretical option having "forgotten in the original thesis that the self was constructed socially."¹¹

But does this critique apply to Butler's constructivist theory? Her thought certainly concerns the "society constructed" individual, but ironically, it is not Butler but her critical interlocutors who determine that her theory lacks a substantial notion of agency.¹² Butler is vulnerable to the opposite claim—especially as she shifts from gender performativity toward a more general linguistic performativity in books like *Psychic Life of Power* and *Excitable Speech*—that there is a diminished concept of agency.¹³ In direct contrast to O'Donovan's claim that for constructiv-

6. O'Donovan, *Finding*, 59.
7. O'Donovan, *Finding*, 59.
8. O'Donovan, *Finding*, 60.
9. O'Donovan, *Finding*, 60 (emphasis mine).
10. O'Donovan, *Finding*, 61.
11. O'Donovan, *Finding*, 61.
12. For seminal criticism, see Benhabib, "Feminism and Postmodernism," 21.
13. For the history of change of agency in Butler's corpus, see Magnus, "Unaccountable Subject," 81–103.

ists it is irrelevant, Butler is entirely concerned with the way the mind frames the world. This means that Butler's social constructivist theory is not vulnerable to O'Donovan's critical observation that "the 'I' appears as a *deus ex machina* lowered onto the stage of the social self precisely to supply what it lacked, which is to say freedom."[14] Butler does not take the easy theoretical option having "forgotten in the original thesis that the self was constructed socially."[15] She does not suppose a sovereign-I, but accepts, in the sense that she acknowledges, the reality of its claim on her. Butler does not achieve agency and freedom by invoking a sovereign-I, or by transcending its claim on her, but by wrestling with it.[16] If "the constituted character of the subject is the very precondition of its agency" then agency is always derivative and therefore simply cannot overreach, but settles for the limited capacity of reforming from the inside out that which forms one's subjectivity.[17] When she poses the question "What speaks when 'I' speak to you?" Butler is asking, what horizon of knowledge frames what I see in the world?[18] This is an ostensible reiteration of wisdom's call to encounter the world as one in the world in such a way that, in practice, my account of myself and others does not evade this reality. Butler avoids "a speculative colonization of society"[19] by treating one's given creatureliness as "a matter of truthful self-knowledge" from the beginning to the end.[20]

Narrating the Self

If Butler avoids O'Donovan's critique, how does O'Donovan respond to the call of wisdom not to overlook where we stand in the world? In the section of the book called "The Objectified Self" O'Donovan pursues the question of how "the self finds itself in the world," yet he struggles to come to grips with what it means to be in the world from the *beginning*.[21]

---

14. O'Donovan, *Finding*, 61.
15. O'Donovan, *Finding*, 61.
16. Magnus, "Unaccountable Subject," 82.
17. Butler, "Contingent Foundations," 46.
18. Butler, "Contingent Foundations," 41.
19. O'Donovan, *Finding*, 61.
20. O'Donovan, *Finding*, 62. There is more to be said concerning agency in Butler's thought that will be explored in chapters 5 and 6.
21. O'Donovan, *Finding*, 53.

O'Donovan's narration of human subjectivity begins by positing that I do not initially view the world and account for myself as part of it. This renders my point of view stable and objective. Only with increased interrogation of the world do I become aware of myself, and my role in the world as an actor and observer.[22] Self-discovery occurs when I observe myself in the world as one who sees the world. At this point, I do not see myself as an agent, but as one piece of the world's created furnishings. This initial moment of observation leads to a more complex discovery of the self, as I further interrogate the connection between myself and the other objects around me. I come to realize by observation that I am not only one of many discrete objects, but one of a kind.[23] As my understanding of the world increases, I come to understand myself in relation to other things, and others who are like me in kind. Thus, knowledge of the part, and its relation to other parts, is dependent on understanding that it is first part of a whole. In other words, placing myself as the object of knowledge—to know myself—I must know I am one of a kind, and that I am one of the human kind.

The neighbor emerges out of this conception of the self. If I know of myself as one of a kind, then, in naming myself thus, I also name those others who are like me—ones of the same kind—as neighbor. The neighbor has always been as myself, but now emerges as such. Hence, to heed Jesus' command to love my neighbor as myself is to love my neighbor as another of the same kind. This is how O'Donovan can say, "Self-love is love of a kind . . . constituted by self-awareness and agency."[24] So, we reach the point of agency.

O'Donovan's last observation is that the reflexive motion allows me to love my self. Because a dynamic of equality and reciprocity characterizes those of the same kind, I view my self, therefore, as an object of their gaze as "other people's other people."[25] From O'Donovan's standpoint, this rules out the popular assertion that how one would like to be loved is how one ought to love the other.[26] The notion of loving one's self emerges

---

22. O'Donovan, *Finding*, 54.
23. O'Donovan, *Finding*, 54.
24. O'Donovan, *Finding*, 54.
25. O'Donovan, *Finding*, 54.
26. "Do to others as you would have them do to you" (Luke 6:31 NIV).

so late in the theorization of self that it cannot form the grounds or the measure by which the love of the neighbor should be conceived.[27]

According to O'Donovan's theorization of the self, this moment of emergent or developed self-awareness is not the moment for moral decision-making. Self-awareness is not enough to think and act ethically. What is required is a better perspective, an objective perspective, which comes with an accumulation of knowledge of reality:

> The objective view can only be formed by one who occupies a subjective viewpoint.... The only way to attain objectivity is to take note of *more*, not to take note of *less* or to take *less note* of what one noted first.... Any fool can change his mind; the difficult thing is to enlarge it.[28]

Knowledge of the world (of me and my neighbor) becomes objective as I *increase* my knowledge of the world, rendering my perspective *less* subjective. As I accumulate knowledge and understanding through realizing how things are connected—the serious task of seeking a "common wisdom"[29]—I pass over the "threshold of moral sensibility."[30] Here, drawing on Romans 12:3, O'Donovan asserts that I can now think judiciously of the selves of me and my neighbor.

Closer investigation of O'Donovan's theory of the agent-self, however, reveals some problematic elements, especially in light of his critique of constructivism. In the first moment of O'Donovan's theorization of the self, who is this person who does not observe their self as one seeing the world? This person is a puzzling creature because their vision is objective by virtue of their vision not being subjected to, or conditioned by, what is other. This person cannot be a baby because a baby cannot conceive of the world in the way O'Donovan describes.[31] This person is not the Edenic man pre-woman, or the man and woman, because in both contexts they differentiate their selves from each other, animals, and God. So, who is this figure who sees the world, but does not see one's self always already as part of it? While O'Donovan does not name or offer a description of this

---

27. This is to observe an otherwise trending Augustinian theme that to know is to love.

28. O'Donovan, *Finding*, 57.

29. O'Donovan, *Finding*, 58.

30. O'Donovan, *Finding*, 55.

31. This object sees a complex world that is named, which a baby cannot do. O'Donovan, *Finding*, 53–54.

person, we learn that it identifies its self with "I" despite the curious lack of a "thou" or "we."[32] In light of this, we must conclude that the human self that O'Donovan *constructs* is a mythical creature that (rather than who) identifies as "I" and sees the world with an objective gaze unaffected by self-awareness. This "I" occupies space in the world God created without participating in it. In short, this self is not a created human. This self that is unaffected by self-awareness is an extra-creation *idea* that "lives" in the world, like that in which we live, but not as one having had any human experience of itself.

O'Donovan's subsequent introduction of a notion of reflexivity permits *building* on the always already world and the mythical sovereign-I he has placed within it. The self stumbles upon their self.[33] The human that O'Donovan is theorizing begins as a sovereign-I, but later *becomes* a subject-I as I observe my self through another (thou), which then enables me to love others as another like me. Agency and selfhood are never a God-given quality, but are emergent characteristics of the human self throughout time despite the perspicuous lack of time.

It should be clear from this critical reading that O'Donovan's response to his own critique of constructivists breaks down in precisely the same way. O'Donovan predicates the self with sovereignty without theological or historical justification. Thus, he constructs a self that is external to where we stand in the world, absent minded, and not self-aware. O'Donovan unwittingly constructs an agent-self that is a purely formal or abstract entity, which does not exist in time. The difference between O'Donovan and the constructivist theorists he critiques is *where* they respectively theorize the appearance of the "I." Problematically, O'Donovan theorizes an "I" onto a stage that does not even exist.[34] Before God sets history into motion, a "person" exists who can say "I" and gaze objectively upon the "world," which causes significant problems when language must eventually transform the sovereign-I (ideal) into human existence as a subject-I (real) without jeopardizing the subject's clear sight. The grammatical strain is evident when O'Donovan equivocates over how best to describe this.

For O'Donovan's pre-social sovereign-I whose sight is unencumbered by self-reflection, to see is to know. A brief investigation into

---

32. O'Donovan, *Finding*, 53.
33. O'Donovan, *Finding*, 54.
34. O'Donovan, *Finding*, 61.

another published version of this section of *Finding and Seeking* called "Know Thyself! The Return of Self-Love," reveals the stark crisis of language that besets O'Donovan's theorized self.[35] For ease of comparison, I have inserted in parenthesis the terms found in "Know Thyself!" into the parallel passage in *Finding and Seeking*:

> As I locate myself in God's world, I observe others like me. For to understand a thing—any thing—is to know [see] it as one of a kind, and to understand oneself is to know [observe] the kind, or kinds, to which one belongs.[36]

Is to see to know? Is to observe to know? O'Donovan cannot give up seeing and observing as knowing because this forgoes the sovereign-I who alone has pure objective agency unencumbered by self-awareness. Yet O'Donovan is aware that to see with our eyes is to see with the mind's eye. To see myself as an object in God's world is not a literal description of the eyes' function, but a metaphorical (though no less real) description of the mind's comprehension or understanding of the self in, and therefore as part of, the good world God created. Eyes, then, describe the organ required to illuminate the world. My self in relation to the world that includes other selves is therefore a form of knowledge—as if to see is to know, which cannot be accepted without criticism. Rather, as a sinful and fallen creature who comes to understand their self via the mind's eye, what I see must be purged of the problematic patterns of knowledge that form what is seen. The call of wisdom is to take up Romans 12:3 to think and act judiciously, but not before taking account of being in the world, which is why the apostle first exhorts the believer in verse 2: "Do not conform to this world." Paul's words imply not only the possibility that I

---

35. The chronology of these two works is difficult to pinpoint. In the preface to *Finding and Seeking*, O'Donovan points to a soon-to-be-published volume that contains an essay of his own that has "an unusual degree of overlap" with the content of the book (O'Donovan, *Finding*, x). In the introduction of that essay—which we learn is called "Know Thyself!"—O'Donovan asserts that the occasion for the essay is not to revise the overlapping content in his recently published book (*Finding and Seeking*), but "to reconsider some reflections I first pursued in my earliest published book," which was published in 2006 (O'Donovan, "Know Thyself!," 268). There is, therefore, good reason to believe that "Know Thyself!" was written prior to the appearance of the modified version in *Finding and Seeking* despite the essay's slightly later date of publication. Notwithstanding the ambiguous chronology of these two works, the argument moving forward concerns the crisis of language that emerges when one tries to describe the nature of human knowing as objective.

36. O'Donovan, *Finding*, 54. The parallel text is O'Donovan, "Know Thyself!," 277.

have been conformed to the world, but that my vision never escapes the horizon that forms the world in which I find myself seeing. My vision is therefore never objective, but is always subject to the world, which is why I must discern the will of God rather than crassly lay claim to it.

O'Donovan's language comes under strain when he seeks to explain how one gains an objective gaze. The problem with developing a reflexive notion of the self is that the self is bound, in some sense, to the world. This means that my view of the world is not entirely mine; my perspective is intersubjective, something akin to the person Butler theorizes. A cursory glance at the world suggests that the integrity of one's agency as sovereign is in jeopardy, but O'Donovan seeks to address this concern by nuancing his notion of the sovereign/subject-I. But he problematically equivocates because of the need to preserve the objectivity of the human gaze to lay claim to objective truth and reality. We see this internal conflict when we compare once again the parallel passages. In one instance in *Finding and Seeking*, the term objective is not in quotation marks. With quotation marks, the text in "Know Thyself" reads drastically differently:

> The "objective" viewpoint, then, can only be occupied by one who still occupies the subjective viewpoint.... The only way to reach objectivity is to take note of *more*, not to take note of *less* nor to take *less note* of what one noted at first.... It is almost perilously easy to alter one's perspective; the difficult thing is to enlarge it.[37]

The reason the term objective is in quotation marks in the earlier piece is that the viewpoint is not objective, but essentially subjective, always becoming and never arriving at objectivity before the eschaton. The reason for taking out the quotation marks in *Finding and Seeking* bespeaks the crisis plaguing this aspect of O'Donovan's notion of self. The problematic point of his formal *theorization* of the self is that the meaning of the term *objective*, regardless of the presence or absence of quotation marks, does not and cannot equate to the pre-social sovereign-I for whom to see is to know. The next line in the passage more than adequately informs the reader that because the human is required to "reach objectivity," the human in view is not a sovereign-I, and therefore can never be one in this age. This means that agency is perpetually fraught, and that O'Donovan should have kept the quotation marks around the term "objective" viewpoint in *Finding and Seeking*, or else use subjective viewpoint.

37. O'Donovan, "Know Thyself!," 281. The parallel text is O'Donovan, *Finding*, 57.

Finally, O'Donovan notes that his theorization of self-knowledge and self-love is purely formal, and so requires substantiation by creation order. This admission occurs at the end of his chapter called "Faith and Meaning," and at the end of the essay "Know Thyself!":

> But these are purely formal notions if we abstract them from the order of creation in which they acquire substance.... Christian understanding, speaking with the voice of humanism made possible by monotheism, has said that my neighbor is my equal *as mankind*.[38]

With Butler's call to depart the human in mind, the argument I am making is not principally concerned with the outcome, but the method. It is theologically inadequate to theorize the self formally and then substantiate it retrospectively with creation. This formal maneuvering indicates that the creation order, which is said to be indicative of creation, is not included in the initial theorizing of creation order. How can we think about what it means to be a human, as man and woman, without speaking explicitly about creation from the beginning? How can we conceive of Christian theology if it is not theologically concerned from the beginning? In an effort to maintain our agential sovereignty over the world—to see is to know—O'Donovan theorizes the self apart from creation, and only after having done so, reverts to the very substance of creation that he has already theorized.

For those who confess that God created the world, time is not dispensable nor a secondary or peripheral property for conceiving the self. The challenge for a Christian theology of gender is to ensure that the human, whether originary or mundane, does not evade the implications of the self in time, but is continually found and considered within it. The human subject is therefore not a single transcendent concept, but is necessarily wrought from the moment within which it is found. This implicates thinking about Adam and Eve, and ourselves as gendered and sexual, but it also concerns ourselves as thinkers about Adam and Eve, and ourselves as thinkers of our own gender and sexuality. Ignoring the historical contingency of the human thinking subject enables one to assume autonomy despite the world that conditions us.

Constructivist theorists are critiqued by O'Donovan for good reason, but he responds by theorizing an ironic mode of sovereign-subjectivity despite the world in which we live. In contradistinction, Butler's

---

38. O'Donovan, *Finding*, 62.

thought does not fall victim to such critique. It is for this reason that she calls for a certain departure from the human, which, while threatening, serves to provoke serious self-reflection. I suggest that her voice does not threaten a conservative account of gender and sexuality, but can be received and heard carefully as strangely redemptive. The human that Butler seeks to depart is precisely those mute timeless "human" images of man and woman who gaze upon the world with Archimedean perspicuity while remaining unaffected by the world and time. A Christian theology of gender need not fear such a departure. Indeed, not only must we not fear such a notion of human being, but we should wholly embrace it by factoring it into our thinking about gender and sexuality in light of Scripture's claim that "God saw *everything* that he had made, and indeed, it was very good."[39]

Created Intersubjectivity

Fighting for Life and the Beginning

Butler's integration of a literal originary story into her gender theory is not wholly surprising. An originary moment grounds human history, thereby providing what we need to make sense of the world and ourselves within it. Butler's thinking about the originary moment gives rise to a challenging and pertinent question: what happens when the originary moment depicts human gendered and sexual experience in ways that are not wholly commensurate with my and others' mundane experiences? Butler reconciles this difference, not by pointing to the problematic fact of a generating originary story, but by pointing to the static lifeless quality of originary images or terms that often populate such stories. How do I reconcile the apparent discontinuities between what God created very good in the beginning as depicted in Genesis 1 and 2, and divergent experiences in the present? What do I make of bodies and desires that are experienced now that *exceed* this originary story? We have seen that Butler suggests making a certain departure from our creation story by remaking the originary form as malleable and open to adjustment to reflect certain present experiences and observable excess.

In *Frames of War* Butler interrogates the apparent alliance between secular French culture and Christian theology. She notes the sexuality

---

39. Gen 1:31 (emphasis mine).

and marriage norms that characterized French culture at the time did not look that different from Joseph Ratzinger's "Letter to the Bishops of the Catholic Church on the Collaboration of Men and Women in the Church and the World" in which he roots a doctrine of sexual difference in Scripture. Butler's "protological" orientation is in full force:

> One could simply reply by saying, yes, the truth of man and woman that you outline is no truth at all and we seek to destroy it in order to give rise to a more humane and radical set of gender practices. But to speak this way is simply to reiterate the cultural divide that makes no analysis possible. Perhaps one needs to start with the status of the story of Genesis itself and to see what other readings are possible.[40]

Unbeknownst to Butler, several years earlier theologian Ken Stone did this in an article called "The Garden of Eden" in which he relies on Butler's methodology. Stone models his reading of the second creation narrative in Genesis 2 on Butler's rereading, or better, Butler's use of the Derridean strategy of double reading of the ancient text of Antigone in her book *Antigone's Claim*.[41] Butler uses this ancient text to bring into question kinship and gender structures that society takes for granted, particularly, the heterosexual contract.[42] Butler's focus on originary structures that found gender and sexuality norms stimulates Stone's focus. Instead of taking up Antigone, he considers the ancient biblical creation myth undergirding current debates over kinship and gender, asking the question: do the Christian creation accounts in Scripture presuppose thought about sexual relations and their perceived links to human reproduction? Having swiftly done away with Karl Barth and Phyllis Trible's respective interpretations of the first creation narrative in Genesis 1, since they explicitly link man and woman with the *imago Dei*, Stone turns his attention to the second creative narrative in Genesis 2.[43] Here he queries the coherent figures in the prelapsarian era that condition (produce and regulate) sexuality and gender in the present.

Stone uses Butler to bring into question the traditional reading of the foundation of compulsory heterosexuality by "focus[ing] upon the

---

40. Butler, *FW*, 117n12.

41. Derrida, *Positions*.

42. Butler, *Antigone's Claim*. Stone draws explicitly on Monique Wittig's concept of the heterosexual contract in Wittig, *Straight Mind*.

43. Stone, "Garden of Eden," 52–53.

instability and incoherence of this textual foundation."[44] Stone does not let his reading overreach by denying that the creation account "*does* offer a narrative of origins for [the marriage] institution" as comprising one man and one woman. Stone's point, however, is that it is "hardly a stable one."[45] Having read the creation myth through a Butlerian lens, Stone asks the pertinent question, "Might a reader not conclude, then, that the story of the Garden of Eden . . . can be read differently?"[46]

The first point Stone raises is the possibility that desire between the primeval creatures does not appear until after their fall in Genesis 3:16. Stone postulates that Eve's desire for her husband is a consequence or punishment for her disobedience to God.[47] By drawing encouragement from the ancient biblical commentators, Stone describes his view as taking seriously the problematic assumption that Adam and Eve desired each other and had sexual relations before the curse.[48] Furthermore, by attending to the textual detail in Genesis 3:16, Stone shows that Eve's desire for her husband is characterized by insecurity, which stands to reason in light of the husband's rule. According to Stone, Eve did not necessarily find herself in an originary moment of blissful heterosexual union, thus "women might have good reason for refusing to submit to the terms of the heterosexual contract."[49] The point is that the heterosexual arrangement, in which the woman finds herself with the man, could in fact be a fallen arrangement from the very beginning.

Stone's second point takes up the Pauline observation that "Adam was formed first, then Eve": if God created primeval man and woman sequentially, then the Yahwist would find it troublesome to describe sexual differentiation neatly.[50] The Yahwist seeks to give the man the preeminent place by having him created first in the narrative, but noting that the man is created first raises the question of what it means to be a man, sexually and in terms of gender, if there is no woman. Is the man a man without a woman? What does it mean to speak of pre-woman man as a sexed creature, which probes the question of whether it is genitalia that makes

44. Stone, "Garden of Eden," 50.
45. Stone, "Garden of Eden," 64 (emphasis mine).
46. Stone, "Garden of Eden," 65.
47. Stone, "Garden of Eden," 55.
48. Stone, "Garden of Eden," 55.
49. Stone, "Garden of Eden," 56.
50. 1 Tim 2:13.

one a man or woman. Stone wrongly enlists Phyllis Trible to defend the possibility that the original human creation could have been "a single androgynous being" from whom God made two beings.[51] Stone, however, unwittingly challenges Trible's actual view when he identifies that such a view requires continuity in the "maleness" of the pre-woman man (*adam*) and that of the subsequent sexually differentiated man (Adam) in order to maintain the thesis that a prelapsarian moment as described in Genesis by a postlapsarian man has not managed to avoid divesting itself of *his* interests.[52] In highlighting these tensions and contradictory possibilities, Stone is suggesting that the male author of the ancient narrative is in a muddle as he tries to narrate the primeval origins of women without undermining his own assumptive notions of male dominance.[53]

Then thirdly, Stone observes that the ancient author's muddle over his preoccupation with male dominance is matched by his attempt to "*buttress* the heterosexual contract," which is in fact what Stone believes is the goal of the ancient text. The creation myth is concerned with "sketching the etiology of 'humanity as male and female.'"[54] The difficult project confronting the ancient Yahwist was to narrate a moment that did not yet exist that reinforced both "compulsory heterosexuality and male domination."[55] In Stone's estimation, it stands to reason that interpretive problems wrack the ensuing text. One such dilemma occurs when the author positions the male as temporally prior to the woman and therefore closer to the divine. The result is an inadvertent same-sex relationship between the man and God, which undermines the normative and originary heterosexuality. The author's narration of the man's loneliness and need of a woman is, therefore, not a *real* male need, but a necessary provision to avoid an unwanted same-sex relation that is built into the originary scene.[56] Averting the possibility of this uncomfortable conditioning of the originary scene entails identifying the pre-woman man as not male until the woman arrives. Drawing explicitly on Butler, Stone deploys this

---

51. Stone, "Garden of Eden," 57. This is an earlier view that Trible explicitly rejects in the book Stone cites. Trible states that "androgyny assumes sexuality, whereas the earth creature is sexually undifferentiated." Trible, *God and the Rhetoric of Sexuality*, 141n17.

52. Stone, "Garden of Eden," 56–57.

53. Stone, "Garden of Eden," 57.

54. Stone, "Garden of Eden," 58.

55. Stone, "Garden of Eden," 58.

56. Stone, "Garden of Eden," 58.

textual moment to "open up spaces for the production of an alternative queer subject."[57] The pre-man-and-woman man is a queer figure that Stone hopes "will challenge religiously grounded heteronormativity."[58]

Having granted in some measure that the creation story does assert a notion of humanity that is sexually differentiated as male and female, Stone challenges the view that coherence lies in the union of the differentially sexed creatures. Looking to Butler, Stone argues that the principle of heteronormativity prohibits using man and woman as categories to identify intelligible bodies and experiences.[59] Stone maintains that those who do not measure up to the man or the woman, including, "for example the intersexed, transsexuals, individuals labelled with the pathologizing term 'gender identity disorder,' and so forth," might find solace in the God-created queer figure who is a man at some points in time, and unidentifiable at others.[60] Ultimately, Stone finds the ancient author in a bind because he cannot cover every possibility: if the figure is a man, then he installs a divine homoerotic relationship, but if the figure is a pre-man and pre-woman androgynous being, then he installs an originary figure who is not defined by gender norms. On either account, the author undermines the heterosexual contract.

Stone makes this rereading of the second creation account to highlight the supposed already existing ruptures in the text to demonstrate its failure to narrate human existence neatly. This is important for Stone because he understands that the creation text is not merely narrating the originary moment, but producing, or better, reproducing someone's idea of gendered and sexual subjects in time. In response, Stone poses the questions:

> What kinds of reading effects, and subject effects, become possible when this reader encounters the tensions and contradictions that fracture the story of the Garden of Eden, tensions and contradictions that I have attempted to highlight here and that complicate the story's presumed contribution to the coherence of the heterosexual contract? How might this gay reader bring his labor on the text to bear on . . . the "improbable" modes of individual and social existence that he is trying to bring about?[61]

57. Stone, "Garden of Eden," 59.
58. Stone, "Garden of Eden," 60.
59. Stone, "Garden of Eden," 63.
60. Stone, "Garden of Eden," 63.
61. Stone, "Garden of Eden," 62.

Along with Butler, who seeks to remake the human by departing the human, Stone understands that Adam and Eve in their originary form are the humans that must be departed in order to justify different mundane notions of good sexuality and gender that exceed the strict formulation in which man and woman desire each other and desire to procreate together.

Stone's Butlerian reading of the second creation narrative gives credence to the possibility that the originary condition functions like a law prohibiting certain modes of desire. That Stone seeks to re-form or rupture the terms of the creation account suggests that this origin story operates as a law that produces and regulates good and normal desire, and gendered being. While Stone is not clear about how the subject is produced, rereading a traditional Christian account of Adam and Eve offers hope to those people who exist outside the terms of the originary law. Stone's hope is not grounded in the bold assertion of the goodness of one's desire, or a notion of gender and expectation that the originary law must be adjusted to accommodate these. Rather, where rupture and incoherence are observed in the originary law, Stone seeks to expose the law as *not* natural or God-given, but as a man's—the Yahwist's—mundane desire that, through sedimentation, has been installed as the foundation as what is natural and God-given.

Finally, like Butler, it is clear to Stone that the originary moment is foundational because that is where the human comes into existence. The reality of a literal beginning is not contested, only how that beginning is structured and the terms used to populate it. Stone demonstrates a desire for particular mundane sexual and gendered lives to be recognized as good and normal, but a traditional reading of the originary "law" does not permit this desire. His rereading opens the door for different interpretations of the originary scene, which subsequently provides the opportunity for different mundane possibilities to be considered good. While Stone, and Butler, do not assume access to the originary moment where the human is created, they bring into question traditional sedimented views of that moment to reveal the possibility of a new law or remade human that can reflect a new range of experienced and observable human mundane desires. The pivotal assumption for Stone, like Butler, is that the originary scene is always installed with mundane desire, meaning that good gender and sexuality can be remade through queering established readings.

In response to this reforming of the human at the originary scene to justify mundane desire, I offer a different reading of the second creation narrative in which the pre-man-and-woman figure is not an androgynous queer figure who more closely resembles Plato's androgyne in his *Symposium*, one who offers possibilities of life and is to be celebrated, but rather as one on whom God's judgement falls—"not good."[62] Stone seizes the only aspect of prelapsarian creation that is not good to justify as good, modes of mundane desire and gendered being that exceed God's originary creation. In fact, the appeal to the lonely queer figure undermines what Butler demands is necessary for conceiving of gender as something more complex than mere solitary existence. Stone, like O'Donovan, stumbles by appealing to a foundation that is constituted by a person who is abstracted from relationship to others in time. In contrast, I offer a theology of gender that has a foundation that, with Butler, is a complex dynamic in which people learn about themselves as sexual and gendered in relation to another in time.

The Good Before the Bad

In Genesis 2—before the fall—troubled embodiment is evident. This originary instance of trouble indicates that what is good does not concern individual Edenic perfection, or being located in Eden, but embodied existence within the entirety of the world God created and continues to sustain.

In the first creation account in Genesis 1:1—2:3, God speaks and creates male and female.[63] Shortly thereafter, God makes the sweeping declaration concerning "all that he had made ... was very good."[64] In the second creation account beginning at 2:4, God brings humanity into existence, but unlike the first narrative, God does not look at it and declare it very good. On the contrary, it is "not good" because it exists in a state of aloneness.[65] In this pre-man-and-woman instance, and despite the presence of every animal, humanity exists, but not in the form that arouses the divine declaration "very good."[66] God's declaration that the solitary

---

62. Blocher, *In the Beginning*, 95.
63. Gen 1:26–27.
64. Gen 1:31.
65. Gen 2:18.
66. Despite points of disagreement with her thought at critical moments, this reading of Genesis is indebted to Phyllis Trible's interpretation of Genesis 2 in Trible, *God and the Rhetoric of Sexuality*, ch. 4.

human is "not good" is not a moral marker, but a more fundamental assessment that what has been made so far is not yet considered a good part of God's very good world.

At this point, there are two important implications about what is good. Firstly, what is good does not necessarily equate to mere prelapsarian existence. Secondly, what is good is not mere human existence. These two implications tell us that God's view of created humanity as good, hinges neither on one's location (being in Eden), nor even on one's undefiled relationship with God. Thus, whatever Stone wants to make of this figure (as male or androgynous), God does not yet recognize this figure as participating in what God declares "very good." With the creation of woman in 2:21–22, humanity comprises man and woman as two, but as one interdependent flesh.[67] What is good, therefore, is human existence that is found in a particular embodied relationship *in* the world *with* God *and* with *this* other (as opposed to another) human creature. God's originary creatures are not self-dependents who exist alone in isolation, because such an existence is not good.[68] Moreover, as created by God and found in relation to God, the other and creation, the man and woman are not self-determinants. This raises the pressing question of agency, which suffice to say is increasingly chastened, though not finally undermined, in this developing theology of gender.[69]

Note also that God does not create a man to help the originary man. Francis Watson states: "Solitary man, this being that in its abstraction is 'not good', needs a helper that God cannot be," and so "pure likeness would be a repetition that would merely replicate the original solitude."[70] James Brownson offers the contrasting view that the arrival of the woman is in fact the arrival of one of the same. The woman stands in contrast not only to God but also to the different animals who provide no respite from Adam's originary predicament.[71] It is indisputable that the woman is of the same *kind* as Adam, but to limit one's interpretation of Adam's not-good state as lacking another of the same kind does not account for her difference as one of the same kind.[72] At times the woman disappears

---

67. 1 Cor 11:11–12.
68. Trible, *God and the Rhetoric of Sexuality* 89.
69. The question of agency is explicitly treated in chapters 5 and 6.
70. Watson, *Agape, Eros, Gender*, 58.
71. Gen 2:20.
72. This supposed originary absence of particularity establishes kinship as the heart of God's desire for humanity in community on which Brownson justifies one-flesh

entirely from Brownson's description of humanity in the garden: "The animals are certainly different from the man, but that is not what the story is interested in. It is pursuing not differences but someone similar to the man, someone similar enough to be 'his partner.'"[73] He continues: "The primary movement in the text is not from unity to differentiation, but from the isolation of an individual to the deep blessing of shared kinship and community."[74] Brownson's interpretation of the creation of Adam's helper means that what God declares good is mere existence: humans in community.

Particularity, however, characterizes originary humanity-in-community kinship. In the form of man and woman they are pleased (or not ashamed)[75] to dwell with and in the other. God did not create two humanoid forms that have features and functions to be identified for our enacting, but embodied creatures to love each other, and together, to love God and the world for which they were created. As Trible claims, "The divine evaluation 'it is not good for the earth creature to be alone' contrasts wholeness with isolation."[76] In the beginning the individuals find themselves beyond their selves as they find themselves in community.[77] Stone overlooks this crucial point while enlisting the figure to underwrite a queer theology of gender and sexuality. Humanity in the form of man and woman, as same yet different, multiple yet united, individuated yet plural, constituting a part of all that God had made, is very good.[78] Let us now expand further on the two claims that make the creatures' lives good apart from their location and mere existence.

Location, Location, Location?

Unlike the real estate market mantra that guides the value or good of a property, the aphorism "location, location, location" does not correspond analogously to embodied existence. From the creator's perspective, embodied selves in Eden are not more or less good than they are following

---

union between people of the same sex. Brownson, *Bible, Gender, and Sexuality*, 107.

73. Brownson, *Bible, Gender, and Sexuality*, 30.
74. Brownson, *Bible, Gender, and Sexuality*, 30.
75. Gen 2:25.
76. Trible, *God and the Rhetoric of Sexuality*, 89.
77. Blocher, *In the Beginning*, 96.
78. Gen 1:31.

the fall and their expulsion from the garden. This does not deny the reality and impact of the fall, which will be taken up shortly, but takes seriously the claim that what God creates is good and that one's embodied reality is to be received as such, regardless of where we find ourselves in history. This claim relies on God's corollary declarations: firstly, that man pre-woman existed in a state that was not good, and secondly, that man and woman are a *part* of creation that God declares "very good."

If the condition that makes humanity good is its constitution as man and woman *in* the world, then at a foundational level humanity's fall into sin does not strip God's creation of its created goodness. Thus, one is not good because of what one does or does not do, nor is the declaration based on what one looks like or does not look like, or who one desires. God's creation, of which each human is a part, is good because one is created and sustained by God the creator. This draws a distinction between being morally good, for which *I* am responsible, and being declared good as a part of God's creation, for which *God* is responsible. God's view of man and woman as good remains true after the fall because God's view of creation is not predicated on humanity's view of itself: how humanity sees itself in the mirror, reflexively in the world, or through others' direct communications with them.

Psalm 139 reinforces this point. God's vision or valuation of embodied existence is decisive for thinking about oneself as good despite existing in a location east of Eden. The psalmist, while groping in darkness, comes to realize this when he states:

> For it was you who formed my inward parts;
> > you knit me together in my mother's womb.
> I praise you, for I am fearfully and wonderfully made.
> > Wonderful are your works;
> that I know very well.
> > My frame was not hidden from you,
> when I was being made in secret,
> > intricately woven in the depths of the earth.
> Your eyes beheld my unformed substance.
> In your book were written
> > all the days that were formed for me,
> > when none of them as yet existed.[79]

While the psalmist does not use "good" or "very good" in this passage to describe creation, one does find the argument offered; that creation finds

---

79. Ps 139:13–16.

its ultimate value as God "sees" it as a part of creation and not due to its mere existence or location. In the preceding verses of this passage, the psalmist reflects as one who exists in the postlapsarian era, who struggles within the numbing darkness of selfhood (vv. 11–12). Yet despite that which surrounds him and his experience of it, he comes to understand himself not merely as wonderful, but as God's wonderful *created* work.

The important aspect of this passage for our purposes is the origin and extent of the human's characterization as a wonderful creation. The psalmist begins to understand himself as he comes to understand the depth of God's knowledge of him, which is a creator's knowledge of his body (v. 15), inmost being (v. 13), and life (v. 16). The point being drawn out here is that a person's creaturely value is not determined by one's perfection or residence in Eden or one's imperfection or residence in the fallen age, nor one's ability to perceive the self as good. God knows each person as wonderful *as a part* of the created world that God declares very good. Such a declaration, again, is not a moral qualification, but an objective description of God's embodied creations despite their location.

This realization impacts a Christian theology of gender. As Brian Brock argues at length in *Singing the Ethos of God*, the psalms are not intended for private devotion, but are to be sung as a public proclamation that takes root in the heart and claims one's affection and actions "internalized as a way of life."[80] This being the case, a corporate or communal reading of Psalm 139 is not merely a recital of an uplifting story of one man's journey out of darkness into a life of light having come to know his worth in God's sight. Rather, the gathered believers who read this piece of Scripture together have God's Word wash over them, each sharing in the renewal of their minds by the Spirit as they come to understand the value of not just their selves, but others. I come to understand not only who I am in God's sight, but also who my wife is as one created good by God, and who my two young daughters are who are created by God as good. Likewise, they come to understand who I am in God's sight. In the corporate reading of this psalm, we learn that our "enemy" is actually our neighbor and is worthy of compassion and love because God deems their embodied existence as good as our own.

We learn from Brock that the proclaimed psalm also has a self-critical function. A Christian theology of gender is impacted when one realizes that one's responsibility *for* the other is not because the other

---

80. Brock, *Singing the Ethos of God*, xvi.

manifests bodily perfection or moral suitability, but because we have come to *know* they are good in God's eyes. The divine performative utterance that man and woman *in* the world is part of what is very good has taken hold of us. The other's existence is worthy of our compassion and care because they are God's wonderful creation, which God sustains. This simple truth is often lost amid the theological infighting over what constitutes the *imago Dei*, which to this point in the unfolding argument has deliberately been avoided because of the speculation surrounding it. Furthermore, it is not necessary to understand the relation of the *imago Dei* to humanity to comprehend God's created humanity as wonderful works.[81] To confess "God created them" is to confess that humanity, *as* man and woman *in* God's world, is God's wonderful work. Human embodiment may be troubled now, which requires further investigation, but one must conceive of such trouble against a backdrop of its primary creaturely goodness.

Embodiment

From the preceding argument, it is theologically problematic for a Christian idea of gender to be reduced to static images. Departing the originary bodies does not jettison the physical body. The body is a present reality and one must pay more, not less attention to it, and to the aspects of gendered embodied existence that is unable to be captured by an image. By integrating the mind into our account of the body and gender, like Butler, we come to understand gender as a complex intersubjective reality. Gender concerns physical bodies, but as part of God's creation, it is also a good social event. To demonstrate that sociality is a good part of God's creation of man and woman and not an effect of the fall, let us take up again the second creation account in Genesis 2. Here we find a notion of sociality that enriches a Christian theology of gender, and possibly points to the reason why gender discourse is baffling.

In Genesis 2:1–20 God creates the earth and the heavens, which is then nourished by water, thereby providing a place for which God can create the man from the dust of the earth. Until this point in the creation narrative, humanity consisted of only one person, which means that the constitution of humanity fundamentally changes in Genesis 2:21. In light

---

81. I agree with Brownson on this point, which is the reason why I defer engaging with the theme until chapter 6. Brownson, *Bible, Gender, and Sexuality*, 31–32.

of God's previous declaration that humanity is not good because of loneliness, what is crucial here is God's creation of a new humanity characterized by a new human reality—*embodied relationality*. With the formation of woman from the man's rib, humanity consists of two different embodiments of the same kind that have breath and life, who relate to each other, to God, and the world. Man and woman are discrete and unique bodied existences, but they are not mere individuals in the world, they are a unity of man and woman (2:22–24). Bodies and minds individuate humans, which also draw them into unity.

It is at this point that we begin to see our exploration of Butler's emphasis on the sociality of the body and intersubjectivity come to the fore for thinking about gender. Man and woman do not relate to each other as two images on a poster, or as two statues side-by-side, or resembling trees with swaying intermingling branches. Certainly, man and woman represent to the other their own limit in that God creates both in physical bodily relation to the other. In Dietrich Bonhoeffer's exploration of the other as limit in *Creation and Fall* he states: "The other person is the limit that God sets for me, the limit that I love and that I will not transgress because of my love."[82] But as much as this new humanity, man and woman, is characterized as limit, they also find with the other a complex relation of mind that renders one's subjectivity an intersubjective corporeality. The other is their limit, but they are also the means of transcending that limit.

The argument unfolding resists assumptive notions of shame that result in a simple notion of the self.[83] Shame is not merely useful but fundamental to a theology of gender because it brings together the body and mind as the originary gendered reality that God ordained as part of the very good creation. I suggest that by looking "behind" shame or at the mechanism that structures shame, we can see that man and woman is a complex and mysterious reality. Shame signals the intersubjective nature of embodiment or names a social dynamic or mechanism by which God intends for the man and the woman to comprehend their respective selves.

In Genesis 2:25, the reader learns that "the man and his wife were both naked, and they felt no shame." This aspect of the creation narrative is usually used to muster evidence to support the claim that creation is

---

82. Bonhoeffer, *Creation and Fall*, 92.

83. For an exploration of the notion of shame as a social event in the Adam and Eve narrative, see Ward, "Adam and Eve's Shame (and Ours)," 317.

good, but to move too quickly to this conclusion obscures humanity's interdependence for self-understanding that shame bespeaks. What is important for our purposes is not shame *per se*, but how the text directs us to what shame tells us about how the man and woman interrelate.

Christian ethics commentators usually focus on shame as a feeling or emotion. When Bonhoeffer attends to this to describe the man and woman's lack of shame, he articulates what shame expresses before explaining what the creatures do not feel. For Bonhoeffer, shame expresses "that we no longer accept the other," our "dividedness," and our discontent with the other.[84] The prelapsarian characters, therefore, did not experience this kind of relational division when they are said to have "felt no shame." In O'Donovan's discussion on shame in *Finding and Seeking*, he notes that shame is "a moment of painful self-discovery" that is not a "fully reflective moral self-awareness" but a "feeling" that "is largely instinctive."[85] He later remarks that "shame . . . establish[es] our existential position" as ones who have lost agency.[86] This is the sentiment driving Augustine in his *City of God* to lament the novelty of his insubordinate pudenda.[87] Yet, however accurate these descriptions are of the experience of shame, Bonhoeffer and O'Donovan do not inquire into shame's mechanism. One feels or does not feel shame, but what human facility enables such feelings? O'Donovan edges toward the facility when he speaks of shame as a "reaction" that can be "inflamed," but is sometimes "unresponsive" when it should be more so. He also states that shame results in "a bewildering attention to the self," but retreats in the next clause when he reflects that in shame, the self is "astonished by the inner contradiction of failed agency." The closest O'Donovan gets to identifying the facility that enables humanity to feel no shame, and to feel shame later, is when he states that "its concern is with the appearance."[88] If shame is concerned with the appearance, then it is concerned with being seen or recognized.

Roger Scruton picks up on this theme. Shame is a form of embarrassment, which is an individual emotion but one that is entirely *social* in structure. Whereas one can recover from embarrassment, shame is

---

84. Bonhoeffer, *Creation and Fall*, 3, 95. Bonhoeffer does explore a notion of sociality, but this is done expressly as a postlapsarian reality in Bonhoeffer, *Sanctorum Communio*. See ch. 3.

85. O'Donovan, *Finding*, 22.

86. O'Donovan, *Finding*, 23.

87. Augustine, *City of God*, xiv, ch. 15.

88. O'Donovan, *Finding*, 22.

terminal. Shame is a self-imposed metaphorical death sentence that is handed down when one is exposed; when one realizes that another knows the truth about oneself. Scruton references Massacio's fifteenth-century artistic depiction of Adam and Eve's expulsion from Eden to capture this *social structuring*. The painting illustrates the torment of shame as Adam covers his *eyes* with his hands while Eve attempts to cover her *body* with her hands. Shame involves the eyes and body, but paradoxically concerns a reflex that is responsive to the other as a mirror of the self. Adam and Eve surely experienced shame when the other looked at them in their bare state, but they experienced shame more deeply when they saw their selves through the other's eyes. Shame concerns self-perception rather than the other's mere perception. The primary issue is not the other's gaze, but *how* the other's gaze facilitates self-knowing. In the painting, Adam does not cover his eyes to avoid gazing at Eve, but to avoid looking at his naked self, while Eve covers her body not to avoid being seen by Adam, but so she can avoid looking at herself.[89] Shame, contra Augustine, is not the result of God's retribution for their rebellion that rendered the body insubordinate to the mind.[90] This would make the structure of shame a mere individual emotional response to a somewhat embarrassing situation of public exposure. Shame is closer to what David Vellemen describes as a negative *self*-assessment; seeing oneself as falling short of an ideal.[91] The desire to cover up, which the artist depicts in the painting, concerns privacy, which in terms of the creation narrative is a self-imposed isolation from the other. This is a return to a state of human

---

89. Scruton, *Sexual Desire*, 141.

90. Augustine, *City of God*, xiv, ch. 15.

91. Velleman, *Genesis of Shame*, 29. Velleman wrongly suggests, however, that the "knowledge" Adam and Eve gained by eating the fruit was privacy or chastity, which manifests in the originary creatures covering up and hiding from each other and God. Rather than obeying God and indulging sexually in each other as they were commanded, they resist each other and God's desire. This reading of the creation account makes little sense, first, because God provides them with longer-lasting coverings after their "private turn." Why would God participate in their sinful state of relating? God also brings them out of their hiding place and engages them in conversation. The second problematic aspect with Velleman's view is that his claim rests on an assumption that an item of sexual knowledge caused their fall rather than the rejection of God's word not to eat the fruit. As I will show in chapter 4, we must be careful not to equate sin and sex because where sex stands synecdochally for humanity's fall, sex is subtly installed as that which redeems humanity. This is seen in Velleman's conclusion in which he suggests we need to recover our shame and modesty, which is an embrace of private sex rather than God's word by faith.

existence that God has already described as "not good." Adam sees himself fallen in the eyes of Eve, and Eve in the eyes of Adam, and themselves in the eyes of God, which drives them to hide from each other and God.

Despite its undesirability, shame reveals the created originary intersubjective nature of humanity. Shame, therefore, can signify a realization that one is not the person one ought to be, but it reveals also that one finds oneself in inextricable relation to others.[92] This relation does not merely help us understand what it means to be human, but is the facility by which we come to experience our humanity. As Jean-Paul Sartre quips, "Shame is by nature *recognition*. I recognize that I *am* as the Other sees me."[93] But whereas for Sartre shame is the genesis of human relationality, I suggest shame in the beginning and presently points beyond itself to that which is an ineradicable feature of human creatureliness.[94] Shame is not ontological and therefore an inevitable human experience to be embraced, but parasitic, which also means that because shame is not something for which humanity is destined, it is something from which it can be saved.[95]

Humanity is created by God in such a way that the self is not known without the other. Graham Ward states that "it takes two to shame" and I would add that it takes two to not live in shame, which is another way of saying that shame (and not shame) "is intrapsychic."[96] Who the man perceives himself to be cannot be known apart from the woman's body *and* her gaze, and who the woman perceives herself to be cannot be known apart from the man's body *and* his gaze. Indeed, that they "felt no shame" only informs the reader secondarily that man and woman truly lived in paradise. One learns that they do not feel shame primarily because they are comfortably naked within the gaze of the other and God, and each person sees his or her self through the gaze of the other and God. In the first instance, this self-perception does not result in a feeling of

---

92. I am not suggesting that shame is synonymous with guilt or even the result of guilt. Shame in the creation narrative, however, is a result of guilt.

93. Sartre, *Being and Nothingness*, 246.

94. Sartre, *Being and Nothingness*, 312. Dolezal offers a rereading of Sartre's conception of originary shame that provokes one to think beyond shame to human bodily vulnerability and interdependence. This reveals that belonging is the driving force behind shame. Dolezal, "Shame, Vulnerability and Belonging."

95. For entry points into exploring how shame is reworked in the existential philosophical tradition, see Sedgwick, *Touching Feeling*, and Guenther, "Shame and the Temporality of Social Life."

96. Ward, "Adam and Eve's Shame (and Ours)," 312.

vulnerability—despite their state of vulnerability—that induces the impulsive feeling of being exposed and the need for privacy. Stone's suggestion that desire for the other could be a postlapsarian experience is undermined by the realization that God created the originary humans with a desire for recognition that the experience of shame or no shame signifies. The presence or absence of shame bespeaks a created human facility to see the self through eyes of the other.

Notice, however, that to experience oneself in the gaze of the other and to feel no shame even though one is naked is not a conscious realization that the man or woman makes. This dynamic describes an absence of awareness of this constitutive gaze. O'Donovan rightly observes that shame is not the result of self-awareness, and we can extend this observation to speak about the absence of shame. The presence or absence of shame is not (usually) realized through self-reflection or conscious deliberation. This is why the phrase "they felt no shame" can be said to reflect the goodness of God's creation. They were naked, and yet as they saw their own body through the eyes of the other, they were not threatened, but felt at peace with the other looking on. Where no facility exists to view the self through the other's eyes, the concept of shame, expressed first in Scripture as "no shame," is a redundant concept.

The point of this inquiry into the concept of shame is to note that human existence is obviously a bodily relation, which less obviously, cannot be divorced from the mind's eye, including the others' eyes. The implication is that one's account of oneself as embodied man or woman cannot be fully realized without the perceived gaze of the other *and* God. The man and the woman are equally subjectified by the other and God in that moment. They do not know their selves apart from how they see their naked body through the others' eyes. Butler is right to formulate a subject that dwells in inextricable relations in the world, in particular with people by whom one desires to be recognized in a particular way. Moreover, as we will see, Butler's notion of gender does not valorize the mind over matter or matter over mind, but attempts, however unconvincingly, to hold them together as one human reality. Shame concerns psychology and physiology; impacting how one feels and how one acts; altering self-worth and one's conduct. Shame not only reveals that the mind cannot be divorced from the body, but that my mind and body are tightly bound up with other minds and bodies.

The wonder of the primeval marriage in the originary moment is therefore a thing of beauty to behold. The man's song in 2:23 must not merely be read as a response to the arrival of another with whom he can keep the garden and procreate. The man rejoices at the arrival of the woman who "is bone of my bones, and flesh of my flesh," which bespeaks a unity so deep and "mysterious," drawing on the apostle Paul's estimation of their unity, that they are "one flesh."[97] The evident joy in this song over the *unity* of the man and woman does not merely give voice to the received physical functional unity that results in "filling the earth."[98] This undermines those views that fixate on sex (often under the pretext of procreation) as the controlling narrative of the creation account.[99] The man's song testifies to the rich unity and goodness of the humanity of man and woman as a deep and mysterious bodily *and* psychic relation.

This rich and complex unity is possible only after the man and woman "leave" their parents, which Brownson interprets literally.[100] He claims that leaving cannot mean departing one's parents for another geographical location because this was economically unsustainable within an agrarian culture. He favors instead an interpretation that sees the man and woman depart one kinship relation for a new one. What we see in the originary leaving and cleaving is not an act of sex, but the building of human community.[101] This reading avoids a hyper-sexualized creation narrative or at least a narrative driven by sex, which frees one to pursue an emphasis on God's desire to build a robust human community. Having said this, sex *and* procreation are a *part* of this new kinship relation. This is not an aspect of human embodiment that can be treated separately. In other words, they do not leave and cleave as mere humans, but as a man and a woman. Their characterization as one flesh is not reducible to sex but nor cannot it be divorced from sex. Their sexual union is not an

---

97. Gen 2:24; Eph 5:29–32.

98. Due to Augustine's aversion to problematic "lust" in marriage, we need to avoid a hasty assumptive conflation of desire, sex, and sin. Despite his reluctance, Augustine confesses that the world and the heavenly city must be populated, which requires Edenic sex. His account of the beginning shows that he did envisage desire in Eden, but this desire was passionless or "without shame of lust." In other words, even if there was no passionate sex, Augustine could conceive of the man and woman as possessing an originary "desire" for each other that resulted in procreation. This was a basic notion of desire in which the man and woman were shown to lack the world outside their selves (here the other) that they needed for new life. Augustine, *City of God*, xiv, 23–24.

99. Wenham, *Genesis 1–15*, 71.

100. Gen 2:24.

101. Brownson, *Bible, Gender, and Sexuality*, 33–34.

addendum nor a metaphor for what is "really" happening spiritually.[102] Disembodied and de-sexualized interpretations of the beginning are just as theologically deadening as conservative accounts that are hypersexual and have no place for the mind for thinking about embodiment as intersubjective. The man and woman are freed from the constitutive gaze of their parents when they cleave to each other. In the marriage of the man and woman, their bodies and minds are inextricably enmeshed physically and psychically in subjection to each other and God.

Beginning with a complex and dynamic originary scene of human embodiment does not foreclose complex and rigorous theological engagement about the body, gender, and sexuality but gives rise to it. My account of the beginning does not resort to either of the triple threats of hierarchy, biology, and procreation to safeguard the goodness of heterosexual sex and marriage now and in the future.[103] On their own these are inadequate for responding to powerful gender theories like Butler's because on their own they do not form a robust theological account of gender. They cannot account for the complex nature of embodied life. But notice also that my account does not seek to reinterpret the beginning with what Scripture subsequently reveals about the body, gender, and sexuality. We should not confuse the beginning with the middle and/or end, and we should avoid confusing the end and/or middle with the beginning.[104] In contrast to both approaches—conservative and revisionist—my approach seeks to account for the complexity of the beginning and the continuity and discontinuity it has with each subsequent age. This means that my interest is the unfolding nature of the canon and a canonical approach that when coupled with redemptive history riddles

---

102. Brownson, *Bible, Gender, and Sexuality*, 86–87. Brownson does eventually bring sex between the man and woman into the frame. When he does it takes the form of a dissection to distinguish the sexual act and their one flesh. This distance is unwarranted because one can affirm that their one flesh is by virtue of their sexual union without foreclosing other aspects that draw them together in unity.

103. Brownson, *Bible, Gender, and Sexuality*, 39–40.

104. I am pushing back against revisionist accounts that use the rest of Scripture to bar descriptive accounts of the beginning. For example, Brownson states: "The physical complementarity of the genders is nowhere else directly affirmed (or even addressed) in Scripture, and thus cannot be sustained as a comprehensive reading of the creation narratives themselves." The logic does not hold up because the first clause is not determinative for reading the creation accounts. Rather than rule out conservative readings of the beginning, the observed discontinuity should alert us to the need for a more nuanced account that takes seriously the observed difference. Brownson, *Bible, Gender, and Sexuality*, 39.

the themes of body, gender, and sexuality with time and therefore the human and divine acts that characterize that time.[105] It is for this reason that we must continue our investigation of embodiment by observing the impact of the man and woman's rebellion on their lives and the world.

Trouble

The revelation that gendered human embodiment is a mystical intersubjective and bodied union means that human gendered existence is not reducible to a simple observation of one's "bits 'n' bobs," that can be represented in a checklist or by an image. It is, rather, a complex and wonderful mystery that incorporates the other. The impact of the fall, however, introduces inexorable trouble into the fundamental pillars of embodiment that God created for flourishing human existence. The trouble introduced by the fall can be seen at the physical level, but just as importantly, can be seen at the level of intersubjectivity. If human embodiment is a complex mystery before the fall, then it stands to reason that the trouble besetting human embodiment after the fall is also complex and mysterious. The complexity of the current crisis concerning gender and sexuality issues in the church and society reflects the bodily and intersubjective fall of God's complex creation of embodied gendered existence.

One is alerted to this when, having disobeyed God's command by eating the fruit from the tree of the knowledge of good and evil,[106] the man and woman "see" their respective selves as naked. What is interesting for this investigation is that the intersubjective and bodily aspects of embodiment become troublingly obvious: they "see" their selves differently as the result of their "eyes" becoming open—the body and mind are caught up in this moment. They see the same thing as they did before—a naked body, but they "see" or understand it differently through the other's eyes. The first part of Genesis 3:7 reads: "Then the eyes of both of them were opened, and they knew that they were naked."

What follows in the narrative cannot be divorced from the prior exploration of reflexivity: the man and woman seek to hide their bodies. But from whom do they hide? In the first instance, they use fig leaves to hide from each other, and then they use the trees of the garden to hide

---

105. Brownson, *Bible, Gender, and Sexuality*, 50–52.
106. Gen 2:17.

their bodies from God.[107] The exposing question comes in 3:11 when God asks: "Who told you that you were naked?" The man and woman do not answer this question because no one *told* them they were naked—their shame was *felt*. Previously, nobody needed to inform the man and woman that "they felt no shame,"[108] and nobody told them they now feel shame. One experiences or feels shame, which is to say that shame is an impulse that reflects an internal state of perceiving the self through the eyes of the other as naked.

Despite their existence as good and wonderful, their experience of their body is now plagued by perverted sight. With the integrity of the man and woman's respective bodies and minds in jeopardy, their given capacity to live as flourishing creatures, or live as the good creation they were made to be, is stripped from them. From that moment, the new humanity of man and woman exists as God's good and wonderful creation, but their capacity to live as that creation is thwarted by their newly fallen state. Their bodies and minds are plagued by disorder and death. *They are now good, yet troubled.*

If we conceive of God's creation of man and woman as pre-relational entities, like O'Donovan and Stone, then one is able to evade the full impact of the fall on gendered existence. If, however, God's creation of humanity as man and woman is a mysterious complex of entwined intersubjective and bodily existence *and* fallen, then a Christian theology of gender must appropriately reflect this. One cannot endorse theological accounts of gender that are represented by two-dimensional images or three-dimensional static figurines. Nor can one accept a concept of gender that denies the physical body as good. Viewing God's creation of humanity as profoundly complex contests overly socialized notions of the body that reduces one's body to mind, whether one's own or society's. This stance also rejects simplistic creation accounts of gender that are reduced to a basic image, or accounts that do not give full attention to the complex notion of intersubjectivity. A Christian theology of gender must consider intersubjectivity as an aspect of good embodiment, and by taking into consideration the impact of the fall on both the body and the mind, must reflect that human life is deeply and necessarily problematized. This means that whatever Butler is doing in her gender theory, she

---

107. Gen 3:7–8.
108. Gen 2:25.

is not problematizing, troubling, or undoing gender because human lives are already and ineradicably problematized, troubled, and undone.

Yet, even after the fall, the embodied human cannot escape its God-given good body and socialized orientation, which means that what God created good is constantly under threat of being co-opted for humanity's own desires. The marred description of the judged originary marriage is indicative, in which the man will "rule" her and she will "desire" him.[109] The body and the mind are jeopardized, which leads to a deeply problematic situation where fallen minds re-narrate problematic bodies according to disordered desires. It is for this reason that the two guiding observations that structure this section are crucial for a theology of gender. The first allows us to hold onto embodied existence as good regardless of one's experience of it, and the second observation prompts us to be suspicious of the subjective experience of embodiment. To find ourselves in time as God's creation and impacted by the fall should induce a measure of humility concerning what I claim of myself and how I speak to you and about you. Gender is troubled, and Christian theology of gender ought to reflect how this is the case and what this means for thinking about the self as gendered and sexual now.

Desiring to Be What I Am Not

The Teacher Called Desire

Butler observes that when we seek to give an account of human desire, we learn that we are characterized by lack (the condition of desiring the world for life) and loss (the condition predicated on a belief that we do not desire as we did originally). While mundane experiences of desire teach us about our lack and thus our need of the world for life, it is a pursuit of desire's lost object that orients us to the distant past. There are significant points at which an explicitly Christian account of gender must depart from Butler's thought. However, it is important not to overlook Butler's attempt to think about how loss and lack structure the human subject, and what kind of theological reflection on gender this might precipitate.

When the apostle Paul reflects on his own desire, he gives an account of himself that is characterized by bafflement and final incoherence. Paul's words in Romans 7:24 are revealing: "Wretched man that

---

109. Gen 3:16.

I am!" conclude his reflection.[110] We read in the biblical text that Paul desires his personal behavior to be different to the way he observes his everyday actions. The incongruence between what Paul wants to do and how he acts finds its full force when we learn that he does "not understand" and "hates" what he does.[111] Paul's life is characterized by an undesired existential discord, which, when self-observed, reveals a state of seeming unquenchable misery; an abiding hope for the redemption of the body that brings his existence, and his desires, into full harmony with God's existence and desires.

A similar account of the experience of the self is described in explicit detail in Augustine's *Confessions*, in which desire functions pedagogically as it does in Paul's account. Augustine personifies his desire: it has its own "voice" and "speaks." Augustine "listens" to the pedagogue, which seeks to convince him of the need to be satiated. In these moments, Augustine learns about himself, namely his need for that which he does not have and which he thinks he needs to be complete. Of the thirteen books that constitute the *Confessions*, the first eight recount Augustine's youth and pre-conversion as he fought King Solomon's allegorical "bold woman" who sat outside inviting him in to "eat bread in secret, and drink sweet, stolen water."[112] Like Paul's account, what troubled Augustine and brought him grief was that he "knew nothing else" except an experience of the self that was utterly characterized by desire-induced incoherence.[113] He could not escape the seduction of the woman because he lived in his "carnal eyes."[114] Augustine was subject to his desires to the extent that when the woman confronted him he did what he did not want to do. Thus, with regard to overcoming his "sickness," Augustine confesses: "I would almost achieve it, but then fall just short. . . . Then I would make a fresh attempt, and now I was almost there, almost there. . . . I was touching the goal, grasping it

---

110. I understand that interpretation of "I" in Romans 7 is heavily contested. Throughout this book I interpret "I" to be referencing Paul, and thus representative of the "anthropological condition" of each Christian believer. This view rests on the recent commanding study in Timmins, *Romans 7 and Christian Identity*.

111. Rom 7:15.

112. Augustine, *Confessions*, 3.6.11. This is a direct reference to Prov 9:17.

113. Augustine, *Confessions*. 3.6.11. I am taking Augustine's use of "I" in Romans 7 to denote one under law and not grace as he himself did at the time. For a brief summary of how Augustine's view of the "I" in Romans 7 changes from signifying life before grace and under law, to signifying life under grace, see Bounds, "Augustine's Interpretation of Romans 7:14–25," 20–21.

114. Augustine, *Confessions*, 3.6.11.

... and then I was not there, not touching it, not grasping it."[115] Augustine desired to overcome desire, but found himself submitting to it. He, like Paul, did what he did not want to do.[116] In this moment, Augustine "shrank from dying to death and living to life."[117]

The gravity of this condition is seen when Augustine explains that when he was not enjoying the "foul deeds," or the "disgraceful exploits," the memories taunted him, "plucking softly at [his] garment of flesh and murmuring in [his] ear, 'Do you mean to get rid of us?'" They later compounded his confliction: "Do you imagine that you could live without these things?" Even when he had the truth in sight, he still heard the voice of desire, albeit only "less than half as loud," as it "muttered behind his back and slyly tweaked [him] as [he] walked away, trying to make [him] look back."[118] For Augustine, desire's *voice* is inescapable and irrepressible, as it is for Paul and Butler, and indeed all humanity.

This inescapable reality of desire is made further complex when one considers the question of the origin of the voice. Eventually, Augustine came to think of this voice not as the personification of evil, a person indwelling the self from outside and able to be expelled from his body like the dressage horse's rider. For he came to believe that "evil has no being."[119] This is an important observation because with it he comprehends the thoroughness and complexity of the subject's embodied subjection to desire. In some sense, desire's voice was indexed to what was exterior to Augustine's self, reflexively impinging on his inner being, but as something without the status of being.[120] This realization enabled him to say "I was at odds with myself."[121]

There is moral valence accorded to being "in love with loving," but where no object is referenced and loving lacks qualification, the moral valence awaits determination. Augustine informs his reader that he does not possess a passionate desire for the other's good, but for "loving"—the gratification of desire. In the case of Augustine, the object of his love is

---

115. Augustine, *Confessions*, 8.11.25.
116. Rom 7:15.
117. Augustine, *Confessions*, 8.11.25.
118. Augustine, *Confessions*, 8.11.26.
119. Augustine, *Confessions*, 7.13.19.
120. Here, I am referring to Augustine's rejection of Manichaeism.
121. Augustine, *Confessions*, 8.10.22.

clear: it is the self.[122] Love, and how love manifests, may be directed to an appropriate or inappropriate object. For Augustine, at that moment the object of his desire was not God, for he was "relishing the freedom of a runaway slave."[123] In this moment of enslavement, desire's pedagogical function manifests repeatedly in *Confessions* revealing to Augustine that desire was not an evil person to be evicted, but "one soul, thrown into turmoil by divergent impulses."[124] Stated more emphatically, "The soul is torn apart in distress,"[125] and later, "All this argument in my heart rages between myself and myself."[126] Augustine's love for loving "split" or "undoes" him because, like Paul, he does what he does not want to do.

But one is split or undone only where an originary scene is incommensurate with one's mundane desire. Butler's often quoted, though rarely explicated, text from *Undoing Gender* presents an interesting point of intersection:

> Let's face it. We're undone by each other. And if we're not, we're missing something. If this seems so clearly the case with grief, it is only because it was already the case with desire. One does not always stay intact. It may be that one wants to, or does, but it may also be that despite one's best efforts, one is undone, in the face of the other, by the touch, by the scent, by the feel, by the prospect of the touch, by the memory of the feel. And so when we speak about *my* sexuality or *my* gender, as we do (and as we must) we mean something complicated by it.[127]

It is true that when we lose someone, we can experience grief in ways that lead to unanticipated personal responses. But accepting loss can prove transformational, which, likewise, is unable to be chartered before it happens. Accepting the loss of someone, Butler counsels, is challenging because the loss arrives in waves that can hinder progress, crafting an exhausting and seemingly directionless trajectory to the newly transformed self. At this point in the process, Butler makes the startling confession that here "one finds oneself fallen."[128] A person has fallen from

---

122. O'Donovan, *Problem of Self-Love*.
123. Augustine, *Confessions*, 3.3.5.
124. Augustine, *Confessions*, 8.10.23.
125. Augustine, *Confessions*, 8.10.24.
126. Augustine, *Confessions*, 8.11.27.
127. Butler, *UG*, 19.
128. Butler, *UG*, 18.

the high heights of coherence into a state where "we are not the masters of ourselves," we are undone.[129]

The passage, however, uses grief as an entry point to reflect on how desire functions in a similar manner. Whereas grief indicates loss and thus one's undoing having fallen into incoherence without the one who is lost, desire signals a similar fall and inability of self-mastery due to one's lack. I might assume desire operates according to my will, but Butler, Paul, and now Augustine show that desire has a different master. The thing that is desirable (i.e., the face, scent, touch, feel, memory, etc.) seizes me despite my attempts to resist it. My gender and my sexuality, Butler is suggesting, are not things that I am and master—uncomplicated things—but complicated modes of being in life that are fallen and foiled, and that, despite my best attempts, are beyond my reach to possess as I desire. My sexuality and my gender, therefore, are not my own, but are in the hands of the other, over whom I have no mastery, and on whom I rely to be recognized as gendered and sexual. Having *lost* the originary object of my desire, and *lacking* the world outside of me that I need for life, I find myself fallen, exhausted, and in unchartered waters, yet, in Butler's own words, cognizant that "something is larger than one's own deliberate plan or project, larger that one's own knowing."[130] In this way a Christian theology affirms with Butler, "we're missing something" if we are not undone by desire.[131]

Desire teaches us that we need the world for life, but it also teaches us that we are at a loss as to where to go or what to do about it. The irony of Butler's account is that she speaks of loss and the need to confess loss in order to be transformed by it, yet according to her account she cannot because she cannot access the beginning to know who or what was lost, or even if something was lost. The suggestion of this book is that God, the creator, is the one humanity has lost, and by continuing to refuse to confess this forecloses any possibility of personal transformation. Butler's account of desire-induced incoherence is a secular counterpart to that of Paul and Augustine's experiences and narrations of uncontrollable, aimless desires that induce wretchedness. One significant difference is that Paul and Augustine live with the hope that this is not their destiny.[132]

129. Butler, *UG*, 18.
130. Butler, *UG*, 18.
131. Butler, *UG*, 19.

132. Butler actively resists a religious notion of hope being read into her work. In response to a question offered after she presented the Sigmund Freud Lecture in

Originary Loss

In W. H. Auden's 1948 Pulitzer Prize winning long poem, *The Age of Anxiety*, Auden uses stunning poetry and prose to elucidate his body of death and the wretchedness that is quintessential to the embodied life that desires. Despite his Christian predilections, under the influence of Kierkegaard, and in opposition to Hegel, Auden crafts the subject's synthesis or final realization of self-certainty as remaining aloof.[133] Instead of narrating one's path to coherence, Auden's non-synthetic description of human existence answers two questions implicit in the title: What is the "Age" and what is the "Anxiety" characterizing that age? Auden's answers to these questions constitute the long poem, which is an exploration of the wretchedly embodied human subject. The poem gives voice to the embodied existence of desire, lack, and loss that is evident in Paul and Augustine's confessions, as well as providing a theological entry point into thinking about hope within gender and sexuality as troubled embodied existence.

It is not immediately evident, even when one has finished reading the poem, what "Age" Auden believes is characterized by anxiety. Jacques Barzun, who was a cultural critic at the time the poem was published, noted in his glowing review in *Harper's* magazine that "the very title roots it in our generation," which was the post-World War II generation.[134] Read in this way, the poem functions as a piercing cultural analysis of the time. But Alan Jacobs observes that those who understood the poem to be depicting a cultural moment, generally struggled to find a clear sociological phenomenon corresponding to the anxiety of that age in the poem.[135]

Vienna in 2014, she says: "He is definitely, definitely with me as I am thinking that through—Levinas. . . . But I don't know if it has to stay within the bounds of religion. It doesn't bother me if it has origins in religion, but it may wander outside this sphere of religion. [ehm] You know it's Kafka. I am closer to Kafka than Levinas, and Kafka says: There is hope infinite hope unfortunately not for us." Butler, cited in Riedl, *Judith Butler and Theology*, x.

133. The subject in the poem comprises four characters who collectively form one self. This collective person is derived from Carl Gustav Jung's *Psychologische Typen*, in which Jung explores Intuition, Feeling, Sensation, and Thought as psychological types. Auden viewed himself as "a Thinking-Intuitive type." Mendelson, *Later Auden*, 165.

134. Barzun, "Workers in Monument Brass." This review is mentioned by Jacobs in the introduction to Auden, *Age of Anxiety*, xli.

135. Jacobs, introduction to Auden, *Age of Anxiety*, xii.

In his commentary on the poem, John Fuller notes that Auden frames the barroom dialogue as occurring on "the night of All Souls," but this does not spur him to make a more theologically informed reading of the poem.[136] He reasons that Auden judges the *spiritual* subservient to the *psychological* (referring to Jung's psychological types).[137] All Souls is the day in the church calendar set aside to reflect on the universal judgment of all sinners, which in the poem, Fuller reads as describing the event of World War II that had purged the world of evil: the world had been judged, but not consumed.[138] But this interpretation of "All Souls night" does not take into account the rest of the prologue, in which the words are situated. In the third paragraph before the four characters are introduced, and before we learn what day it is, we come across the term "anxious." Auden pens these words:

> But in war-time, when everybody is reduced to the *anxious* status of a shady character or a displaced person, when even the most prudent become worshippers of chance, and when in comparison to the universal disorder of the world outside, his Bohemia seems as cosy and respectable as a suburban villa, he can count on making his fortune.[139]

Anxiety refers to a state of being, which takes on specific meaning when we learn about Auden's personal life. When Auden wrote this poem, he was a confessing Christian,[140] and had begun to reflect deeply on his homosexuality.[141] His reflection on love, broadly speaking, is set against the backdrop of his separation from the man he loved, Chester Kallman, who refused to commit to a monogamous sexual relationship with Auden, despite Auden viewing his homosexuality as sinful.[142] In light of this biographical information, the above passage is theologically instructive. A brief exegetical inquiry demonstrates, firstly, the value of this poem for our theological inquiry, and secondly, the context for

---

136. Fuller, *W. H. Auden*, 6.

137. Fuller, *W. H. Auden*, 373.

138. Fuller, *W. H. Auden*, 370–71.

139. Auden, *Age of Anxiety*, 3 (emphasis mine).

140. In October 1940, Auden reaffirmed his faith at St. Mark's Episcopal Church in New York. Kirsch, *Auden and Christianity*, 21.

141. Jacobs, *What Became of Wystan*, xvi–xvii.

142. Isherwood, *Christopher and His Kind*, 346; Jacobs, *What Became of Wystan*, particularly ch. 5; and Mendelson, *Later Auden*, 148–204.

inquiring theologically about lack and loss in Auden's reflection on his own desire-induced incoherence.

In the passage above, the term "anxious" is expressed in such a way that it cannot be confused with a passing emotion or fleeting sensation. Anxiety is a "status" that no one escapes, that is, "everybody" experiences life as such. Whatever anxiety is, for Auden, it is an inescapable human reality, a feature defining every human within a world characterized by "universal disorder." Moreover, the anxious one is "shady" *or* "displaced," which could bring two subjects into view, or one subject who is the perpetrator *and* victim having been "reduced" to a life of inner conflict. This unwholesome character has fallen from the height of reputability and order into a situation described sardonically as "cosy." The disorder associated with the cultural playground "Bohemia" has become "respectable as a suburban villa"—normativized—rather than being seen for what it is: a place of chaos or as Mikhail Bulgakov pens in *Master and Margarita*, "In a word, hell."[143] Finally, one notes that this describes an epoch or *age* that within the passage is "war-time."

Through exegesis of the poem, and the possibility of a theological allusion in mind, the age and anxiety in *The Age of Anxiety* becomes evident. The age is that time in which we live—the *postlapsarian* age—which bears the marks of having been "reduced" and "displaced" from Eden, represented in the poem as Arcadia, the place to which the four characters are seeking to return. Nonetheless, however disordered and dislocated from the original location one might be, the place one finds oneself, from Auden's perspective, has become harrowingly accepted as respectable despite the war raging around it. Auden masterfully describes the world in which humanity suffers. The *age* of anxiety Auden explores and articulates in the poem then, is a limited, bound, particular bodily existence lived outside of Eden. The poem describes a journey back to Eden that failed, thwarted by one's sinful or *anxious* existence.

Jacobs interprets the poem in a similar way, but from extra-textual evidence. Concerning the term *anxiety* in the title, Jacobs concludes that it is "a moral and spiritual predicament."[144] He arrives at this interpretation after observing a review by Auden in 1941 of Reinhold Niebuhr's *The Nature and Destiny of Man*. Jacobs observes:

---

143. Bulgakov, *Master and Margarita*, 76. I am grateful for Michael Morelli for pointing me to this text.

144. Jacobs, in Auden, *Age of Anxiety*, xxxi.

> Auden had written of "the temptation to sin, [which] is what the psychologist calls anxiety, and the Christian calls lack of faith." At this point the characters experience a reinterpretation of their own condition: what had been named psychologically as "anxiety" comes home as a moral and spiritual predicament, "the temptation to sin."[145]

Jacobs mistakenly creates a false dichotomy between spiritual and psychological, where Auden is seeking to use the psychological types of Jung as a means of "getting to" a theological explanation of human reality as spiritual. Biographically speaking, we know Auden found himself in existential angst, similar to that experienced by Paul and Augustine. However, the terms he uses to describe the existential angst do not correspond one to one with how the ancients' predicament is described. Anxiety could be synonymous with wretchedness or incoherence, and temptation to sin would represent desire adequately, but Auden makes anxiety and temptation to sin synonymous. This shows that the difference between the account given by Paul and Augustine and that given by Auden is that *The Age of Anxiety* is not describing a form of confliction that entraps by acting on desires, but depicts being entrapped *by desire itself*. Paul does what he does not want to do, and Augustine "knew nothing else" but loving to love. Auden's anxiety is more fundamental: he desires not to desire.

The *Age of Anxiety*, then, does not narrate *humanity's* quest to overcome desire, but is a *personal* inquiry and quest to understand and come to terms with the reality of one's own desire. This offers additional information for consideration. It is well known that Auden's experience of same-sex attraction was lifelong, which to invoke Augustine's reflection, means that Auden too loves loving. So Auden is not so different from Augustine in that he was also entranced by the "bold woman" who sat outside inviting him in to "eat bread in secret, and drink sweet, stolen water."[146] But while this metaphorically describes Auden's basic troubled experience of desire, it does not accurately represent Auden's experience. The particular nature of the predicament Auden brings to light is that, whereas Augustine did not deem his desire to be wrongly ordered, but wrongly directed, Auden describes his desire as both wrongly ordered and wrongly directed. That is, Auden did not desire a "bold woman," but a bold man. Auden's anxiety was temptation to sin, but he desired not

---

145. Auden, *Age of Anxiety*, xxxi.
146. Augustine, *Confessions*, 3.6.11.

to desire a man. This desire to not desire testifies to his dissatisfaction with how "Bohemia" had become or threatened to become "cosy" and "respectable"—normal—which caused him grief. The temptation to sin was to live in anxiety, which, as Jacobs observes in Auden, was not only a moral predicament, but also a spiritual predicament.

The *Age of Anxiety* depicts the fallen era in which bodies of death figure prominently. Auden's depiction of his own desire in this age is not only a material or psychological reality, but also spiritual reality. Auden's recognition of the raging war and Bohemia as an orderly neighborhood demonstrates theological awareness of the problematic nature of this age, which is realized in his own life of desire—the normativization of desire as the epistemological ground for moral discernment.

Who Will Rescue Me?

While Butler does not desire to be rescued from her body of death, which is her desire-induced incoherent self, Auden does. This difference identifies the gulf separating what Butler offers in her gender theory, and what Christianity confesses (1) in acknowledging the desire to "overcome" mundane desire (2) through faith in one from the outside who is personally encountered. Paul is clear that his desire to be rescued from the body of death is futile when it takes the form of rescuing oneself. The ineradicable truth that humans are stuck in the world in their anxiety and incoherence, and that salvation comes from outside the self, is the irreducible point of the poem.

In "Part Three: The Seven Stages," the four characters begin their quest for "a common goal,"[147] "our common hope,"[148] which is summarized in prose as a search for "that state of prehistoric happiness, which, by human beings, can only be imagined in terms of landscape bearing a symbolic resemblance to the human body."[149] The subject goes on a journey to find happiness by escaping its own body, which results in despair once one realizes that the body is the finite and limited reality of human existence.

The four characters begin their journey in darkness, poignantly, walking alone, having lost their way. They subsequently meet up and

---

147. Auden, *Age of Anxiety*, 57.
148. Auden, *Age of Anxiety*, 52.
149. Auden, *Age of Anxiety*, 46.

travel together, and at other times break off and walk alone through forests, valleys, up mountains, and into towns, but they are hindered in their quest by being rendered hopelessly (in spite of their hope) "obedient to their own mysterious laws of direction."[150] Their obedience is determinant—they could not resist seeking out Arcadia for personal happiness, that is, they have a proclivity[151] to overcome desire. However, despite acting on impulse and searching in all directions for Arcadia, their tireless trekking is futile. They find themselves in "reunion at the forest's edge."[152] They do not enjoy what is before them, but "stare at what they see."[153] This is the beginning of the end of their journey where "for the first time fear and doubt dismay them."[154]

The reality of their predicament is unearthed as they begin to doubt ever escaping the landscape that is the body. The body signals existence in this "age" as the limit of possibility and the reality of condemnation. The spiritual, rather than the mere moral dilemma, is outlined and confronts the characters: "Is triumph possible? If so, are they chosen? Is triumph worth it? If so, are they worthy?"[155] This raft of questions probes the means of escape from the body of desire, and the answers seem wracked with despair: "their fears are confirmed, their hopes denied."[156] It did not matter how hard they tried, or how far they traveled, or what they did, they stood condemned in the landscape that was the body. As the characters stood looking out over Arcadia questioning how one could enter, Auden's realization is like that of Augustine, who, at the end of book 7 of *Confessions*, seizes on the writings of the apostle Paul and asks, "What is a human wretch to do? Who will free him from this death-laden body?"[157]

Auden then seeks to describe the existential human condition theologically. Quant's mundane observation of the back garden is theologically rich: "God's in his greenhouse, his geese in the world."[158] The force of this observation is not merely that the geese are alienated from God, but that the geese are "his"; the geese, as God's possession, remain in the

---

150. Auden, *Age of Anxiety*, 74.
151. Perhaps "natural instinct," but I'm cautious about using the term natural.
152. Auden, *Age of Anxiety*, 74.
153. Auden, *Age of Anxiety*, 74.
154. Auden, *Age of Anxiety*, 75.
155. Auden, *Age of Anxiety*, 75.
156. Auden, *Age of Anxiety*, 78.
157. Augustine, *Confessions*, 7.21.27.
158. Auden, *Age of Anxiety*, 80.

world estranged from *him* who dwells in the shelter, warmth, and light of the greenhouse. This is a watershed moment in the poem because as the geese, so to speak, come within reach of the greenhouse, the depth of their predicament is revealed:

> For the world from which their journey has been one long flight rises up before them now as if the whole time it had been hiding in ambush, only waiting for the worst moment to reappear to its fugitives in all the majesty of its perpetual fury.[159]

The subject is an alienated fugitive that cannot escape. *The Age of Anxiety* describes the self, trying to escape the world, which, in light of Auden's same-sex attraction, can be otherwise narrated as trying to overcome the wretched body of desire. It has already been shown that Augustine thought of his own life as a journey that was a failed escape despite becoming tantalizingly close to the desired destination. Again, toward the end of book 7, he describes the possibility of the scenario remaining tragic, which finds strong terminological and thematic echoes in Auden's account above:

> It is one thing to survey our peaceful homeland from a wooded height but fail to find the way there, and make vain attempts to travel through impassable terrain, while fugitive deserters marshalled by the lion and the dragon obstruct and lurk in ambush.[160]

Auden's own fugitive subject closes in on Arcadia, the place where the subject desires to dwell in peace with God, only for the world to rear up and close in on the subject like a tidal wave of embodied reality, swamping the subject in darkness. The journey-goers set off in darkness and they end in darkness: "They woke up and *recognized where they sat and who they were*. The darkness which had invaded their dream was explained, for it was closing time and the bartender was turning off the lights."[161] For Auden to recognize that one dwells in darkness is to realize that one is stranded *in* the age of anxiety *outside* the "greenhouse" where God dwells. Auden's desires teach of his need that he is in lack and in need of something outside of himself for life. But by tracing his desire, he realizes that his life is wretched because he has suffered significant loss.

---

159. Auden, *Age of Anxiety*, 78.
160. Augustine, *Confessions*, 7.21.27.
161. Auden, *Age of Anxiety*, 81 (emphasis mine).

Auden is clear that one does not know *where* one is or *who* one is until one comes to terms with this age and the anxiety that wracks it due to its loss. The theological interpretation given here argues that for Auden, Arcadia represents *the coherent body*; an existence in which one desires out of lack but not loss. As one *outside* Arcadia, the body of desire suffers wretchedness, which must be overcome, but which in the end we cannot accomplish on our own.

Comparing Auden and Butler's desires reveals how they handle their respective incoherence. First, both Auden and Butler have the same(-sex) desire, and both experience their desire as transgressive according to the originary humans. Secondly, while Auden desires to overcome his sexual desire to be coherent, Butler desires to be coherent without overcoming her sexual desire, even if she thinks it is impossible in the end. Their subsequent move is telling: Auden acknowledges that the beginning is unable to be entered, which means that for him the beginning offers no hope in overcoming his desire. Butler, on the other hand, like Stone, enters the beginning to change the originary law to overcome that which makes them incoherent. However, this description of Butler and Stone is not entirely accurate because both do not enter the originary moment: how can they? The origin exists in another time and place, out of reach and out of sight. In fact, both respect the otherness of the originary moment as Auden does. But as Butler and Stone make clear, and as Auden depicts in the poem, the world offers little hope, which explains Butler and Stone's persistence in tampering with the beginning, despite its inaccessibility.

Turning back to Scripture, Paul's exclamation, "Wretched man that I am! Who will rescue me from this body of death?" does not seek to treat incoherence by re-forming the law that brings to light his desire as transgressive. From a personal point of view, Paul's voice is characteristic of the Christian's plea while standing at the edge of Arcadia being swamped by one's own reality having traveled through the symbolic landscape of the body. Bound by the body, we longingly gaze out at Arcadia, and together we recognize where we sit and who we are, our fears are confirmed, and our hopes are denied. This situation is the reality of the earlier picture of God in his greenhouse, while his geese are in the world. While it may be a quaint picture, its reality is one of dislocation and condemnation. To recognize that one is in the world is to recognize that each human is constituted as a body of death, dislocated from God, and in need of being rescued from it.

At the beginning of this inquiry into *The Age of Anxiety*, I investigated how in the prologue Auden framed the poem theologically with the terms "age" and "anxiety." It was shown there that the age and anxiety referenced this war-torn postlapsarian age and the anxiety of living in this age as desiring subjects, prone to temptation to sin. We saw in "Part Three: The Seven Stages" of the poem the four characters' vain attempt to reach Arcadia, and their eventual cognizance of their condemned embodied status. While I have not explored "Part Four: The Dirge," the shortest chapter in the poem, Auden portrays the characters bemoaning their confined and limited place in the world. Then in "Part Five: The Masque," two of the characters engage in a mock wedding. What is interesting is that before the wedding begins, the narrator describes the value of the events to unfold thus: "In times of war even the crudest kind of positive affection between persons seems extraordinarily beautiful, a noble symbol of the peace and forgiveness of which the world stands so desperately in need."[162] Here the condemned embodied subject in the poem is given hope, but it does not come through an appeal to one's own work or initiative. This possibility was thwarted when, at the border of Arcadia, the wayfarers pondered how they would enter, but realized there was no way by virtue of their own capacities. Auden recognized what Augustine described as "the difference between presumption and confession." Augustine argues: presumption sees "the goal but not the way to it," whereas the one who confesses, sees the goal and "the Way to our beatific homeland, a homeland to be not merely descried but lived in."[163]

Despite Auden's same-sex attraction, which he did not desire, he narrates the possibility of his own redemption being through marriage. The marriage he depicts in the poem is an earthly marriage between one woman and one man (Rosetta and Emble), but the marriage that brings peace and forgiveness is not that earthly marriage. The earthly marriage of Rosetta and Emble is a "noble symbol" that illustrates the means by which "peace and forgiveness" are realized. Marriage is not a form of self-re-creation, nor does it equate to entering into Arcadia and eating from the "tree of life."[164] For Auden, marriage is redemptive because it requires an encounter with an-other body. While the other with whom one is united and who brings peace and forgiveness remains at that stage

---

162. Auden, *Age of Anxiety*, 88.
163. Augustine, *Confessions*, 7.20.26.
164. Gen 3:24.

unnamed, Auden communicates that this encounter provides what one desires—to be rescued from the body of death.

Conclusion

Our first attempt to reflect theologically on Butler's queer gender theory has proved fruitful. The first highlighted question concerning the relationship between the beginning (originary) and the present (mundane) has prompted us to see the radical discontinuity between Adam and Eve in Eden and how we experience ourselves today. Moreover, we have been challenged to account for the view that Adam and Eve are a beautiful vision of God's humanity, but one that is out of reach, that we cannot inhabit or access. The originary humanity functions in the present as a perfect image that highlights our loss and lack, and thus our desire for completion. *Adam and Eve reveal our desire-induced incoherence and need for life apart from them.*

The second point that was raised for theological reflection concerned the origin of the originary images. Like Butler, I presented a literal reading of the beginning that is foundational for conceiving gender and sexuality in the present. My reading, however, diverges from Butler's (and Stone's) who considers the originary scene to be a description of a human idea rather than a narration of divine creation. Despite being in agreement with Butler that we cannot access the beginning, she enters the beginning to observe the way in which bodies come into existence. Butler's (re)creation myth seeks to justify as good, bodies that are not presently justified, which stands in contrast to my reading of Scripture's accounts of human origins and Auden's autobiographical account in which not only some but *everyone stands outside of Eden in need of being saved from our desire-induced incoherence.*

The final point of inquiry that Butler's theory prompted thus far concerned the extent to which embodiment is limited to materiality. We have seen that Adam and Eve were created with the capacity to "see." This notion of perception was demonstrated by looking at how God created the man and woman for each other, which was a material relation but one that could not be divorced from another relation that was mysteriously intersubjective. We came to see that their bodies were re-narrated in light of the fall such that they needed to cover them from each other and God. In this moment we see that *gender and sexuality are not simple material realities* that are easily observed, but modes of perceived existence in time as matter that are (in)formed by the other's constitutive gaze.

As we look forward to the next phase of Butler's theory, we are well positioned to consider the ethical implications of Butler's desire for a "certain departure from the human."[165] This is a deeper inquiry into the unjust use of the beginning to justify some (often ourselves) in their bodies, while giving just cause to use force to discipline others to manifest Edenic lives in the present.

---

165. Butler, *UG*, 3–4.

Chapter 3

Diagnosing Gender Violence

Introduction

It is common for people to experience hurt from violent acts even though the acts themselves are not understood as such. Slavery is perhaps the most obvious example. It was a legal and widely accepted practice in many societies, yet over time we have come to see that slavery was and is a gross manifestation of cruelty driven mostly by greed. We can reflect similarly on how we discipline children in schools today. No longer do we see the leather strap or cane as an appropriate means of correcting behavior. In retrospect, our experience of hurt at the hands of a frustrated teacher or principal is now deemed a violent act and worthy of its own discipline. Simply because an act is not deemed violent does not mean it isn't.[1]

Where violence escapes a formal diagnosis, the burden of reclassifying an act as violent usually requires a tremendous shift in understanding in society. This shift is often a costly and time-consuming exercise. Reflect further on what was (and continues to be) needed to purge Western society of slavery and racial prejudice. Whether our mind goes to the US civil war, the Holocaust, or legal reform in Australia to recognize its original landowners, reforming how we *think* about people and the way we *treat* them is slow and costly work. Violence in society is often concealed as

---

1. The point I am making is not that gender and slavery are analogous forms of cultural oppression. My intention is more basic: to draw on slavery to show the difficulty of moving society to recognize what is not considered violence to be violence.

normal life, which not only requires a critical eye to identify but also humility to recognize where we have been complicit in implementing it. We catch a glimpse here of the greatest threat to social movements that seek to reclassify nonviolent acts as violence, namely, ourselves, as we seek to preserve our innocence in the face of guilt, whether personal or collective. The possibility of gender violence in society and the church faces this complex dynamic of concealment through processes of normalization and the pressure of vested interests, not least our own.

Butler's gender theory is founded on a notion of subjectivity that functions as a critique of gender violence. Whereas nineteenth- and twentieth-century feminist movements pressed for a different shape for society, one of legal and social inclusion of women, Butler desired to impact society at a different point: its *foundation*. Her focus on the beginning reveals that gender violence is a mundane event but one that is grounded in the beginning or at the originary scene. The slavery parallel is again helpful. A society can formulate laws to make slavery illegal and make policies to rule out racism, but lingering racist attitudes betray a problem that lies much deeper in our "hearts." Similarly, Butler sees the formulation of laws and policies as not dealing with the real issue. Gender violence was not merely a social structural issue, but one that ran much deeper in society's foundations. Observing hurt is one thing, diagnosing it as an effect of gender violence is another, while locating its origin is the ultimate goal. Butler seeks to show that treating mundane gender violence requires a much more radical interrogation of the originary man and woman that establishes and justifies the hurt inflicted by mundane violence.

Observing Normative Violence

Treating the Weapon, Not the Wound

Violence is central conceptually to Butler's thinking about gender, but this manifests late in Butler's writing, sometimes retrospectively. For example, it is toward the end of *Undoing Gender* that Butler explains that she "would like to consider this theory of gender explicitly in terms of the questions of violence."[2] More striking in this regard is Butler's retrospective reflection on violence in her 1999 preface to *Gender Trouble*, nearly

---

2. Butler, *UG*, 207.

a decade after its first publication. In this reflection Butler describes how she "grew up understanding something of the violence of gender norms."[3] This included having "an uncle incarcerated for his anatomically anomalous body," as well as watching "gay cousins forced to leave their homes because of their sexuality," and ultimately her "own tempestuous coming out at the age of 16."[4] From Butler's perspective, the "strong and scarring condemnation" to which she was subjected revealed violence as the issue to be interrogated.[5] Yet, having pursued pleasure and "insisting on legitimating recognition for [her] sexual life," the problem Butler faced was that "it was difficult to bring this violence into view precisely because gender was so taken for granted at the same time that it was violently policed."[6]

These autobiographical moments reveal another more abstract instance of violence—a foreclosed life. In this idea of violence, gender is a placeholder for conditions or terms used to adjudicate who is named as living or not, and how non-living or death in life must be experienced.[7] Butler cites her uncle as an example of "one whose incarceration implies a suspension of life, or a sustained death sentence."[8] From these insights, Butler illustrates that gender violence is complex, and her primary concern in *Gender Trouble* is bringing into view what I call originary violence. This is opposed to mundane violence, which is inflicted by bigots, homophobes, etc.[9] Butler continues to reflect:

> The dogged effort to "denaturalize" gender in [*Gender Trouble*] emerges, I think, from a strong desire both to counter the normative violence implied by ideal morphologies of sex and to uproot the pervasive assumptions about natural or presumptive heterosexuality that are informed by ordinary and academic discourse on sexuality.[10]

---

3. Butler, *GT*, xx.
4. Butler, *GT*, xx.
5. Butler, *GT*, xx.
6. Butler, *GT*, xx.
7. Butler uses Sartre's "zombie" to describe the colonized one who lives in a state of non-living. Butler *SS*, 175.
8. Butler, *GT*, xxi.
9. Chambers makes a similar distinction between first- and second-order violence. In Chambers, "Normative Violence after 9/11," 49.
10. Butler, *GT*, xxi.

Butler's gender theory is characterized by "de-naturalizing gender" for the interlocking reasons that violence implies the normativization of ideal gendered bodies, which is due to the authorization and regulation of the assumptions that establish gender ideals through sexuality discourse.

What is occurring in these post-publication reflections is an explicit retrospective investment into the text of *Gender Trouble* of a term and category distinction that is otherwise largely absent. The term "violence" does not appear until the thirteenth chapter (of fifteen chapters), where Butler takes up Monique Wittig's thought, which indicates the centrality of Wittig's notion of violence in Butler's gender theory. Sanna Karhu observes this and points out that it is only after exploring the concept of violence that Butler begins to use the term "norms."[11] The observation of particular experiences as effects of violence is an observation of the reality effect of norms. Butler's reflections note that violence is a latent category in the text of *Gender Trouble*, which she makes explicit in the 1999 preface by making clear the link between what is violence and what is normative.

These reflections by Butler also mark the beginning of a category distinction between the mundane and originary. Following the claim that she doggedly pursues the de-naturalization of gender, Butler continues to reflect on the content of *Gender Trouble*:

> "Normative" clearly has at least two meanings in this critical encounter, since the word is one I use often, mainly to describe the mundane violence performed by certain kinds of gender ideals. I usually use "normative" in a way that is synonymous with "pertaining to the norms that govern gender." But the term "normative" also pertains to the ethical justification, how it is established, and what concrete consequences proceed therefrom.[12]

The term "normative" describes two forms of gender violence, which Butler initially conflates. Here she reflects and identifies that violence occurs due to the mundane "performance" of norms and that which grounds (produces) and sustains (polices) them. The terms "violence" and "normative" are synonymous: they both name the normativization (production and policing) of norms. This is not to say that norms are violent, but that norms can be violent when they are beyond contestation

---

11. Karhu, "Judith Butler's Critique of Violence," 833.
12. Butler, *GT*, xxi.

and social intervention. Chamber's pithy summary and distinction is apt: "Normative violence points not to a type of violence that is somehow normative, but to the violence of norms."[13] Butler's principal concern, therefore, is not with the mundane, but the originary: that which produces and polices the mundane. It is therefore apparent that Butler's attempt to denaturalize gender is predicated on an implicit, which later becomes explicit, exposure of normative violence. Normative violence is retroactively thematized by Butler, which helps the reader to comprehend her gender theory and its political utility for contesting assumptive and compulsory heterosexuality, and the terms that underwrite its discourse.[14] One may therefore summarize Butler's theoretical intention as principally concerned with those in society whose bodies are inflicted with normative violence.[15] Butler's gender theory treats bodies being inflicted by violence, not by attending to the wound or the perpetrator, but by critiquing gender norms and ideals, and the originary terms by which the wound is inflicted through discourse.

Didier Eribon and Observing Violence

Gender and sexuality violence at the mundane level is visible and invisible. On one hand, gender violence is obvious for the reason that the subject, object, and instrument of violence are readily identifiable. To illustrate this: in February 2017, a peer of an eleven-year-old transgender schoolgirl fired on the girl with a pellet gun.[16] In this incidence of gender violence, the subject is the pupil who fired the gun, the object is the transgender girl, and the instrument of violence is the pellet gun. Gender and sexuality violence is readily observable in these kinds of lamentable events.

On the other hand, gender and sexuality violence is not always visible or obvious, which is Butler's explicit concern in her corpus. She desires to highlight complex forms of violence and the tacit operation of power underwriting them. For Butler, gender violence is rarely something uncomplicated, but a complex operation of power: "a complexity

---

13. Chambers, "Normative Violence after 9/11," 44.
14. Chambers, "Normative Violence after 9/11," 56.
15. Butler, *UG*, 9.
16. A report on the incident can be found at http://www.bbc.co.uk/news/uk-england-manchester-38909360.

which is not easily named."[17] Before exegeting Butler's texts to show how gender and sexuality violence is a complex and often obscured phenomenon, I will illustrate this by exploring the theme in Didier Eribon's book *Insult: The Making of the Gay Self*.

Eribon poignantly narrates the story of one who comes to learn of their homosexuality.[18] Even before a person identifies as homosexual, they understand insults like faggot, dyke, and poofter, and their intended target. Eribon, a homosexual, describes the horror of becoming a target as the realization of one's same-sex attraction increases. This autobiographical detail gives a glimpse of the making of the gay self as one subjectified by insult. The insults that once referred to others—those who were openly gay and those whose gay self was realized though hidden by the "closet door"—are now understood by the person to be targeted at *them*.[19] Eribon testifies that in this moment of designation, the child is inflicted with violence and the associated trauma for life.[20]

The scope of the designation is an integral aspect of Eribon's Foucauldian view of subjectification. When a child realizes they are gay, they do not need to wait for the insults for the violence to set in. By identifying their gay self, they immediately absorb the historical collective weight of the designation.[21] Gay insults apply at an individual level because they apply collectively, that is, gay insults are personally hurtful not just because the words are derogatory, but because the specific terms used are employed to identify through social categorization. They are originary terms or, reflecting on a previous metaphor, a cookie cutter that reveals the "truth" of a gay person's existence. Insult is therefore an effective means of perpetuating homophobic discourse because it takes away the individual's ability to identify as anything else. What replaces an individual's self-description is an identity comprising a caricatured discourse of images, metaphors, and states of wellbeing, etc. This discourse imposes itself on the gay person such that they understand themselves to be a

---

17. Butler, *ES*, 35. For a concise explanation of power and violence in *ES*, see Brady and Schirato, *Understanding Judith Butler*, 91–97.

18. I use the terms "homosexuality" and "gay" because these are the terms Eribon uses. Eribon, *Insult*, 11.

19. Eribon, *Insult*, 61–62.

20. Eribon, *Insult*, 16.

21. Eribon, *Insult*, 79.

member of a transgressing, and therefore condemned, "particular species" of society even before the world knows who they "really" are.[22]

How insults hurt the gay person can be explained in part with the term "shame." According to Eribon, the shame that becomes characteristic of the gay person is not happenstance, but something for which they are destined.[23] To begin with, Eribon attributes the shame of being gay to the exterior world. Drawing on a Foucauldian paradigm, Eribon narrates shame, not as a personal production that is indicative of a weak constitution, but as something produced externally and inscribed onto the subject, or more accurately, deep within the subject. Think again of the metaphor of the dressage horse. Shame is an impulsive response to an insult that comes from the outside, disciplining the mind's understanding of the self. Eribon speaks of the marked and shamed conscience, and the soul that shame subjects.[24] Here we begin to see how insult comes to determine the inhabited existence. Insult does not simply describe the individual, but explains to them who they are. We note here Butler's point that the terms conditioning the mundane experience of shame "predate" the individual's subjectivity. It becomes clear why Eribon asks the rhetorical question, "How can the intensity of this shame be understood by those who have never experienced it?"[25] The heterosexual is not only normal in the eyes of wider society, but also in the eyes of the gay person. The gay person, on the other hand, is not normal in the eyes of the heterosexual person or in their own eyes because of their relationship to normative heterosexuality.

At this point, a poignant line of inquiry is revealed: who is served by staying in the "closet"? Whose interests are being safeguarded by keeping secret one's transgressive and offensive homosexual existence? Eribon reveals that the child keeps the heterosexual assumption firmly in place in order to prevent being judged as having transgressed the heterosexual principle. In this sense, self-preservation is the function of the heterosexual "mask." One wants to avoid offending the normal order, for fear of inciting the charges of legal, mental, physical, or spiritual illness. The mask, or the closet, is therefore crucial in the early stages of managing the shame of the gay self. The close connection between the closet and shame

22. Eribon, *Insult*, 70–71.
23. Eribon, *Insult*, xv.
24. Eribon, *Insult*, 15, 16.
25. Eribon, *Insult*, 29.

becomes evident: to be ashamed of oneself is to remain in the closet; to be proud of one's self is to reject the closet: hence Eribon's description of the closet as a "symbol of shame."[26]

Finally, Eribon describes shame as that self-understanding resulting from being dominated through socially structured oppression.[27] The gay person lives a life dominated by the shame and knowledge of an illegitimate life. This illegitimacy is reinforced by exclusion from natural processes that characterized their own family. Eribon refers to the loss of a heterosexual lifestyle as melancholy—an endless sadness "of the loss homosexuality causes homosexuals."[28] The gay person's sexuality disqualifies them from participating in a life that is "normal," which Eribon identifies as mostly bound to the notion of the natural family. Often one has had to leave one's family after either being expelled or deciding to leave in order to find a context where one can live outside the closet as a person with pride. Thus, by virtue of not being heterosexual, the homosexual person's experience of their immediate family is characterized by rejection and exclusion instead of love and belonging.[29] This is compounded by the loss experienced from being denied the possibility of having a family by natural means. Eribon postulates that this could be "one of the most deeply rooted aspects of psychological 'suffering' in homosexuals of both sexes."[30] Finding oneself outside heterosexual normative reality renders the normal impossible, and Eribon notes that while the laws about gay marriage and adoption are slowly changing to rectify some of these issues, the notion of the natural family still looms large, always threatening the validity of the gay family.

Eribon's (self-)narration of the gay self describes the invisibility of violence, the observation and analysis of which can extend to those who do not identify with their bodies according to traditional gender categories, as in cases of gender dysphoria. Invisible, in these cases, refers to those "inside" the closet who are hidden by the "normal" heterosexualized body. From the outside, a gay person or someone with gender dysphoria does not appear to be subjected by terms that make them disappear. On Eribon's reading, no visible instrument inflicts violence—there is no

26. Eribon, *Insult*, 49, 107–9.
27. Eribon, *Insult*, 108.
28. Eribon, *Insult*, 37.
29. Eribon, *Insult*, 35.
30. Eribon, *Insult*, 37.

visible subject wielding an instrument, and no visible wound resulting from the violence. Gender and sexuality violence was observed as a concrete reality in the case of the transgender girl, and here violence is no less concrete, only hidden.

Having illustrated a complex notion of subjectivity as an effect of violence, the task remains to grasp the "frames through which we apprehend or, indeed, fail to apprehend the lives of others as lost or injured."[31] From within Butler's schema, what are the power operation and terms that condition the observed violence so it can be confirmed as such and appropriately addressed?

Weapon of Violence

The Law of Man and Woman

Butler asks the question at the beginning of *Gender Trouble*: "To what extent does the category of women achieve stability and coherence only in the context of the heterosexual matrix?"[32] The first part of the question asks the reader to think about the "category of wom*en*" and not wom*an*. The second part of the question probes the extent to which a category made up of such a diverse number of people could possibly find "coherence *only* in the context of the heterosexual matrix."[33] If the matrix is "that grid of cultural intelligibility through which bodies, gender and desires are naturalized," then Butler's question is rhetorical in that it seeks to highlight the non-universal scope of the category of woman.[34]

At this early stage of her corpus, Butler is targeting feminist identity or representational politics, which she deems is largely predicated on a problematic universal category of woman.[35] The question reveals that no such universal category or image of woman (or man) can underwrite forms of representational identity politics. The reason for posing this question, therefore, is to draw attention to the inapplicability of a gendered form for realizing individual or societal coherence. Butler's conclusion is that *humans are more diverse than the heterosexual matrix suggests.*

---

31. Butler, *FW*, 1.
32. Butler, *GT*, 7.
33. Butler, *GT*, 7 (emphasis mine).
34. Butler, *GT*, 208n6.
35. Butler, *GT*, 8.

Butler attributes her notion of the heterosexual matrix mostly to Monique Wittig, which Wittig calls "the heterosexual contract."[36] We see Butler's reliance on Wittig in the early stage of her seminal work, although it takes some time before Butler explicitly engages with her thought in the book. When she does, her intention is to theorize violence in such a way that it makes the originary body/bodies disappear. This means theorizing the body as the biologically ordered controlling mechanism that underwrites the authority of the heterosexual matrix as operating violently on those who do not or cannot conform to it.[37] Butler's idea of making the body disappear does not amount to a more radical claim or desire to eradicate categories of gender and sex, as Wittig desires, but, as we have already explored, is a more nuanced claim that is better reflected by her desire to make a certain departure from the human. Here Butler does not desire to *eradicate* gender and sex, but undermine the categories of gender and sex that underpin *unjust universal notions of sex and gender*. A pertinent question to ask is whether undermining traditional notions of gender and sex does away with the categories of gender and sex. Certainly, they have been done away with as categories that do any work in their traditional "hard" form. However, Butler emphatically rejects Wittig's suggestion to do away with the binary categories. Rather, she asserts: "The more insidious and effective strategy it seems is a thoroughgoing appropriation and redeployment of the categories of identity themselves, not merely to contest 'sex,' but to . . . render that category, in whatever form, permanently problematic."[38] To reform gender, Butler employs an undermining strategy, which amounts to taking hold of the very substance that constitutes the foundation and reassigning it. In this passage, Butler shows how this can be achieved by taking up the preexisting terms that structure gender and redeploying or re-forming them to render gender in its traditional form fundamentally and therefore permanently problematic. In Butler's thinking, norms are *not* fundamentally problematic nor dispensable aspects of subjectivity, but are foundational and necessary, which means that norms imposed from the outside on people, while not necessarily violations, must always be susceptible to disabling.[39] In this sense, the critique Butler's theory exacts does not *do*

36. Butler, *GT*, 208n6.
37. Karhu, "Judith Butler's Critique of Violence."
38. Butler, *GT*, 174.
39. Butler, *UG*, 214.

away with gender categories or norms, but *opens them up* to perpetual re-evaluation and therefore recalibration, reconditioning, or *reform*.

Butler's use of Wittig's thought to formulate a notion of discursive violence is grounded in a line of questioning precipitated by Simone de Beauvoir's use of the term "become" in her famous quip from *The Second Sex*: "One is not born a woman, but rather *becomes* one."[40] Butler states: "Are there ever humans who are not, as it were, already gendered?"[41] The logic behind this question probes the implied meaning of "becoming" gendered, where to become gendered means that one is not already gendered. Butler gives the example of a baby being "humanized when the question 'Is it a boy or a girl?' is answered."[42]

Signaling Butler's use of Wittig's notion of discursive violence is a fundamental question regarding the parameters of human being: what is the relationship between being a boy or girl and being a human? If to be a boy or girl is to be human, then what is implied if a new-born is held up by the midwife, and instead of hearing—"It's a boy" or "It's a girl"—there is silence and a look of confusion? The midwife's silence would denote the baby's inability to enter into the category of human because it cannot meet the bodily criteria required to be a boy or girl. The law invoked to adjudicate that the baby is transgressive and therefore not (yet) a part of humanity is the law of heterosexuality or the law of man or woman (biologically conceived).[43] Here we see why Wittig refers to this matrix or law as a "contract" because it regulates what it means to be human. If the baby does not satisfy the law or fulfill its contractual obligations in order to be human, it is deemed transgressive, thus requiring, in this case, medical disciplining.

In this scenario, the baby's body is submitted to the process of heterosexualization on two occasions. In the first instance the process operates to rule the baby (or its body) out as being human, and in the second instance, the process is once again engaged to remake the body through medical means so it can meet the requirements to be human. Before one is able to attain full citizenship within the category of human, Butler asks the question whether the baby first needs to "become" a boy or girl.

40. Simone de Beauvoir in Butler, *GT*, 151.

41. Butler, *GT*, 151.

42. Butler, *GT*, 151. Looming large yet not explored in any depth is Jacques Derrida's theorization of the rupture between signs and what they signify.

43. Butler, *GT*, 100.

Notice that the originary human produces and regulates the mundane human. Regarding this process of humanization, which is in fact a system of heterosexualization, Butler observes, "The mark of gender appears to 'qualify' bodies as human bodies."[44] Again, the point Butler is pressing home is that mundane humanity is more diverse than the heterosexual contract, heterosexual matrix, or law of man and woman suggest. Because the categories of boy and girl or man and woman are not universal in their representational coverage, Butler deems them to be the means to justify violent normative processes of heterosexualization. "Boy-or-girl" functions as a law of gender that condemns some in their bodies and justifies their disciplining. Butler is exposing the law of man and woman as a mechanism of assimilation. The law of man and woman is a way of processing the heterosexualization of society, which disciplines transgressing bodies and minds.

Undoing the Law of Man and Woman

If a law is found to be unjust, it is incumbent on society to change that law. However, this response is susceptible to a knee-jerk reaction that runs the risk of installing another law as unjust as the one in need of reform. Instead of seeking merely to reform the existing law of gender by changing its terms, Butler problematizes the unjust law in play. She does this by pressing de Beauvoir's notion of gender as "becoming" to make two related claims about the relationship between gender and sex. First, "sex does not cause gender and," second, "gender cannot be understood to reflect or express sex."[45] If sex does not ground gender, then gender is not dependent on the shape and function of one's internal or external genitalia. Undermining the biology-is-destiny thought paradigm equates to a simultaneous undermining operation of the biology-is-gender paradigm. The result is an inversion of sex and gender whereby gender is understood to inform sex.

In Butler's thinking, the body is not a substance with inherent meaning that instructs society on who is what gender. Rather, drawing on Butler's subject of desire for recognition, gender is an idea or concept that instructs society on how to recognize a body in a particular way. In other words, to say that a person is a particular gender is not to say

---

44. Butler, *GT*, 151.
45. Butler, *GT*, 152.

that they have a particular body, but that they are recognizable against a particular *idea* of gender. Thus, returning to the example, boy and girl are not bodies but two *ideas* (gender) against which the baby's body is measured to see if it is recognizable. Once recognized as the idea of boy or girl, they possess the *vocation* of continuing to become that gender by conforming to the idea by which they are initially recognizable by virtue of their appropriate iteration of codes of dress, language, gestures, hobby, vocation, and desires, etc.

Butler describes as radical the consequences of thinking about gender as something one is entered into and becomes. If gender does not describe what someone is essentially, but is the reference by which someone can be recognized, gender, conceptually speaking, is not necessarily limited to a binary, but *malleable* and therefore able to cater for more diverse forms of gender recognition:

> Gender is something that one becomes . . . a kind of becoming or activity, and that ought not be conceived as a noun or a substantial thing or a static cultural marker, but rather as an incessant and repeated action of some sort. If gender is not tied to sex, either causally or expressively, then gender is a kind of action that can potentially proliferate beyond the binary limits imposed by the apparent binary of sex. Indeed, gender would be a kind of cultural/corporeal action that requires a new vocabulary that institutes and proliferates present participles of various kinds, resignifiable and expansive categories that *resist* both the binary and substantializing grammatical restrictions on gender.[46]

Butler makes two theoretical moves to undo the law of man and woman. First, drawing on de Beauvoir and extending her thought further than originally considered, Butler fractures the causal, reflective, or expressive relationship between sex and gender by positing "becoming" as gender's fundamental characteristic. Secondly, drawing on Wittig, Butler qualifies the idea of the gender binary as an idea or an effect of political discourse and therefore susceptible to resistance via social intervention.

Butler's proposal of resistance in the above passage as the means of precipitating change avoids the real danger of slipping into "an impossible and vain utopian project," which is an inferred critique of Wittig.[47] The kind of gender reform to which Butler subscribes is not the

46. Butler, *GT*, 152 (emphasis mine).
47. Butler, *GT*, 152.

reconstitution of the law of man and woman with another idea of man or woman, or the addition of a third gender, following Wittig, or no gender, as is popularly suggested of Butler and queer theory in general. The lesbian does have subversive potential, not as a third sex, but as "a category that radically problematizes both sex and gender as stable political categories of description."[48] The lesbian, as one example of transgressing embodiment, manifests a gendered existence that challenges the universal claim of the heterosexual couple. By living out and pointing out lives that do not exist (despite existing), lesbians, for example, demonstrate that conceptions of sex and gender that reflect the law of man and woman are constructed abstractions that hold sway only by virtue of their previous naturalization. The task of queer gender politics is to interrogate the present conceptions of gender and sex in order to root out and expose meaning that is received as natural or essential by drawing attention to those who exist but are not represented by the present conceptions.

Inscription or Description

Perceiving Bodily Violence

The reformation of gender and sex in Butler's gender theory reconstitutes the body as a site of political contestation, which has been Butler's goal all along. Yet this formulation threatens to position the body as preexisting discourse like a canvas (the body) on which an artist applies paint (terms). Butler asks, "Is there a 'physical' body prior to the perceptually perceived body?" She answers her own question, though not decisively: "An impossible question to decide."[49]

The grammatical framing of the question locks physical bodies into a regime of knowledge that facilitates their recognition. In Butler's own words: "As both *discursive* and *perceptual*, 'sex' denotes an historically contingent epistemic regime, a language that forms perception by forcibly shaping the interrelationships through which physical bodies are perceived."[50] Notice that Butler does not displace the physical body, but its inherent meaning. The collusion between the body and inherent meaning

---

48. Butler, *GT*, 153.
49. Butler, *GT*, 155.
50. Butler, *GT*, 155.

is shattered, rendering each body subject to perception for which one appeals to culturally and historically embedded ideas about gender.

This is a significant moment in our reading of Butler's gender theory. In order to narrate gender violence as a reality effect, Butler does not simply scream, "Violence!" but seeks to demonstrate how an uncontested binary notion of gender was not *describing* people, but *forcibly shaping* (however unsuccessfully) people's desires and bodies into a binary mold, despite pleas to stop.

On this reading of Butler's gender theory, I suggest there *is* a physical body prior to its perception. But Butler is alerting us to the horrific historical reality that while we *see bodies* when they come into view, we do not *perceive* them as recognizably *human*. The way Butler chooses to use body and human often goes unnoticed: "the matrix of gender relations is prior to the emergence of the 'human.'"[51] Of course, that these bodies and minds were and are subject to the "matrix" or the "law" of male and female through medical, legal, social, or spiritual means, in order to make them perceptibly good humans, betrays the fact that they were initially perceived. They were recognizable according to the law of binary gender, but as wretched and in need of salvation from their bodies of death. Unfortunately, this perception did not prompt society (and the church) to reflect on humanity's relationship to the law of gender, but caused panic and hasty decisions to "bring them quickly into line" with the law or to remove them altogether from society to maintain the façade of integrity of the law. Instead of encountering these wretched bodies and making ourselves and society susceptible to them, society and the church upheld the law in the name of what is natural, good, normal, and even righteous.

Historically, the physical body was not conceived as either good or not good, but became either by being recognized as such by exhibiting or not exhibiting that which was determined by the regime of knowledge as good. Gender violence is fundamentally concerned with these terms that determine and regulate what and therefore who can be perceived or recognized as normal and abnormal. The human is always perceived according to a set of terms, the question is, *what terms?*

---

51. Butler, *BTM*, xvii.

Foucault's Glitch: Death by Inscription

In the final moments of her published doctoral thesis in conversation with Michel Foucault, Butler notes the need for a "history of bodies" to be written, because bodies are not given things that simply are gendered, but are conceived as sites where "history encodes itself."[52] In this context, Butler poses the question: "How, for instance, are we to understand the body as the inscribed surface of gender relations?"[53] The body in this thinking is a site that suffers the fate of being inscribed with meaning. But this is the beginning of Butler's published journey to think about gender, which she qualifies in a little-known article called "Foucault and the Paradox of Bodily Inscriptions."[54] Butler makes clear that she differs from Foucault on the point of inscription. For Butler, the very thought of a body as a surface that can be inscribed with meaning suggests that Foucault "assume[s] a materiality to the body prior to its signification and form."[55] What is this body before it is given meaning? This, it has been shown, is an impossible question to decide. But concerning the location of a body prior to the attribution of meaning in the thought of Foucault, this is much easier to decide: it exists outside of history—unreality—and therefore beyond political contestation. This claim is devastating for Foucault's own schema because it creates the originary conditions he seeks to refute: "a pre-discursive ontology of the body and its drives."[56]

---

52. Butler, *SD*, 238.

53. Butler, *SD*, 237.

54. This is a common and persistent misreading of Butler's gender theory. For example, Joseph Sverker's final critical account of Butler rests on this very claim. See Sverker, *Human Being and Vulnerability*. Such readings seem to latch on to a question Butler utters at the very end of her own 1987 published doctoral dissertation. Foreshadowing her future direction of research, Butler does speak of inscription, but even here she realizes that the term is troubling, which is why she couches the term in quotation marks. Butler, *SD*, 237. In time, Butler repudiates or at least undermines the integrity of this early claim as the very thesis of her gender theory. Butler, *GT*, 11, 175–78; *BTM*, 171. Sverker also overemphasizes a view of the body as a site, which is a term Butler uses, but only as understood through other terms and ideas like the body as a process of materialization. Butler, *BTM*, xv, xii, xxii–xxiv, 7–10.

55. Butler, "Foucault and the Paradox," 604.

56. Butler, "Foucault and the Paradox," 604. Also, in Foucault, *Discipline and Punish*, Foucault states: "It would be wrong to say that the soul is an illusion, or an ideological effect. On the contrary, it exists, it has a reality, it is produced permanently around, on, within the body by the functioning of a power that is exercised on those who are punished" (29).

Butler is careful to avoid letting her thinking about the body slip into a notion of construction that gives ostensible support to a pre-discursive body. She does this by noting the paradox of speaking about a culturally constructed body. The question "What is 'the body' that it can be constructed?" identifies the body that exists *prior to* its construction. How can the body be theorized to exist prior to its construction without installing a pre-discursive body? Butler states: "'The body' would not be constructed, strictly considered, but would be the occasion, the site, or the condition of a process of construction only externally related to the body that is its object."[57] Butler rejects the possibility of the constructed body in the first clause, but invokes the paradigm that I have already set up between the originary and the mundane. Butler can be read as speaking of the body as having two dimensions: the subject and object, which means that she refutes the polarized possibilities of the body as a *material* object or an *idea* subject. This would create two bodies, reiterating the problematic view that an external idea writes itself in a Foucauldian manner onto a material body. Rather, Butler inverts the subject/object relation, wherein the material is subject and the idea is the object. In this way, the originary body is the object that is externally related to the subject who is the occasion for becoming the object in the gaze. I am where the object of man is slowly lived out, becomes, or is constructed from my birth to death. The trouble arises when my living out conflicts with the object man.

The distinction between the originary and mundane reiterates the juridical nature of gender-objects that frame (or foreclose) what counts as a good life to be celebrated and what forms of gender-subjects are worthy of condemnation and discipline.[58] Butler is concerned that Foucault's "constructed body" can be used to justify unethical violent action by virtue of appeal to the object of man or woman, which operates in time as a law of nature (material body), and as a law of the normal (cultural body). For Butler, nature and culture are the processes by which the originary object of man and woman are consolidated as the measures of mundane good and not good sexuality and gender. Butler is seeking to undo the situation wherein a material body that escapes time, that is enculturated as normative within time, manifests to distribute life and death in life unequally.

57. Butler, "Foucault and the Paradox," 601.
58. In her more recent work, Butler frames this as the unequal distribution of violence, grief, or precarity. See Butler, *FW* and *PL*.

First, the law of nature: the pre-time material body tends to assume materiality and therefore functions as primary for thinking about good sexuality and gender. For Butler, this kind of bio-logic inscribes or confers intelligibility onto the body, even though this body does not exist in time. Butler states: "By maintaining a body prior to its cultural inscription, Foucault appears to assume a materiality to the body prior to its signification and form."[59] This body is problematic for Butler because bio-logic functions as a transcendent and binding law that is located in an originary moment beyond contestation. The material body that is conferred with bio-logical meaning conceals the mythical nature of its inception. Its authority to determine what is good and not good is grounded in an appeal to itself as natural and as such is beyond question.

The ethical ramifications of the law of nature tend to affect only some because not all the bodies and desires of people appear to fall outside the range of justified function and desire. That is, some bodies do not properly image the object that structures the law of nature—morphologically, chromosomally, functionally, or desirously—and therefore acquire the labels ab-normal, un-natural, and transgressor. The reaction, often by those who are normal, natural, and law abiding, is to discipline them so that their bodies and desires align with the law's demands. Historically, men have been subject to aversion and conversion therapies, partial lobotomies, and electric shock therapy, for example, to make them desire women, as the law demands.[60] These are medical interventions, but such un-natural and ab-normal men have also been subject to legal, physical, emotional, or spiritual disciplines to correct errant desire. In addition to Butler's ethical appeal, she anticipates the law of nature's dogged resistance to attempts to construct the body in ways that better account for the diversity of embodied experience.[61]

The second law that emerges from reflection on Foucault's notion of inscription concerns the productive and regulative power of culture, which Butler also resists. If the body is a socially mediated reality, then the social context is the limit of the body's possibility. In this schema, the normal body is not determined by bio-logic but socio-logic: sedimented

---

59. Butler, "Foucault and the Paradox," 604.

60. This is a heavily documented social phenomenon. For literature that documents this in the United States, see https://www.apa.org/pi/lgbt/resources/therapeutic-response.pdf. See specifically, "A Brief History of Sexual Orientation Change Efforts," 21–22.

61. Butler, "Foucault and the Paradox," 607.

cultural thinking over time. But according to Butler, this logic is no less problematic than the law of nature because it poses as a paternal law by which transgressors can be identified, measured, and disciplined, ostensibly for their own good. Finally, this form of socio-logic is problematic because it offers no entry point for resistance or possible re-construction because what is inscribed universally is an inescapable "single drama."[62]

The Sovereign "I"

In light of the foregoing, for Butler, the body is not a given reality one simply has, that one autonomously en-genders, sexualizes, and dresses at will in the morning. Rather, Butler argues that iterated language authors and authorizes the body. This finally explicitly broaches the topic of performativity in Butler's gender theory. In *Gender Trouble*, Butler thematizes performativity as the reiteration of terms to effect being, or to become, but this was received critically as being overly voluntarist principally due to her description of drag as a means of subverting gender.[63] In *Bodies That Matter*, Butler addresses this critique by confirming the contingent nature of gender as "the forcible reiteration of those norms."[64] The prospect of new gendered possibility theorized in *Gender Trouble* is significantly chastened by this move to make gender a more sedimented existential reality, as my reading of Butler hopes to make clear.

Butler develops a notion of gender performativity in the last chapter of *Bodies That Matter*, "Critically Queer," by identifying the utility of language, conceiving it as iterative practice. The term "queer" is the example given to show that what was once "the mundane interpellation of pathologized sexuality," which caused "the discursive regulation of the boundaries of sexual legitimacy," could be redeemed by "being subject to an affirmative resignification."[65] But recalling Nietzsche and Foucault's views on the ubiquity of power, Butler highlights the problem of agency and finds hope in asking the question: "And yet how are we to understand their convergent force as an accumulated effect of usage that both constrains and enables their reworking?"[66] Our previous usage of "reality

---

62. Butler, "Foucault and the Paradox," 604.
63. Butler, *GT*, 183–89.
64. Butler, *BTM*, xii.
65. Butler, *BTM*, 169.
66. Butler, *BTM*, 170.

effect" is nuanced because the effect is not hiding what is, that is, what lurks beneath. The reality effect is what really is, which means that reality—death in life—is the sedimented sequence of practiced discourse throughout time. Drawing on Eribon's account of the gay self, shame in life is the gay person's reality. Thus, two questions are posed, first, in terms of the mundane, and then the originary: "Here it is not only a question of how discourse injures bodies, but how certain injuries establish certain bodies at the limits of available ontologies, available schemes of intelligibility."[67] This line of interrogation prompts Butler to assert that gender is a psychic reality, but one that cannot be thought apart from bodies.

The "speech act" Butler uses to help comprehend the process of becoming gendered is the marriage ceremony. For J. L. Austin, marriage as a reality effect is reducible to the utterance, "I pronounce you . . ." Butler notes that the reality effect sedimented over time but that such an utterance not only effects marriage but, vitally, "the relations that it names."[68] Butler defines performative acts as

> forms of authoritative speech: most performatives, for instance, are statements that, in the uttering, also perform a certain action and exercise a binding power. Implicated in a network of authorization and punishment, performatives tend to include legal sentences, baptisms, inaugurations, declaration of ownership, statements which not only perform an action, but confer a binding power on the action performed. If the power of discourse to produce that which it names is linked with the question of performativity, then the performative is one domain in which power acts as discourse.[69]

We see in the paradigm of marriage that the performative utterance, "I pronounce you . . ." is an utterance with consolidated power that authorizes and so binds the heterosexualization of social bonds.

But on what grounds does the performance affect this reality? Butler invokes this line of questioning to highlight problematic naturalized contingent foundations. Butler offers the example of a judge's binding performative utterance, which "cites the law that he applies."[70] This point is pertinent for Butler's argument because the judge appeals to the law

67. Butler, *BTM*, 170.
68. Butler, *BTM*, 170.
69. Butler, *BTM*, 171.
70. Butler, *BTM*, 171.

to justify his judgement, which further establishes the authority of the law and the judge. Power is not latent in the person of the judge, nor does power reside in the judge's will, "but in the citational legacy by which a contemporary 'act' emerges in the context of a chain of binding conventions."[71] Legal precedents in modern law further establish this performative principle. The person who performs the utterance is, in Butler's estimation, merely an actor repeating words, or one engaged in "reiterated acting."[72] Butler's theory of performativity invokes previous discussions of Hegel and Freud: "That one comes to 'be' through dependence on the Other—an Hegelian and, indeed, Freudian postulation—must be recast in linguistic terms to the extent that the terms by which recognition is regulated, allocated, and refused are part of the larger social rituals of interpellation."[73] The social ritual of marriage performs an interpellation in which the "I" that utters the performative "I pronounce you..." in the marriage ceremony is not a person but the discursive law that binds the utterance.[74]

The implications of this view of marriage, according to Butler, are a matter of life and death in life. Because the "I" precedes the celebrant's pronouncement of "life," the celebrant "births" people, thereby regulating who can become a human "I." Referencing Althusser's notion of interpellation, Butler states: "the 'I' only comes into being through being called, named ... and this discursive constitution only takes place prior to the 'I'; it is the transitive invocation of the 'I.'"[75] To say that "I" live is not to say that I am recognized, but that I am recognizable according to terms that constitute what is recognizable. Returning to the earlier scenario, the midwife is confused, not because the baby cannot be recognized, but because the baby is unrecognizable against a set of preexisting terms that structure recognizability. Butler states: "the address constitutes a being within the possible circuit of recognition and, accordingly, outside of it, in abjection."[76] The baby is abject because it cannot (yet) be named boy

71. Butler, *BTM*, 171.
72. Butler, *BTM*, xviii.
73. Butler, *ES*, 26.
74. Austin's theory is deficient according to Butler because the utterance assumes the subject. Butler offers a corrective by drawing on Louis Althusser's notion of interpellation in which "the speech act that brings the subject into linguistic existence precedes the subject in question." For a fuller description see Butler, *ES*, 24–28.
75. Butler, *BTM*, 171.
76. Butler, *ES*, 5.

or girl. This unrecognizable "not-I" (my term) is therefore a transgressor and so must live as a transgressor or be disciplined legally, socially, spiritually, medically, etc., to be a recognizable "I."

Butler's mature account of gender performativity in *Bodies That Matter* is much more pessimistic that agency can be achieved, and when speaking of the possibility in *Excitable Speech*, she is circumspect, noting the "peculiar bind" that results from "speak[ing] a language that is never fully one's own."[77] The depth of one's discursive formation by virtue of the contingent foundation of the "accumulating and dissimulating historicity of force" hinders any attempt to name one's self autonomously. The self is bogged down in the discursive "I," which ironically Butler does not desire to overcome because the violent discursive formation is the grounds for or foundation of existence, and therefore the substance of Butler's paradoxical politics of gender re-form. Repudiating discursive history is not a possibility because that discourse permits one's emergence as an "I." *That discourse is therefore the only means for possible re-signification.*

The prerogative to remake oneself *ex-nihilo* is not a possibility in Butler's view. Discursive terms totalize the self, which undermine one's autonomy to self-name. Butler resists identity politics for this reason, noting the fetishization of authorship as a "presentist conceit":

> It may be that the conceit of autonomy implied by self-naming is the paradigmatically presentist conceit, that is, the belief that there is a one who arrives in the world, in discourse, without a history, that this one makes oneself in and through the magic of the name, that language expresses a "will" or a "choice" rather than a complex and constitutive history of discourse and power which compose the invariably ambivalent resources through which a queer and queering agency is forged and reworked.[78]

The critique that Butler's gender theory amounts to a voluntarist activity drives Butler to take her theory to its logical conclusion. Not only does she reject that her theory of performativity is voluntarist, but makes the counter-claim that the alternative to her theory is a voluntarist notion of gender. This is the conceit that characterizes late modern liberal identity politics. At best, one is naïve, and at worst, one is arrogant to think one can enter the world and escape the discourse that dictates and allocates who gets life or death in life.

77. Butler, *ES*, 140.
78. Butler, *BTM*, 173–74.

If the always already terms that condition sex, gender, and sexuality circumscribe each person, then autonomy is a vain utopian quest. Where autonomy as self-description is claimed, one is more vulnerable than ever to reiterating the violent terms that constitute the conditions and limits of sex, gender, and sexuality. In sum, there is no sovereign "I," simply the belief in one.

Conclusion

Butler's critique of gender violence brings to light several issues for theological consideration in the following chapter. The first concerns the nature of gender violence and its effect on people's lives. From our reading of Butler, gender and sexuality violence is subtle and the wound it inflicts is often invisible. Coupled with Eribon's narration of invisible wounds, Butler's theorization is a poignant revelation of the terrifying experience that some people endure. "Violence!" is a catch-cry that is used by some to fend off accountability and avoid rigorous inquiry, but this is not the case with Butler or Eribon. They bring to our attention a form of violence and pain to which Christians should be sensitive and responsive rather than tone-deaf and dismissive.

The second issue for theological reflection concerns the weapon that Butler claims inflicts invisible violence. The specific point is that gender violence is mundane, but this is only because it is predicated on what lies in the beginning, that which is deemed originary: gender norms. These normative terms function as a law in the present to determine not only who is allowed to enter or appear in society but also what form of gender or sexuality change is required for these same people to appear as intelligibly good to gain entry. Furthermore, Butler suggests that this law is problematic because it is not universal and because it does not represent all people.

In response I will suggest that Adam and Eve is a theological counterpart to Butler's originary law. Formulating Adam and Eve as a law constitutes a theological reform of gender insofar as the originary creatures are stripped of their capacity to narrate all human gender and sexuality experiences neatly. This raises further questions about how we should relate to Adam and Eve as God's willed creation in the beginning as expressed, for example, by Jesus in Matthew 19:4–6, which we will addressed in due course. For now, however, the task to be engaged concerns accounting for the terms in the beginning that function in the present to justify only some people as good.

The final point for theological reflection that Butler's thought has precipitated concerns whether gender is an object or subject. Within the theological re-narration of Adam and Eve as a law, we come to see gender as an object that we do not, indeed *cannot*, inhabit. Rather, gender, as we experience it today, is a mode of subjection to the law of Adam and Eve. The body, as we have already seen in chapter 2, does not exist outside of history. As such we always find ourselves in time in subjection to the law of Adam and Eve.

Chapter 4

Eden's Seduction

Introduction

REFORMING A THEOLOGY OF gender is necessary because we need to account for a certain departure from the human. This was narrated theologically as humanity's departure from Eden. We confess that we do not dwell in Eden, and as it currently stands, we cannot enter Eden to enjoy the grace God offers there. Outside of Eden people can only approximate what God created in the beginning, revealing to us that further reflection is needed on what it means to be gendered today, which must include how we relate to the humans we have departed. The theological critique of gender violence I offer amounts to unmasking the idolatry and false righteousness that lies latent in theologies of gender that are characterized by a disordered orientation to Adam and Eve. In other words, theological reflection on Butler's critique of gender violence leads us to see how the humans we have departed continue to operate in the present as a seductive site of pilgrimage for idolatrous worship *and* as a righteous law that justifies some and condemns others.

In *The Romance of Innocent Sexuality*, Geoffrey Rees's view of the beginning is ultimately incompatible with a Christian confessionally grounded account. Despite this, his critical analysis of the human gaze at the departed images provides the theological traction needed to chasten the overreaching force of Adam and Eve in Christian dialogue about gender and sexuality. Rees offers at least two points that are worthy of serious consideration. The first is whether we are right to think about sex as fallen, and if so from what and to what extent. The second point concerns the worth ascribed to Adam and Eve, which Rees calls "ideals of orientation," as the means for personal and social coherence.[1]

Rees's critique of innocent sexuality has wide-ranging implications for thinking about the beginning *and* now. Augustine's perspective on the creation and fall of the man and woman preoccupies Rees's theological reflection, but the nature of this reflection can be extended to reflect on a conservative vision of gender and sexuality in the present, specifically, the merit of narrating the sexual revolution as an ostensible fall of sex from innocence that characterized the age prior to it. This leads to the pressing issue of the worth of heterosexual marital sex and nuclear families for undoing the effects of the fall of sex and returning to the state of societal innocence. Regarding this specific inquiry, Rees's critique of the fall of sex is entirely consistent with a conservative theological position on sexuality and gender, namely, that the body, desire, and its expression prior to the fall of sex marked by the sexual revolution does not represent Edenic innocence. This begs the question of whether "right" sex and marriage is a credible means of achieving individual and societal coherence today.

This gives way to a more fundamental discussion about the fall of sex in the beginning, and whether innocent sexuality preceded it. Aspects of Rees's critique of innocent sexuality break down at this point. Despite this, some aspects remain, which provoke theological reflection on how God's good creatures in the beginning can operate oppressively in the world today. By upholding the confession that Adam and Eve were a part of God's very good creation in the beginning, they are reconceived upon humanity's departure from Eden as an image of bygone human innocence *and* a righteous law that stands over and against fallen humanity. As innocent images and a righteous law, Adam and Eve can therefore be misconstrued as a means for self-justification and a means by which some can condemn the troubled bodies of others. I argue that the problematic issue in need of treatment is not that the law of Adam and Eve is unjust because it justifies only some forms of gender and sexuality, but that some, even most, stand self-justified in their bodies despite their guilt before the law. When the full scope and force of the law of Adam and Eve is revealed, we learn that Adam and Eve do not bring life, but death, and thus the news that *everyone* stands condemned in their bodies of death and thus their need of saving.

---

1. Rees, *Romance*, 51.

While Rees, following Butler, would rather "undo" the law of Adam and Eve rendering it possible to reflect emergent forms of mundane gendered and sexual life, I suggest we take this claim of Rees seriously:

> The promise for theological investigation, admittedly risky, of confession of the inherent sinfulness of all human sexuality is that it offends equally. It succeeds by pleasing no one. It comprehends the entire landscape of theological discourse of sexuality and places at its center not the morality of any particular sexual activity but instead the morality of the discourse itself.[2]

A theology of gender is subject to reform when it is driven by a theological engagement about gender (along with sexuality) that does not hide behind human traditions that appeal to God as the author to justify only some (often oneself) as rightly ordered or good.[3] Learning to take seriously the force of the law of Adam and Eve is about learning and beginning to live out the reality that *everyone* is condemned in their troubled bodies of death, and that returning to the edge of Eden to gaze upon the bodies of Adam and Eve to instruct our body-work will not result in achieving life in our bodies. The beautiful bodies of Adam and Eve do not hold out hope, but point to our need of being saved.

The Fall of Sex

Revising the Beginning

In *The Romance of Innocent Sexuality*, Rees argues for the fall of the *myth* of innocent sexuality. Humanity has not fallen from originary innocence, but from the *human idea* of sexual innocence. Expanded even further, humanity has not fallen from the God-ordained and perfectly ordered creation of Adam and Eve, but from the human ideas of Adam and Eve. If there is no divinely ordered innocent sexuality in the beginning, then there is no form of sexuality in the present that deserves to be given a higher moral standing over another.

---

2. Rees, *Romance*, 4.

3. In view here is Mark 7:1–23 in which Jesus is patrolled by the Pharisees and is accused of impurity on the grounds of transgressing "the tradition of the elders," to which Jesus responds with the claim, "You abandon the commandment of God and hold to human tradition."

Rees's queer theology of sexuality levels the playing field of what counts as good sexuality.[4] But instead of allowing the discussion to descend into a notion that all sexuality is good sexuality,[5] he argues surprisingly for the opposite, that all sexuality is fallen or sinful. If human history is utterly circumscribed by the fall, then the beginning is a narrated tale about someone's fallen sexuality rather than God's creation of innocent sexuality. And if God "created" the beginning, then God is co-opted for the purpose of "re-creating" their fallen sexuality thereby giving it the appearance of God's perfectly willed creation. Using God in this way not only justifies a form of sinful sexuality as good, but also universalizes it as the standard to determine what is good and natural.

According to Rees's account, Adam and Eve in the beginning is therefore an installed myth or fiction that, rather than confirm the inherent goodness of heterosexuality, disguises its inherent sinfulness. Rees describes this retrospective creation account with the pithy claim: "As an effect of sexuality, the fiction of sex secures the efficacy of sexuality."[6] The beginning is an effect of mundane sexuality that a person can enact to realize self-coherence.

This interpretation of the beginning seeks to deconstruct the traditional categories of sex and marriage that are said to be unjustly inhospitable. For Rees, this is "to protest in charitable anger against the unjust distribution of the shame of unintelligibility of original sin."[7] Drawing on Butler's thought, Rees understands Adam and Eve to be an unjust law that promises identity and coherence only for those who measure up to it. It is unjust because the promise of Adam and Eve in the beginning is only for those who see in those images their own bodies and desire. But if as Rees argues all sexuality is sinful, why do only some people experience shame when they look to the beginning? The promise that some find in the argument of Rees is that if all sexuality is fallen then Adam and Eve do not offer a divine blessing to only some, or justify some people as good and others in need of becoming good.

---

4. Rees, *Romance*, 287.
5. Rees, *Romance*, 198.
6. Rees, *Romance*, 42.
7. Rees, *Romance*, 271.

Sex in the Beginning: A Political Drama

Rees employs Butler's queering strategy to undermine the images of Adam and Eve in the beginning that falsely and therefore unjustly represent the limits of what is good sexuality. Rees deconstructs a traditional notion of gender and sex by drawing attention to the importance ascribed to heterosexual sex and marriage for achieving individual and social coherence. Drawing explicitly on Foucault's notions of subjectification and bio-power in *The History of Sexuality*, Rees outlines the collusion between marriage and sex: "The power of marriage as it inappropriately organizes theological discourse on sexuality relates directly to the ways in which sex is experienced practically as a solution to the desire for unity thwarted by original sin."[8] Marriage is the social form of power that prescribes how sex remedies the de-unifying effect of sin which Rees describes as the body's disobedience or rebellion against God.[9] If Adam and Eve are a fiction then so is the whole complex of fall and redemption in which sex is bound up. Rees concludes that marriage-ordered sex is a pseudo-solution to the problem of desire-induced incoherence, calling the bluff of Adam and Eve's promise of coherence through heterosexual marital sex.[10] In other words, heterosexual marital sex as represented by the image of Adam and Eve does not describe some people's coherence and provide a means for others to become coherent, but is a refusal by some to take responsibility for their sin along with the others.[11]

The theological view that the fall and sex are inseparable is sewn deep into the foundations of historical Christianity. Rees uses two passages in Augustine's *The City of God* to develop this theme.[12] In one of the passages, Augustine describes Adam's shock at his disobedient organ of shame and his spontaneous desire to cover himself. Rees comments that Augustine saw "humanity's collective fall from grace in the fact of an original disobedience by Adam and Eve in Eden" which "concentrates in a 'novel disturbance' of the 'organs of shame.'"[13] In this very graphic scene, God's grace is removed from Adam and Eve and they began to see and feel their desire-induced bodily disobedience. Their previous perfection

---

8. Rees, *Romance*, 42.
9. Rees, *Romance*, 196–97.
10. Rees, *Romance*, 31.
11. Rees, *Romance*, 34.
12. Augustine, *City of God*, 13.13 and 14.20. Cited in Rees, *Romance*, 3, 7–8, 14.
13. Rees, *Romance*, 3.

in God did not differentiate between the private and the public. Now they are seen, and their shame at being seen leads to covering up their sinful sexuality literally, by making coverings, and metaphorically, by finding a way to justify their sexual sin as good, thus deflecting the gaze off their sinfulness onto others.

Humanity's utter distraction by their sinful sexuality hinders them from seeking to return to God. Their confounded effort for embodied completion is redirected into the pursuit of restoring their fallen innocent sexuality, which leads them to do the previously unimaginable: to justify sinful sexuality as good to experience embodied completion again. The degradation of human relationships and the pursuit of sexual coherence leads to an agonistic context in which humans wrestles with each other for the right to control the terms that structure the "beginning." Human pride will not allow submission to another's will, and nor does humanity desire to live in unintelligibility and shame according to a beginning that does not justify them. Even if the beginning is a self-deception, the myth of innocent sexuality eventually sediments, convincing the self and others that unity with another in the order of marriage brings completion, which also pacifies the shame of their sinfulness. Adam and Eve are redemptive when a person is found in their likeness, that is, in a heterosexual marital union. This is a dual union: with a marriage spouse and thus with Adam and Eve. What belongs to Adam and Eve belongs to the married person. The trouble is that the married person does not experience the kind of embodied sexual coherence that is imagined and promised in the blissful union of Adam and Eve. Moreover, the guilt and shame of their stubborn sinful sexuality remains.

For Rees the "personal is political," and this is why he narrates sexual shame working its way out of human consciousness by means of the *agon*.[14] The "beginning" is not an image of what God ordains as good in the beginning. It is, rather, a "false start ... an opening of insight into the relation of sin to creation that arises *within* politics."[15] If the "beginning" is a human idea, then Rees's creation narrative is best described as a record of an ancient political drama depicting the victor of a political struggle for the right to install their own sexual images in the beginning to justify their own fallen sexuality. According to this ancient myth, Adam and Eve are not a God-given gift, but the politicization of sexuality by some to

14. Rees, *Romance*, 208.
15. Rees, *Romance*, 209.

avoid the shame of their own sinful sexuality and lack of coherence in the face of the other and God.

Is Sex Worth Dying For?

Rees's critique of innocent sexuality lies in his observation of the investment of sinful life into the "beginning" that takes an incontestable final form in the images of Adam and Eve. The life they represent—heterosexual marital sex—is thereby installed as the space in which a man and a woman are divinely encountered, which therefore privileges that sexed space as where God is encountered for unity and coherence in the present.[16] But if that originary site is not a picture of innocent sexuality, but an indicative projection of what all humans desire—peace and satisfaction with the world and God—then the disproportionate allocation of guilt and shame based on one's (in)ability to enter that space or measure up to Adam and Eve's coherence is not only unfounded, but manifestly unjust.

The critique lands a final theological blow when Rees observes that one's desire for coherence is found in the mythic sinful images of Adam and Eve rather than God. Rees states emphatically:

> More productive theologically is the fantasy of a communal existence where sex doesn't exist, where the fictional expression of the fallen self's dream of wholeness in a sex never arises, where the self projects no sex to image its completion, especially in another human being, instead finding completion in God.[17]

Rees is not suggesting that sex does not exist, but that the *idea* of sex does not exist. His suggestion is that if the Christian's pursuit of flourishing and coherence is in union with God, then the politicization of heterosexual marital sex will be exposed as the historical means of eschewing the inherent sinfulness of heterosexuality and thus the unjust distribution of shame on those who desire those of the same sex. Moreover, Rees suggests that flourishing and coherence of people and societies will not be indexed to one's sexual approximation of Adam and Eve, but one's union with God.

The provocative scenario that Rees creates forces the person to choose between God and Adam and Eve, where God represents life and Adam and Eve represent sex. Sex saves! But according to Rees's doctrine

16. Rees, *Romance*, 12.
17. Rees, *Romance*, 198.

of creation, to choose sex is to choose the myth of innocence, which equates to sinful sexuality and therefore death. Sex kills! Playing with the notion of the Faustian pact, Rees likens this scenario to Foucault's claim that perhaps "sex is worth dying for."[18]

The Sexual Revolution and the Fall of Sex

This reading of the fall of innocent sexuality and consequent death and vision of life through sex is not as antagonistic to conservative Christian ears as it might initially sound if we defer theological reflection on Adam and Eve. Another fall of sexuality closer to our time—the sexual revolution—exposes a conservative view of sex to the full weight of Rees's critique of innocent sexuality. Even though Rees does not ultimately believe in originary Edenic sexual innocence, the way he brings together a theory and theology of sexuality fosters an opportunity to consider the value ascribed to an idea of sex in the present. In other words, if we read Rees as interrogating conservative convictions on sex after the Edenic fall of Adam and Eve, we face the possibility of the politicization of a controlling idea of sex "as an effect of fallen human avoidance of responsibility for original sin."[19] This is to confess that "the wages of sin is death" and that this confession must be thoroughly accounted for in a conservative theology of gender.[20]

In the 1960s, social attitudes toward sex changed dramatically. Sex was ripped out of heterosexual marriage as the environment that previously justified it as good. Through various means, the sexual revolution may have broken the shackles of marriage that domesticated sex, not least with the introduction of safe and reliable methods of contraception, but it came at the expense of life, as expressed earlier with the Faustian pact.[21]

From many conservative perspectives, the terms of this bargain reflects a fair price or at least is in step with conservative interpretations of the era: the sexual revolution was the point at which the fall of sex precipitated the "death" of society and even some parts of the church.[22]

18. Foucault, *History of Sexuality*, 156, in Rees, *Romance*, 14.
19. Rees, *Romance*, 16.
20. Rom 6:23.
21. Rees, *Romance*, 14.

22 The news of a Christian teenage son or daughter having premarital sex (or worse, the news of teenage pregnancy or coming out as gay), represents a similar fall

But for many, including Rees following Foucault, the trade-off is worth it: sex is worth dying for, especially if the *idea* of sex that society is said to be falling from is *not* innocent.

Rees does not deny the fall of sex, but we must remember that for Rees, sex is an idea: he does not deny the fall of the *idea* of sex. Understandably, what he contests is the possibility that sex is a means of saving society from death. More fundamentally, he contests the merit of returning to the idea of sex from which society has fallen, and for good reason. If the environment from which sex has been unmoored was not innocent, but in fact was a context of predation and coercion,[23] in what sense can we legitimately speak about sex as having fallen? Sex certainly fell, but what idea did it fall from and was that idea of the human will or God's? Specifically, was the idea of sex (and gender) that dominated Western society pre–sexual revolution as innocent as the proposed Faustian pact presumes? Did the 1950s social attitudes toward sexuality and gender characterize Edenic perfection, or are they better described as a sinful and oppressive social construction? Rees's critique of innocent sexuality can be read as probing the precise context from which sex fell. On this account, if the time prior to the sexual revolution is not as innocent as the term "fall" implies, which the catastrophic impact of the fall on humanity and creation in the beginning does suggest, then the stakes of the wager are surely not as high for the side that chooses sex.

For Rees, however, the idea of sex is not a life-and-death issue, simply because by choosing sex, death is not at stake. One does not give up life for sex, because death already rules; this is not in dispute. Ironically, when society chose sex, innocent sex fell, but here we are not speaking about the Edenic reality, but a *human* idea. The *romance* of innocent sexuality rightly demands critique because it names a cathexis on human

---

into death from virgin/sexual innocence. For examples of narrations of the sexual revolution as a fall of sex into "death," see Harrison, *Better Story*. C. S. Lewis preempts the effects of the fall (or falling sex) in *Mere Christianity*, 78. Kuby, *Global Sexual Revolution*; Jones, "Sexual Perversion," 257–73; and Post, "Love, Religion, and Sexual Revolution," 405–7.

23. However contested such a claim might be, there is much to be said about the languishing attempts by a society and a church that were controlled predominantly by men and that limited education and vocation opportunities for women. Furthermore, the image of "woman" that women felt the need to conform to was man-made. Betty Friedan comments in her ground-breaking book *The Feminine Mystique* in 1963: "The new image of . . . 'Occupation: housewife,' had hardened into a mystique, unquestioned and permitting no questions, shaping the very reality it distorted." Friedan, *Feminine Mystique*, 44.

ideas of sex that circumscribed society before it fell despite already being marked inexorably by the fall.

We misinterpret the sexual revolution (or any other moment in history that narrates the fall of sex as the cause of death and rejection of life) when it is not conceived first as an effect of another sin-framed context. There is *no* innocent sexuality this side of Adam and Eve's fall from innocence, which renders vast aspects of the sexual revolution and its fruit as not befitting God's desires for his creatures. This claim, however, is different to the problematic one that is revealed when we take seriously our seduction by a problematic notion of innocent sexuality that emerges only in light of the fall of sex in the 1960s.

The romance of innocent sexuality demands critique because it not only valorizes a moment in the prelapsarian era as though it is not thereby glossing over the sinful patterning of sex installed therein. Much worse, however, is the pseudo-redemptive possibility of heterosexual marital sex and the nuclear family as a means of returning to innocence for society. Rees speaks prophetically into the conservative church when he observes the contradictory claim that sex saves even though sex is blamed for society's fall.[24] One has been seized by "a fantasy of liberation from sex without ever achieving consciousness of sin."[25] To get back to the beginning (if that is even possible), society is not encouraged to turn to God to be redeemed, but to its own capacity to engage in sex work, particularly, heterosexual sex in marriage and its institutionalization in society by law and policy decisions, which equates to a politico-religious mode of self-righteousness or sex-works-based righteousness.

Returning to Rees, he calls out the logical fallacy of appealing to authority to justify a claim. Deferring to God to justify the installation of sinful sexuality only masks the true locus of power for justifying means to purity and life. In other words, before the sexual revolution, the point on the horizon that is invoked to be gazed upon, and valorized for others to gaze upon, is not what God calls to be gazed upon for life, but is a projection of our own respective desires where *we* desire to find coherence, goodness, and purity. In Rees's interpretation of Augustine, all

---

24. The conservative Catholic Christian ethicist Lisa Sowle Cahill makes a similar point when reflecting on the goal of "postmodern" thinkers like Judith Butler, Catherine MacKinnon, and Michel Foucault. She states: "Postmodern ethics is not at bottom nihilistic, but positive and prophetic, for it identifies and seeks to overturn real injustices in the world as 'dominations.'" Cahill, *Sex, Gender, and Christian Ethics*, 29.

25. Rees, *Romance*, 200.

sexuality is installed as an authoritative fictitious point on the horizon of knowledge that we look to for coherence.[26] The danger of human ideas of sex that are dressed up as good and even said to be ordained by God for life and flourishing is that they promise life, but in the end can only reinforce our need to be saved from our desire-induced, incoherent bodies of death. The person fixated on sex, whatever its form, is therefore caught up in a relentless pursuit of an illusion, which puts them in an unforgiving bind to sex, which leads to eternal incoherence. The desire for coherence through sex is a "death instinct."[27]

Dashing the Hope of Innocent Sex

The repudiation of originary innocence by Rees limits the critical import his thought can have on a conservative theological view of gender because we confess an originary human innocence in which God's desires for humanity are manifest. Despite this limitation, Rees's critique of innocence continues to impact conservative theological reflection on gender because the sinful predilection to dwell on images in the past for coherence is not limited to those that humans construct.

Rees's critique of innocent sexuality brings to light the possibility that even God's innocent creation of Adam and Eve in Eden is vulnerable to idolatrous fixation. In the previous section we explored the notion that the environment prior to the sexual revolution was not God's desire, but a human construct. We saw that valorizing a notion of pre-fall sex as the background against which to understand sex since its revolutionary fall is theologically problematic. Now we confront the persistent voice that insists on that time before the sexual revolution as not being characterized by a sinful human construction of moral conservatism, but God's originary desire for humanity. In other words, the vision for society that was drawn into the present (or lingered from previous eras) in the post–World War II era reflected the good creation of God that we find in the images of Adam and Eve in the beginning. Before we erroneously assume this to be a theologically defensible mode of moral theology, we must consider what it means to draw Edenic images of Adam and Eve into the present.

---

26. Rees, *Romance*, 15–16.
27. Rees, *Romance*, 15.

The notion that the innocent images of Adam and Eve are of any use to people or society today implies that humanity has departed from them. The impact of the images and the very reason they are brought into the present implies this departure: humanity has lost originary innocence, which it needs to recover. The presentation of the innocent images articulates the responsibility of recreating the beginning in the present: with messianic overtones, the images of Adam and Eve come to us for us to enact. The names of Adam and Eve, therefore, represent humanity's departure from our God-ordained innocent state and the implied divine imperative and means of our return to it.

But this narration dismisses the incontrovertible force of *time* on our relationship with the beginning. The exploration of W. H. Auden's poetic commentary on the body's desire to rid itself of anxiety in chapter 2 provides a more faithful theological account. One cannot draw the images of Adam and Eve into the present because they remain in the beginning. Briefly, Auden's travelers search for Arcadia to be released from their bodies of death, but they learn in the end that they cannot enter Arcadia—or more precisely, cannot exit their fallen embodied predicament. In the end, they sit on the outside of the garden, gazing at what *was* on the inside, now but a memory of innocent sexuality. Eden and humanity's God-created originary innocence lie in the *past*, and so Eden cannot be conceived as coming to us. Rather, we must make a pilgrimage to the edge of Eden to gaze upon the memory of coherence that is lost.

Rees's critique extends to the creation scene of Adam and Eve because his theology of sex is based on the concept of loss. He contends that people are incoherent not only because they lack something, but because they lost something. The human impulse is to recover what was lost so as to enjoy unity by being reunited with what was lost. Here we see Rees's explicit use of Butler's Freudian notion of gender as melancholic loss to construct a theology of sex. The questions for theological reflection come to the fore: can humanity's lost innocence be recovered via the images of Adam and Eve? That is, do the images of Adam and Eve offer humanity a valid means for recovering what was lost due to sin? Or are the images of the bodies of Adam and Eve a seductive site of pilgrimage that reveal humanity's desperate desire for coherence through a problematic union with created things? Does the perpetual conjuring of the images of Adam and Eve to be gazed upon for individual and societal coherence betray an idolatrous fixation on images of beautifully sexed bodies, something akin to pornography? Do the images of Adam and Eve function as a site of holy communion: a place to consume or participate in *their* bodies as a means of grace for life now? We must begin to entertain the very serious possibility that invoking the images of Adam and Eve for individuals and society to enact does not lead to human flourishing and coherence, but to idolatrous worship of seductive images of created things and therefore to condemnation and death.

A Seductive Image

Adam and Eve: Idols of Death

A conservative theology of gender confesses that the bodies of Adam and Eve do not justify some and condemn others while providing a means of redemption. This reveals two points that require theological attention: the first is the claim that Adam and Eve represent a goal and standard by which humanity can determine who is "naturally" justified and who still needs to be justified in their bodies. The second relates to the first in that in this scheme of salvation there is no need for repentance to God for life in death-ridden bodies.

A Christian view of gender and sexuality that is devoid of God's grace and human repentance reduces Adam and Eve to a beautiful image to be gazed upon idolatrously. They are idols that seduce and captivate the heart and reveal what really matters to the viewer. Foucault's theological instincts are on track when he quips that sex "has become more important than our souls."[28] Rees takes up this claim to reflect on the problem of humanity's dis-orientation and the irrepressible desire for sexual coherence:

> [Foucault] presumably isn't worried that his readers risk the loss of their soul in their desire for sex. Yet in theological terms the affective orientation he describes of the self to sex connotes idolatry. Sex—a creation of human imagination—has been wrongly invested with maximal importance at the expense of return to God. Like any other idol, the ultimate truth of sex turns out to be an ultimate anti-climax: the non-necessity of sex to the desire it promises to fulfill.[29]

---

28. Foucault, quoted in Rees, *Romance*, 45–46.
29. Rees, *Romance*, 46.

While we have rejected Rees's suggestion that Edenic innocent sex is a human idea, we can agree with his associated claim that innocent Adam and Eve is problematically proposed as the path to desire's fulfillment: sex in the form of Adam and Eve is not necessary to answer desire's call for fulfillment. Foucault certainly is not worried about losing souls, but where a desire for Adam and Eve for fulfillment is the affective orientation of a theology of gender, sex and gender do connote idolatry, putting souls at stake.

A theology of gender is reformed when it roots out an affective orientation of the self to sex by challenging the idolatry of the Edenic man and woman. The image of Adam and Eve has been explored as an image on the horizon, like a vanishing point in a painting that organizes the whole landscape. This organization is a malevolent patterning of the mind and heart by a false-messianic figure that (rather than who) is always coming but never arriving. Images don't connote presence but absence. A theology of gender cannot entertain a pretender that offers life but holds people in an eternal sex/death drive. When we properly integrate the image of Adam and Eve into a theology of gender, the question of gender violence is not a thorn in one's side or a pandering to this ideology or that lobby group. Apart from gesturing toward the broad Christian principles of love and mercy, at present the conservative theological warehouse for grounding resistance to gender violence, as we explored in the previous chapter, is bare. Before we turn to the image of God in Jesus Christ in the next chapter, the work must be done first to purge the idolatrous gaze of the static beautiful bodies of the Edenic creatures.

A theology of gender that is serious about treating gender violence must take seriously the often-heard Old Testament exhortation to take down the images. This is worthy of further consideration. The scriptural ground for such a claim is Deuteronomy 4:15–16: "Since you saw no form when the LORD spoke to you at Horeb out of the fire, take care and watch yourselves closely, so that you do not act corruptly by making an idol for yourselves, in the form of any figure—the likeness of male or female." This is a pertinent passage because the author speaks about the LORD who was encountered at Horeb as without form, which stands in contrast to idolatrous images that have the form of male or female. In other words, confusion between God and images of male and female is certainly possible, hence the command: "watch yourselves closely," but the following words are clear that confusion is not justified. It remains to be seen what it means to take down the images of Adam and Eve, certainly a form of deconstruction, and whether this requires a more heavy-handed iconoclastic response. The posture of reform rather than wholesale deconstruction that characterizes the developing theology of gender of this book suggests that iconoclasm is not the course to be taken.

Rejecting an iconoclastic response might appear to go against the aforementioned scriptural counsel to watch ourselves closely, but a brief reflection on Scripture and the content of this book reveals that our relationship to images demands a much more nuanced response. In Scripture we learn that humanity is commanded not to bow down to images, while made in the image of God, yet called to conform to the image of Jesus Christ, and as Butler herself shows, and as we are seeing, constantly captured by the images of the originary man and woman as they linger on the horizon.[30] We cannot escape images nor can we live without them.

This paradoxical relationship to images is what Bruno Latour calls "iconoclash" which is a moment of confusion of not knowing where to look or what to do with the images we see.[31] Iconoclash manifests in uncertainty not only about the efficacy of the image's capacity to mediate the reality to us, but also about the motivation or purpose of their author.[32] For example, as we begin to see Adam and Eve as a troublesome image, disorientation emerges and we lose faith in them, though not entirely. We begin to look elsewhere, but where are we to look? We glance back to Adam and Eve only to reestablish the reason we departed them in the first place. Iconoclash names this ambivalence. How can we be *against* images? How can we be *for* images? Can we be for *and* against images? Latour brings some relief by confronting an image's power and resisting their desire to be captured, framed, and hung. He desires to fight "*freeze-framing*, that is, extracting an image out of the flow, and becoming fascinated by it, as if it were sufficient, as if all movement had stopped."[33] This "flow" is what I call time or the context in which Adam and Eve are situated and which we have departed. In a sense, we have already begun to resist freeze-framing Adam and Eve. The call to watch ourselves closely therefore alerts us to the power of *installed* images and their power to recreate or de-animate the most vital among us.

---

30. Rom 8:29.
31. Latour, "*What Is Iconoclash?*," 16.
32. Latour, "*What Is Iconoclash?*," 20.
33. Latour, "*What Is Iconoclash?*," 21.

The author of Psalm 115 carries out a technical investigation into idols and idolatry. The description of idols given in the psalm is psychoanalytic in so far as the goal of the description is to bring to consciousness the way idols function on the unconscious (or the heart or soul) and therefore how they fundamentally recreate who one is in the world and with God. The psalmist teaches that idols are not powerless and inconsequential lumps of carbon, but powerful pretenders that seductively hang on the horizon as a messianic promise of individual and societal fulfillment.

The psalmist begins his instruction about idols by pointing out their creaturely beauty despite their clear limitations. They are made of silver and gold, but cannot speak, see, hear, smell, feel, or walk despite having mouths, eyes, ears, noses, hands, and feet.[34] Augustine's account of this moment in his commentary on the psalm is graphic:

> From that metal which the true God made, you want to make a false god *or, rather, a false man*, whom you then venerate instead of the true God! If anyone were to mistake it for a real human being and try to make friends with it, such a person would be accounted mad. A likeness of the human mortal shape, with its members disposed in an orderly fashion that imitates the human body, attracts fickle hearts and sweeps them along into gross passion. But if you can indicate the several organs in this copy that bewitches you, O human vanity, show us also how they work.[35]

Augustine's "false man" is not merely a replica of a human body but is a "false god" that seduces hearts into worship. Replacing the true God with an image of a false man does not lead to reverent praise of the creator and savior, but the satisfaction of "gross passion"—sex. What is shocking for Augustine is that the seduced worshiper is not counted among the "mad." The vulgarity with which the passage concludes does not indict Augustine, but those who justify their sex-lives by appealing to inanimate images.

The moral outcome is important for the psalmist, but it is of secondary importance. In the same way that we have seen in Rees, and even Foucault though only ironically, the principal concern with being transfixed by images of humanity is that we become like them. But is this not the

---

34. Ps 115:4–7.
35. Augustine, *Sermons on the Psalms 99–120*, 313 (emphasis mine).

point of pursing Adam and Eve, to become like them, creatures of God's desire? The psalmist's point is sobering in that the problem with becoming like images of God's creation, even very good ones, is that we do not take on their appearance but their life (or lack thereof). To become like them means that the worshiper becomes lifeless—like them. The lifeless idol becomes a permanent vanishing point on the horizon that orients the entire landscape of the self. This worship and deadening are not an occasional or intermittent experience depending on whether one is prostrate before the idol or not, but all-consuming. The ancient votive practice of placing a statue of oneself in the temple to remain perpetually present in servitude to their god demonstrates their inability, unlike the psalmist, to name the totalizing nature of their dead gods.[36] The psalmist writes, "Those who make them will be like them" (v. 8a).[37] Those who install these inanimate objects as focal points of life, experience a radical transformation regardless of their physical or representative proximity. They, like God's creation which they worship as an idol, are also objectivized, that is, they re-create their selves through a process of self-objectification. Here is the irony: the God-sensitized human hands that manipulate created matter to form idols with features that cannot sense God's world, become de-sensitized or de-animated like the idols' features. The once animated body parts undergo a transformation resulting in the loss of their senses. Having desired the objectivized and inanimate image they re-created from God's earth, the re-creators inadvertently re-create their selves as "dead" objects. Here one can see the insight Rees offers through his appeal to Foucault's notion that where sex is an idol, sex is a technology of power that (re)makes bodies.

The impact of the objectification of God's creation extends further than those who orchestrate created matter into idols. Those who turn to idols and trust in them also undergo a transformation through de-animation. That is, "all those who trust in them" will also "be like them" (v. 8b). Those who create images to be worshiped in fact create society-deanimating machines. Finally, the force of holding the image of Adam and Eve up to society is revealed: it does not save society, but further roots its heart in patterned worldliness. Augustine chastises such foolishness:

36. For example, "So Esarhaddon: 'I had a statue of me as king made out of silver, gold and shining copper . . . (and) placed (it) before the gods to constantly request wellbeing for me.'" Clines, "Image of God in Man," 83.

37. Images are not "illustrations of faith, but objects of faith." Clines, "Image of God in Man," 82.

"let people with open and seeing eyes gaze at images that neither see nor live, and let their minds become closed and dead as they worship."[38] The psalmist and Augustine's insight makes it clear that images of God's good creation are not powerless. Indeed, these idols are powerful enough to render the worshiper and society dead and blind to each other and God, the one who does have the power to save society from its bodies of death. God's originary creatures that manifest innocent sexuality are never far from being recrafted into lethal instruments of death.

Practitioners of Purer Religion

The persistent challenge to the call to chasten one's use of the images of Adam and Eve is the refrain that they are God's perfect and ordained creatures. They represent God's desire for humanity and so when I hold them up to society, I am not inducing idolatry but right living, which is what God desires. In response to this kind of thinking, Augustine in the same passage draws attention to how mistaken they are: "Now when a humanoid form is skillfully wrought to serve as some sign (as idolaters claim) and placed on a raised platform, and when the crowd begins to worship it and pay homage, it engenders in each of them a most foul misapprehension."[39] Augustine is right to observe that worshipers find no movement in idols. They are artefacts, and therefore lifeless, but for the worshipper to have "life," he or she is required to believe in the life of the images. In terms of the Edenic creatures, despite the fact that Adam and Eve are dead and long decomposed and therefore necessarily absent from our present lives, they too must be (re)invested with life in our minds—a resurrection from the dead. The figures on the horizon have a messianic character as those who come with salvation for the true believer. Where the worshiped messianic figures take the form of a human, even a very good sinless human who is not Christ Jesus, "it engenders . . . a most foul misapprehension." Likewise, Adam and Eve do not bring life, but a foul misapprehension of life. This delusion is the false redemption of which Rees speaks. The psalmist reminds us: "Those who make them are like them; so are all who trust in them" (v. 8). All created things are powerless as sources of life and salvation, and in this sense can be seen to be as de-animated and senseless as idols made of gold, silver, or wood. Those who

---

38. Augustine, *Expositions of the Psalms*, 316.
39. Augustine, *Expositions of the Psalms*, 314.

put their trust in such created things, rather than in the living God, also become spiritually de-animated and senseless.

Furthermore, recalling the confession "God created them" does not justify idol worship, that is, the worship of the created. Augustine decries those who claim: "I worship neither an idol nor a demon, I regard the image as a physical sign of what I ought to worship." Augustine calls out the flawed reasoning of such "practitioners of purer religion."[40] He states: "When the worshippers begin to be embarrassed by the charge that they are adoring material things . . . they have the temerity to reply that they are not paying cult to the physical objects themselves but to the deities who preside over and rule them."[41] Of course, Augustine is referring specifically to the pagan cults, but his examples are examples. Where the images of Adam and Eve (as reproductive heterosexual sex in marriage) take on messianic redemptive significance, it is not satisfactory to claim: "I am not worshipping dead material things nor demons, but God who created them." Referencing Romans 1:25 and the Pauline description of idolatry as the exchange of the creator for the created, Augustine notes the subtle exchange of truth for a lie where created things become the object of worship in the place of the creator under the guise of pure or purer religion or the confession, "God created them."

The charge of idolatry should be a surprising revelation because it unmasks obvious and self-evident good as merely pretending to be so. In this sense, the charge of idolatry reveals God's judgement for being seduced by the "artificiality of convention."[42] In the moment of revelation, all that obfuscated the true nature of the idol is stripped away revealing the truth and how it managed to evade detection for so long. Bernd Wannenwetsch observes that idolatry is not revealed by virtue of a slow and steady unfolding argument but by an explosive flash of force that amounts to a predicate: "here you have it, *idolatry*."[43] A surprise can be momentary, as in the case of a surprise birthday party, but it can also be a post-event reflection. We see this when a weak football team triumphs over the "unbeatable" team. The game must play out before the surprise dawns consciously as a surprise. The charge of idolatry of Adam and Eve in this book takes the form of a predicate, but this is the result of a slow

---

40. Augustine, *Expositions of the Psalms*, 315.
41. Augustine, *Expositions of the Psalms*, 315.
42. Wannenwetsch, "Desire of Desire," 316.
43. Wannenwetsch, "Desire of Desire," 316.

unfolding rather than an apocalyptic inbreaking. It has been necessarily slow because it is unthinkable that Adam and Eve would take the form of an image to be worshiped.

In this steady investigation, we learn something about our gullibility and propensity for false worship. We also learn that idols "appear in a form different to that which we expect. Moses was concerned with the idolatry of false promises, we are threatened by the common place, the prosaic, the familiar."[44] I would add that we should also be concerned with ourselves. Adam and Eve are the supreme idols because they take the form of me and you. Like Butler's feedback loop that installs mundane desire in the beginning to justify mundane desire in the present, we install a mirror in the beginning so that when we look there, we see ourselves in the garden as God's innocent embodied delights. The originary man, who is in fact a mirror image of me, justifies my fallen existence as good rather than revealing my need for life from my body of death. Adam and Eve in the mirror—ourselves—communicate that we are alive when in fact a proper purchase on God's originary creatures reveal that we are dead in our bodies. There is very little difference between Butler's self-serving re-creation myth and the Christian's perverted sight that envisions one's self in Eden.

The Law of Adam and Eve

The good lives enjoyed by the creatures in the beginning and from which humanity has since departed can be idolatrously fixated upon as a means of achieving false unity in the present. These same originary good lives can also be recast as a law. While seldom conceived as a law, Adam and Eve are a divine institution of holy life and therefore a righteous standard by which all are measured, and by which only some are usually found in want. This, however, is an unjust application of the law.

The theological concept that Adam and Eve is a law from which *all* have fallen is not a new innovative theological conception.[45] We see something similar in the Gospel of Matthew in Jesus' response to questioning about the legal justification of divorcing women for any cause.[46]

---

44. Wannenwetsch, "Desire of Desire," 316.

45. I explore this in more depth in Patterson, "Law of Adam and Eve," in *1968: Culture and Counterculture*.

46. Matt 19:3–12.

Jesus does not respond by appealing to a right interpretation of the law to counter its (mis)use by the Pharisees to justify abuse of women by men for their own satisfaction. The men have undermined the law, and so restating the law would only reiterate the terms they are using to justify the normalization of divorce and the ill-treatment of women.[47] They have undermined the force of the law and so Jesus appeals to the righteous standard of Adam and Eve to carry out the same critical function.[48] Jesus says: "It was because you were so hard-hearted that Moses allowed you to divorce your wives, *but from the beginning it was not so.*"[49] Jesus appeals to God's ordained Edenic good creation of male and female in the beginning to expose their sinfulness. The law which is liable to misinterpretation is interpreted by Jesus against the backdrop of another righteous law, Edenic innocence, which is beyond contest, contra Rees.

Humanity's departure from Eden therefore amounts to a fall from innocence before the *law of Adam and Eve*. The implication of Jesus' invocation of originary innocence did not however equate to a general characterization of general embodiment, but the specific coherence and fulfillment that came through the marital union of Adam and Eve that God created for them to live out and enjoy. The men might be able to twist the law to justify their desire to discard women, but it flies in the face of the beauty of the creation that God created in Adam and Eve.

Must a conservative theology of gender agree with Rees that all sexuality is sinful, especially in light of humanity's universal guilt under the law of Adam and Eve? Rees makes the point of clarification when he claims that all sexuality is sinful, he is not suggesting anything inherent about sexuality.[50] Caution must be exercised, however, because on closer inspection Rees is simply reasserting the already-explored idea that sexuality is a myth that is always a replication of someone's sinful humanity. He is referring to the ground in the beginning on which sexuality can be adjudicated as moral or not. On this account, a conservative theology of gender departs Rees and cannot for that reason conclude that all sexuality is sinful.

But a theology of gender must account for the basic Christian conviction that sexuality and gender is a part of what it means to be human

---

47. Matt 19:7.
48. See the apostle Paul's discussion of torah in Rom 3:19–20.
49. Matt 19:8 (emphasis mine).
50. Rees, *Romance*, 144.

after Eden. In this we can agree with Rees that sexuality is sinful as an implication of a broader Christian truth about the fallenness of human nature. This does not justify panning back so far that we lose the clarity of the defining characteristics of what it means to be a fallen human. It is important that a theology of gender is grounded on the claim that humanity in the beginning was good, but that humanity has departed from that beginning. Clarity about the kind of gaze with which we look upon Adam and Eve now is crucial for how we continue to think about ourselves and others as fallen approximations of them and how redemption is possible from our bodies of death. Enacting Adam and Eve's innocent marital sex is not a means of a possible return to unity, even if that is the kind of life God created in the beginning.

The claim that all gender and sexuality is sinful does not imply there is no good to be found in the world in which we live as male and female. There is a common grace that God imparts to humanity when they live into God's good originary social orders, but this should not be confused as a life that God accepts as pure and holy. Confusing one's "natural" state for what is righteous is what Augustine elsewhere warns against: "Although people may claim to perform good work before faith . . . they look to me like someone running with great power and at high speed, but off course."[51] Likewise, the often-cited prophet who decries those who refuse to discriminate between righteous deeds and filthy rags.[52] If humanity is characterized by *fallen* sexuality and gender then appealing to one's good desire or gendered or marital life to demonstrate one's righteous life before God, only serves to obfuscate the reality of one's guilt before the law of Adam and Eve and thus one's need to be saved from one's body of death.

A theology of gender must account for the human *departure* from what God created in the beginning and must resist the seductive force of Adam and Eve that invites us to return to them for coherence and life. Instead, by understanding Adam and Eve as a law, they are instructive like the law of Moses, revealing not only humanity's fallenness, but also the need for salvation from bodies of death. The image of Adam and Eve, when rightly integrated into a theology of gender, does not become the focal point, but *points beyond itself to the body of Christ*, which does bring the hope of coherence in life, even to our bodies of death.

---

51. Augustine, *Expositions of the Psalms*, 365.
52. Isa 64:6.

Conclusion

We arrived at this chapter provoked by Butler to reflect theologically on gender violence, particularly the weapon that inflicts it, and that which or who justifies its use. What makes this provocation difficult to pursue is the way violence and its justification are often concealed by what is normatively good. In this chapter we have seen that the good originary creatures of Adam and Eve can function in this way. While God created them good as a part of a very good universe, we have seen that when time is not considered, they can take the form of an originary law that can be used to unjustly justify some, yet justly condemn others. In other words, reforming humanity's relationship with Adam and Eve in terms of law reveals the uncomfortable truth that the historically conceived transgressors are not justified but are joined by those of us who justified ourselves as good. *Adam and Eve do not justify any person's sexuality or gender, but reveal everyone's need to be rescued from their bodies of death.*

There are at least four implications that emerge from this reform of Adam and Eve. The first is the confronting and humbling realization that *Edenic Adam and Eve have propped up and at times have even constituted the ideal of heterosexual man and woman as a vision for a good society, which has underwritten and justified forms of gender violence to attain the vision.* Those whose desires, bodies, and minds did not conform to the social vision were subject to cruel and unjust legal, medical, social, emotional, or spiritual discipline.

A second implication relates to the first. The disciplining of the transgressor is unjust but not because the transgressing person is innocent or because the law is unjust. This signals a radical departure from Butler's negotiation of the law that resides in the beginning. For Butler the originary law is unjust because it does not justify mundane desires and for this reason requires reform. This implies that the person has wrongly been labelled a transgressor but is in fact innocent. By contrast, a confessional Christian account maintains that the beginning is inaccessible and descriptive of what God created in the beginning. This originary humanity that represents God's expressed will for creation is not an inherently unjust expectation but is prone to unjust administration. The disciplining of transgressing desires, minds, and bodies is unjust because it manifests gross hypocrisy whereby certain people are forcibly conformed to God's originary creation by people who evade the reality of their own body of death and thus their need to conform to God's originary humanity. *The disciplining of the transgressor is unjust because historically only a few are subject to the verdict of transgressor.* The just administration of the law of Adam and Eve is a verdict of universal guilt, that all people fall short of meeting God's originary expressed desire in Adam and Eve. This reveals that *all* human lives are subject to bodies of death. Cruelty, or gender violence, is produced when the good law of Adam and Eve is administered unjustly.[53]

Another implication of reforming how we conceive our relation to Adam and Eve in the beginning is that we become acutely aware that *the originary embodied lives of Adam and Eve do not equate to pre-sexual revolution era moral conservativism.* When we truly consider humanity's relationship to Adam and Eve, it becomes apparent that there is *no era of innocent sexuality and gender*—apart from the inaccessible beginning—that should bewitch the Christian imagination. A return to the time before the fall of humanity in the beginning is not possible, and the desire to return to the time before the fall of sex in the 1960s is a return to another era of fallen human embodiment. The former desire is an impossibility, while the latter is, at best, misguided naive idealism, and at worst, a sin-bent, death-driven, and self-justifying enterprise. Society's redemption is *not* a program of human social-engineering that is focused on what is lost or what can be found on a pre-1960s billboard, however much it reminds us of Edenic beauty and coherence.

The final implication of reflecting on Adam and Eve as a law is that it reveals that *gender is simultaneously what I am and what I desire to be.* This means that gender must be understood grammatically as a noun and verb, an object that lives in a mode of perpetual subjection. If Adam and Eve represent God's desire for man and woman, yet also a human reality we cannot access, then human embodiment always remains in a mode of being in subjection to these objects. I am a man, but I am not the man God desires me to be, which renders manhood a mode of *becoming* but *never arriving*. Likewise, a woman and her relation to Eve renders womanhood a state of *becoming* a woman. So Butler is right to observe that a baby comes into a world in which its first act is to justify "itself" against an originary law. This is the beginning of a life of desiring to become what it will never be. The regulating force of this law is powerful and normative, which must be chastened.

---

53. This argument mimics the theological movement of Jesus' engagement with the Pharisees and the woman in John 8:2–11.

A common response is that some of us approximate Adam and Eve more than others. But using this line of reasoning underestimates the gravity of *merely approximating* God's originary desire as expressed in creation. It obfuscates where one gazes for life and the means for self-justification. Where all humanity finds itself transgressing the law of Adam and Eve, it is inadequate to say that I don't transgress the law as badly as that person does. This kind of thinking reveals that we are caught up in the rat race of trying to justify ourselves before God by ourselves. When we confess that the law of Adam and Eve reveals that our lives are characterized by bodies of death, we come to terms with the reality that not only is Adam the man I can never be, but that I need to find life outside of myself and apart from the law.

Chapter 5

An Ethics of Gender: Finding Hope in Desire

Introduction

THIS CHAPTER FURTHER EXPOUNDS Butler's theory of gender by investigating what it means to live in a community that is characterized by her subject of desire and critique of gender violence. The result is an ethics of gender that is not a final declaration of what a man or woman is and thus an account of how one should live as such, but a personal response to the realization that I am unintelligibly gendered without other people and society.

So far, we have explored Butler's theorization of a person's subjectivity as *desire-induced incoherence*, which now forms the basis of her ethics, which is characterized by *incoherence-induced responsibility*. She reveals that the nature of our individual striving for life binds us together to form one striving body-corporate. This unveils not only my susceptibility to the other and the body-corporate who wield the power to grant me life, but also the power I wield as one who participates in the body-corporate to grant life for which others strive. An ethics of gender that results in responsibility is not imposed, but revealed as the nature of a society constituted by people with a mutual desire to live.

The "body" is a prominent and often confusing feature in Butler's ethics of gender, which for the purposes of clarity can be interpreted as taking four forms. The first is the crude *material* body. The second body is a *concept* that forms the content of my individual experience of the material body. The third body is the *social union* of bodies which I call the "body-corporate." The final body is an *agreed concept* (norms) that characterizes the body-corporate's belief about the material body. We can see from the way these four forms of the body relate that the material body is not a prominent feature. Butler is more concerned to show how the body-corporate supplies a person's body with conceptualized material. So even when she speaks about a person's body, Butler is usually referring to how one comes to understand oneself according to the body-corporate's conception of the body.

The significance of this circular theorizing about the body for an ethics of gender is that it reflects Butler's ultimate goal to denaturalize gender.[1] A common assumption about Butler's gender theory is that it seeks to unleash desire as a celebration of possibility itself, yet this overstates the task Butler explicitly sets herself. A more modest description is that Butler is attempting to bring to light possibilities of embodied life that already exist yet remain hidden in plain sight. She is not trying to create anything, but reveal what—or better, *who*—is already there. In her own words, the task of denaturalizing gender was taken on "from a desire to live, to make life possible, and to rethink the possible as such."[2] From Butler's perspective, an ethics of gender is about observing the conditions that give or take life, rather than articulating what is moral or immoral embodiment. An ethics of gender, even a Christian ethics of gender, must account for embodied lives that *already* exist.

One must therefore resist drawing a premature conclusion that Butler's tendency to bypass the material body is a rejection of biological difference between men and women. The trouble with biological difference for Butler is not functional difference *per se*, but the ease with which bio-logic becomes a bio-law that justifies the (ill-)treatment of transgression, and rules out of life those who do not or cannot satisfy the bio-legal demands. Assuming the body functions often in predictable ways, Butler is concerned with how society treats those whose bodies do not function predictably, and moreover, to analyze the conditions that enable categorization in the first place.

Butler mobilizes ethical inquiry to see how society can be a more hospitable place for those whose bodies and desires transgress bio-legal

---

1. Butler, *GT*, xx.
2. Butler, *GT*, xx.

demands. This kind of inquiry usually results in "cultivating a will" to allow *their* entry into *our* presence, but this problematically prioritizes ourselves over them.[3] The goal of Butler's ethics of gender is not the integration or inclusion of the transgressor into normal society, but to *reveal* the existing nature of things; that we are already an integrated body-corporate body that shares the desire to live. Rather than reform what is good embodiment to include others, Butler desires to induce the body-corporate to consider what is presently conceived good embodiment as a matter of enduring debate as already existing people emerge from within us to challenge what we conceive to be a valid desirable life.

The principal theoretical motor driving Butler's ethics of gender is Baruch Spinoza's notion of *conatus*, which is a desire of a thing to persist in its being. The importance of this concept for Butler is its double valence: one does not merely desire to *be*, but also *to persist* as one is. This concept will be explored in depth, but suffice to say, Butler sees *conatus* as a universal individual drive to live that is relentless in its pursuit to be what one is. This means that the goal of one's persistence might not be the same as another's, which renders the body-corporate a site of inextricable contest. Moreover, it means that we are all implicated in the lives of others to the extent that we all desire to persist in our respective beings, and so are all equally susceptible to the other's lack of recognition of one's own desire to persist as such. When we come to see our mutual susceptibility, and when we come to see our participatory role in the body-corporate's recognition of a person's desire to persist in their being, we all find ourselves in a state of being responsible *for* the other.

Butler's ethics of gender is not reducible to the "monoprinciple" of Jesus' command of love or the golden rule.[4] A secular approach to this guiding principle is self-serving, which is what Butler finds especially problematic and what her ethics of gender seeks to undermine: I act in a certain way toward the other so that one day, perhaps, they will treat me similarly. According to this view, my action toward the other is not because they are worth it, but so that I might get something in return later. Butler's use of *conatus* turns oneself and society from focusing on their own conception of what is good. This means that her theorization of *responsibility for the other* chastises an ethics of gender that is self-serving, wherein my desire determines whether I will recognize another's desire

3. Butler, *GAO*, 91.

4. I borrow this term and its implied critique from Brock, "On Generating Categories," 49.

to persist in their particular life. Democratizing gender is therefore not a chance for me to exercise my particular desire, but to exercise *our* desire for life by recognizing another's desire to live. Butler therefore submits that the question "What is a man or a woman?" is to be brokered within the breadth and complexity of human community and its complex matrix of desires. While this is risky, Butler is doggedly realistic in her attempt to denaturalize gender, which she understands as lying not in the hands of God, but society. A risky union with the other and the body-corporate is not an option but the very nature of reality and thus the only path to life.

God, Desire, and Hope

Salvation from God: Desiring Spinoza's God

In his *Ethics*, Spinoza demonstrates a basic distrust in humanity's capacity to discern what is true and good. The premise of this distrust is that we cannot know the origin or end of things, which makes possession of such knowledge prejudicial.[5] Spinoza claims that trouble arises when one's worship of God is thought to be a free act[6] of the pursuit of a divinely ordained good, when in fact it is a prejudicial manifestation of "blind desire and insatiable greed."[7] Spinoza's God is not the uncreated God of Scripture whom one must worship, but ourselves and the world around us. Whereas the uncreated God is susceptible to the human propensity of fiction-making and thus self-justification, Spinoza's God is not open to manipulation because it is circumscribed by matter, bound by laws of logic, and accessible through reason.[8] By advancing this doctrine of God, nature, or substance, Spinoza is able to turn what appears to be a cause into an effect and *vice versa*.[9] There is no external cause that determines what is good embodiment, only an infinite series of causing effects.

In Spinoza's God, Butler finds a god *that* (not whom) she can trust because perfection is not a precondition of existence.[10] Perfection does not describe the uncreated God in contrast to imperfect sinful creation,

---

5. Spinoza, *Ethics*, I, App, 110.
6. Spinoza, *Ethics*, I, App, 110.
7. Spinoza, *Ethics*, I, App, 111.
8. Spinoza, *Ethics*, I, App, 109.
9. Spinoza, *Ethics*, I, App, 112.
10. Spinoza, *Ethics*, I, P11S, 92–93; IV Preface, 198–99.

which Spinoza views as another moment of fiction-making.[11] God's perfection is recast as the simple reality of things.[12] This addresses the problematic aspect of slippage between perfection and reality. Spinoza was not interested in refining a set of theological truths, but accurately describing reality as it is. He seeks to treat the problem where what naturally appears is unable to be reconciled, at times, with what is purported to be natural. Spinoza makes this observation:

> For although human bodies agree in many things, they still differ in very many. And for that reason what seems good to one, seems bad to another; what seems ordered to one, seems confused to another; what seems pleasing to one, seems displeasing to another, and so on.[13]

It comes as no surprise that in *Undoing Gender* Butler recounts how she read Spinoza's *Ethics* as a teenager as she sought to make sense of her own nature as one attracted to women that was apparently not natural.[14] By reading his *Ethics*, Butler desired to have passions explained to her, and there, in her Jewish roots and through a Jewish thinker, Butler finds a god in whom she could believe: not the God of Scripture, but a god that provides salvation from the God of Scripture who was (morally) perfect and cruel. Anticipating Beth Lord's view that reading Spinoza's *Ethics* "might change your life,"[15] Butler discovered in this text an "exposition of human passions"—*conatus*—that "signaled . . . a form of vitalism that persists even in despair."[16] In this exposition, the traditional uncreated God of Scripture was stripped of the power to will what was a good, embodied life for each person and community. It is for this reason that Butler takes up Spinoza's concept of *conatus* as the driving force in one's own life and the life of the community.

The early discovery of Spinoza in her teenage years was not a momentary fad, but would become central to Butler's developing work.[17] In her last thorough treatment of gender, Butler states that "the Spinozan

---

11. Spinoza, *Ethics*, IV Preface, 199.
12. Spinoza, *Ethics*, IV Preface, 199; II, D6, 116.
13. Spinoza, *Ethics*, I, App, 114.
14. Butler, *UG*, 235.
15. Lord, *Spinoza's Ethics*, 3.
16. Butler, *UG*, 235.
17. Butler, *UG*, 236.

conatus remains at the core of my work."[18] While this is often hard to detect, the terms Spinoza or *conatus* do not need to be present in order for his thought and concept to be working, even foundationally.[19] Only after a reluctant turn to ethics subsequent to much of her thought on gender having been published does Butler explicitly reveal how *conatus* is functioning in her thought. *Conatus*, we come to see, represents the naturalization of God's will for human life.

A Supernatural Foundation for an Ethics of Gender

A generous interpretation of Butler's gender theory is that she is permanently wrestling with the mind/body question in which she refuses to valorize the mind or body.[20] This wrestling, we should recognize, is reminiscent of the church's own wrestling over the last two millennia concerning the relationship between God and creation. Are they separate entities or are they one, or should they be conceived in a more nuanced way to account for the dynamic complexity of the relationship? These theological questions reach a crescendo in the tricky task of Christology where Christians seek to make sense of and use words to describe Jesus as fully God and fully human. What Butler finds in Spinoza's doctrine of God is an incarnation, of sorts, that treats the problematic uncreated/created dualism: Spinoza de-abstracts God by theorizing God *into* the creation *as* creation.[21] This reform of the God of Scripture means that

---

18. Butler, *UG*, 198.

19. The absence of Spinoza's thought, or where present its dismissal, in Butlerian scholarship is striking. In a compilation of essays called *Butler and Ethics* (edited by Moya Lloyd), for example, Spinoza is mentioned, but only in a cursory manner and only critically. A recent in-depth investigation by Spinozan scholar Hasana Sharp is exceptional. Sharp, *Spinoza and the Politics of Renaturalization*, ch. 4.

20. For example, Carl Trueman's recent interpretation of Butler's thought (*The Rise and Triumph of the Modern Self*) suffers from this kind of reductionism, despite his desire to be careful (30), when he concludes of Butler that "gender is doing, not being" (363) and that "gender possess no prior ontological status" (362). Such interpretations not only fail to give credence to the main critique of Butler's gender theory that it *is* ontologically grounded, but they also fail to recognize that Butler's concern is a historically valid theological concern and worthy of debate and rigorous conversation rather than blithe dismissal. One does not need to subscribe to Butler's gender theory to engage her theory seriously from a theological standpoint, which I try to model in this book.

21. Spinoza uses God, nature, or substance to speak about everything that there is, but I continue to use creation as a subtle signal that we are still speaking about that

God no longer exists apart from creation, acting on creation from outside of it, but is one substance with creation. If God is indistinguishable from creation, then creation does not point beyond itself to what is true—the eternal idea, ideal, or mind of God—but *is itself* what is true.

The presupposition grounding Spinoza's thought is that being is to exist.[22] Like an orthodox doctrine of God, Spinoza conceptualizes creation as not caused, but the "cause of itself," which means that it does not require another thing to exist, and never had a beginning, nor has an end.[23] In short, for Spinoza, creation does not exist in dualistic relationship with the uncreated God, but is one with God as a perpetually self-causing and infinite single substance.[24]

The final idea to add to this brief explanation of Spinoza's God that Butler takes up is that the one substance of creation expresses itself as an infinite number of attributes.[25] Each thing in the world, like a person, water molecule, or chair, does not constitute part of the whole, like a chair in an auditorium, but should be considered as one moment on a continuum of infinite continuity. Spinoza states: "The whole of nature is one individual, whose parts, that is, all bodies, vary in infinite ways, without any change of the whole individual."[26] God, substance, or nature, then, is a unifying principle that binds everything together, and so implicates everything in the existence of everything else. Damage to one thing always implies damage to another thing. Lord summarizes this constitutive characteristic of the world when she says that "physical bodies—your body, the chair you are sitting on, the floor beneath you, the air around you, the person next to you—are really one continuous physical object."[27] A person in this account is therefore not inherently special or good. Instead, they represent a moment of individual facticity that is constituted by and constitutive of other individual things, including other people.

---

which has been created, and also because the word "creation" has a broader use that signifies the universe and all that is in it.

22. Spinoza, *Ethics*, I, D1, 85.
23. Spinoza, *Ethics*, I, D3, 85.
24. Spinoza, *Ethics*, I, D2, 85.
25. There is a wide-ranging discussion concerning how attributes are expressed as thought and extension in Spinoza's thought, but these are not applicable here as Butler's focus centers on *conatus*.
26. Spinoza, *Ethics*, II, L7S, 127.
27. Lord, *Spinoza's Ethics*, 61.

Spinoza's doctrinal reform of God "kills" the creator God who, as Christianity confesses, bestows life on creatures, which is a divine power that is now conferred on creation. Creation, we must now observe in Butler's thought via Spinoza, is not a natural phenomenon with theological import, but supernatural: each thing is characterized simultaneously by singularity and multiplicity. This enlivens the possibility for Butler that being human is not based on nature or theology. Instead, humanity, by virtue of becoming "divinized" or supernatural, accommodates an ethics that emerges in concert with human desire—*conatus*, which is a thing's desire "to persevere in its being."[28] *Conatus* redirects the ethicist's traditional focus from theorizing what independent sovereign acting agents should do to revealing *how* humans live as interdependent subjects in community.

The Potential of *Conatus*

Conatus is not a specifically human drive, but characterizes all things. Notice in Spinoza's definition just mentioned that perseverance is indexed to a thing's ("its") being. A chair, water molecule, and a dog all have this drive, but a chair's desire to persist in its being is much different to how a water molecule or dog desires to exist in their beings. *Conatus* is therefore particular to each thing (not each kind), which means that *each* chair, water molecule, dog, and person have their own particular desire to exist in their being. This draws attention to the ontological quality Spinoza gives to *conatus*: "The striving by which each thing strives to persevere in its being is nothing but the actual essence of the thing."[29]

The complexity of this situation ramps up when we narrow the scene to include only people.[30] For example, where two people who are striving to persevere in their own respective beings encounter each other, they find themselves in a Hegelian originary stand-off wherein each conscious person's desire for life may or may not conflict with the other's desire. If we populate this scene with a family, town, country, or all of humanity, then it becomes a highly charged situation of conflicting

---

28. Spinoza, *Ethics*, III, P6, 159.

29. Spinoza, *Ethics*, III, P7, 159. Commentators of Spinoza do not necessarily view *conatus* as ontological. For example, Williams, "Unravelling the Subject with Spinoza," and Sharp, *Spinoza and the Politics of Renaturalization*.

30. I have limited this example to humans because Butler is concerned with people even though the intersection should accommodate the entire field of desiring things.

desires to persevere in being. The result could be a negotiated hospitable community of different desiring people, or it could end in shunning, a massacre, suicide, or even genocide. *Conatus* renders any encounter of two or more people as a moment of inherent ethical significance.

This scene that is saturated with encounter and *conatus* points to the ethical relationship that everything has to the rest of the universe which reveals that persevering in one's own being is not purely self-referential. Desiring to persevere in my being does not necessarily result in my life. I desire to persevere in my own being when I encounter you, but for this to be realized, you are required to recognize and respond to my desire. In other words, my desire to live implicates my desire for you to desire my life. Butler observes this when she states: "This being is fundamentally responsive, in emotional ways, suggesting that implicit in the very practice of perseverance is a referential movement towards the world."[31] The possibility of life is indexed ultimately to the body-corporate in which a person lives, and its desire to "reflect and further the possibility" of the person's desire to live.[32] Butler does not merely swamp the self with the desires of others, but draws attention to the complex scene of encounter in which desire to persevere in life is a universally shared desire. This is not an ethical imperative that Butler is calling people to live out, and nor is it an attempt "to change the social relations in the world for the better," as Roland Boer critically suggests of Butler, but is a grand unveiling or revelation of the inner workings—*the* social relations—of human life in community.[33] The ontological structuring of human life in community should be a conscious aspect of negotiating how we see ourselves relating to others in community who, like ourselves, desire to exist in being.

The *conatus*-charged community of encounter gives rise to what Butler observes to be a logical ethical implication rather than imperative. The originary Hegelian stand-off wherein each person desires to live but faces the challenge of the other's possible lack of desire for their life, reveals that each person has the power to diminish or enhance the other's desire to persevere in their being.[34] Furthermore, Butler claims

31. Butler, *SS*, 64.
32. Butler, *SS*, 65.
33. Boer, *In the Vale of Tears*, 260.
34. Boer, *In the Vale of Tears*, 260. Butler does not take Hegel's recognition and Spinoza's *conatus* as antithetical conceptions because she deems Hegel was "extrapolating upon" Spinoza. Butler, *UG*, 31. The exact relation between Butler's Hegel and Butler's Spinoza is found in *Giving an Account of Oneself*: "Indeed, a certain desire to persist,

that reflecting the other's desire to live manifests a desire for one's own desire to live. She summarizes *conatus* with its social implications: "'To persevere in one's being' is thus to live in the world that not only reflects but furthers the value of others' lives as well as one's own."[35] Butler therefore challenges Boer's critique that ethics falls into an either/or notion of either response to the other/s or self-care.[36] Or as Butler articulates in *Frames of War*: "The possibility of being sustained relies fundamentally on social and political conditions, and not only on a postulated internal drive to live."[37] Perseverance in one's being is not principally the self's task, but that of the body-corporate of which one is a constitutive part. One cannot care for the self without caring for the other, and one cannot care for the other without caring for the self. Butler does not therefore go beyond Foucault as Boer suggests.[38] Butler's ethics of gender therefore invokes Spinoza's rationalist and materialistic unifying God that unifies all *as* one and one *as* all in an ethical encounter that calls for recognizing our own and the others' desire for life, and thus an ethics of *responsibility for* the other.

When it comes to the theme of gender, originary static norms are identified by Butler as threatening *conatus*. In *Undoing Gender*, Butler makes this link when she states that "norms of recognition function to produce and to deproduce the notion of the human."[39] Finally, that one's human-ness can vary in degrees according to its representation of norms is otherwise articulated in *Senses of the Subject*: "the *conatus* is enhanced or diminished" at the point of encounter with others.[40] Thus we can surmise that my desire to live can be dampened when others do not desire my life. In such a scenario I turn against my desire to persevere in my being by capitulating to the body-corporate's desire for me. The

---

we might say, following Spinoza, underwrites recognition, so that forms of recognition or, indeed, forms of judgment that seek to relinquish or destroy desire to persist, the desire for life itself, undercut the very preconditions of recognition." Butler, *GAO*, 44.

35. Butler, *SS*, 65.
36. Boer, *In the Vale*, 248.
37. Butler, *FW*, 21.
38. Boer, *In the Vale*, 267. Boer's interpretation of Butler's ethics is limited by the fact that he only consults one of Butler's texts, *GAO*. But even with this text, as this chapter demonstrates, Butler makes clear the link, however creative, between Foucault, Hegel, Freud, and Spinoza.
39. Butler, *UG*, 31–32.
40. Butler, *SS*, 65.

malleable originary form is therefore crucial for Butler's developing ethics of gender. If we are going to be responsible and recognize people's desire to live, then this cannot be informed by an originary notion of human that does not permit us to recognize another's desire to persevere in their own particular way.

What is evident in this investigation into Butler's use of Spinoza's God and the emergent theme of *conatus* as a mode of revealing the task of ethics is that Hegel comes firmly into view, along with her other interlocutors. Butler states as much in *The Psychic Life of Power*: "If desire has as its final aim the continuation of itself—and here one might link Hegel, Freud, and Foucault all back to Spinoza's *conatus*—then the capacity of desire to be withdrawn and to reattach will constitute something like the vulnerability of every strategy of subjection."[41] This passage justifies the structure of my account of Butler's gender theory because desire's beginning and end, according to Butler, is *conatus*, which cannot be conceived or thought through without her interlocutors' notions of power and subjectivity, originary and mundane desire, violence, and finally, the ethical implications of realizing the self in relation to others as vulnerable and dependent for life.

In a quest for the hope of life, Butler began reading about Spinoza's God in his *Ethics* in the basement of her house when she was a teenager. Now at the end of her theorizing on gender, she returns to deploy Spinoza's God to figure *conatus* as an implied ethics of gender to induce universal humility and the possibility of hope of life.

Vulnerability and Nonviolence

Affirming and Grieving Lost Life

Thus far, it is not obvious how Butler's ethics of gender deals with loss-induced desire. Within metaphysical systems such as Hegel's, loss can be disavowed by pointing to the end when all things are brought into harmony. A telos permits one to deny or justify loss, or explain it away. However, where there is no possibility to appeal to the end to manage loss in the present, which is what we find in Butler's thought, loss can be confessed as the reality of things, which might induce disillusionment and resignation, or perhaps a pursuit for what was lost, but not without

---

41. Butler, *PLP*, 62.

vulnerability. But to confess loss and pursue what is lost are two distinct responses. For Butler, what has been lost cannot be found: "We cannot endeavor to 'rectify' this situation. And we cannot recover the source of this vulnerability, for it precedes the formation of the 'I.'"[42]

This chastened posture about loss and the beginning contradicts Butler's theoretical entry into the originary scene to depart the traditional human that resides there. This departure was an attempt to install a subject constituted by the loss of the originary object and orientation of desire. In the exploration of Butler's Freudian stubborn attachment and melancholy in chapter 1, we saw that her subject of desire suffered desire-induced incoherence due to a speculative loss of desire's object by prohibition. On this ground Butler developed a notion of individual sexuality and therefore gender that is originally other than one's mundane experience. For example, I desire people of the other sex because I was prohibited at the originary scene from desiring people of the same sex. Despite calling for the de-heterosexualization of the Oedipus mechanism as the structural condition of the originary subject of desire, Butler in the end confesses that one cannot return to the originary scene to find and know what is lost that causes such incoherence and grief in the present. This does not stop Butler from promoting the embrace of one's grief, and therefore loss, to see what forms of life emerge from it. This embrace of the death drive is not murderous or suicidal, but nonetheless destructive because the posture of "tarrying with grief" functions to sanctify one's own inability to grieve the loss of life.[43]

In the first chapter of *Undoing Gender*, Butler broaches the notion of "tarrying with grief" for which she gives an example that curiously does not concern gender or sexuality issues, but international relations. The reason for this could indicate that Butler believes she has already addressed this issue concerning gender elsewhere and deems it unnecessary to labor the point. Indeed, loss figures prominently throughout her corpus, and so this is a reasonable possibility. But if this were the case, why would she bother with the argument itself? In contradistinction, I suggest the international political example signals a rhetorical maneuver that if conceived as macro-politics will assume into its orb other conceptions of human loss, like Freudian loss associated with gender and sexuality. Butler's example seeks to assert the *universality* of her developing

---

42. Butler, *UG*, 23. See also Bulter, *PLP*, 194–95.
43. Butler, *UG*, 23.

ethical paradigm, which is principally concerned about "the question of the human."[44]

The trouble with gender that Butler is targeting with this example is that gender violence is something that many only hear about in the news—a gay bashing or a transgender child being shot with a BB gun at school, etc. The trouble with such violence is that I do not personally carry it out and so my existence is not caught up in the problem *or* the solution. By using the global scenario, Butler locates everyone in the life of everyone else, which echoes our earlier reflection of Spinoza's concept that human "singularity becomes implicated in the singularities of others" which "produces a mode of being beyond singularity."[45] By panning back to take stock of a global issue, Butler seeks to show that everyone is equally vulnerable and therefore equally vulnerable to each other. Again, this recalls her notion of "differential allocation of grievability":[46] "That our very survival can be determined by those we do not know and over whom there is no final control means that life is precarious."[47] Butler here enlarges the scope of who may be implicated in a discussion about gender and violence, gender and grief, gender and vulnerability, and therefore gender and possibilities of life.

Another rhetorical maneuver to note in using this example is Butler's *crossing* over from one side to the other: from being politically culturally oppressed (lesbian)—the one not grieved—to being a political and cultural oppressor (United States of America)—the one who does not grieve the lost. Butler now stands with "us." The rhetorical maneuver is that Butler places herself in the position of those who do not grieve her by inhabiting a place where she can genuinely model grieving the loss of life suffered by people, like faceless Arab "terrorists" held in detention indefinitely.[48] Butler is modeling how to grieve her ungrievable self. We see this when she states: "To grieve, and to make grief itself into a resource for politics, is not to be resigned to a simple passivity or powerlessness. It is, rather, to allow oneself to extrapolate from this experience of vulnerability to the vulnerability that others suffer."[49] Instead of saying, "Grieve

---

44. Butler, *UG*, 17. For a concise description of this thematic move, see Lloyd, "Ethics and Politics of Vulnerable Bodies," 167–92.

45. Butler, *SS*, 65.

46. Butler, *PL*, xiv.

47. Butler, *UG*, 23.

48. See the chapter called "Indefinite Detention," in Butler, *PL*.

49. Butler, *UG*, 23.

me!" or "Grieve others like me!" Butler takes up her vulnerability and uses that as a political resource to grieve for others who suffer. Butler may be writing genuinely about international issues, but she is deploying the need for loss-induced grief in this way to communicate about gender, and to convey that socially constituted embodied vulnerability is universal.[50]

The challenge confronting Butler's ethics of gender is the problem of abstraction. Even though Butler takes up a notion of creation as desiring to live *via* Spinoza's naturalization of God and *conatus*, what does this means when it comes to embodied lives? A raft of questions is confronting, especially for the Christian, who confesses to loving God and one's neighbor as oneself: Which human life do we grieve? Which human life are we permitted to grieve? For Butler, the answer is the same: those people who are deemed to be alive. The one whose life is recognizably human; the one who does not transgress the contours of what it means to be human. This is why many do not grieve the lives of people who are bashed on the street or in homes for being lesbian and gay. This is why society and the church broadly speaking did not grieve the lives of those who died from AIDS in the 1980s. In addition to these un-living people, Butler describes people who are transgendered that have been harassed and murdered. And what about the loss of these lives in the communities and families they leave behind? Do parents grieve their "disappearance"?[51] Such lives are not grieved in many contexts because no life was lost. One is shown to not desire another's desire to persevere in being where one does not grieve their loss of life (literally and metaphorically).

Butler's ethics of gender incites one to tarry with grief, which is a form of death drive in the sense that dwelling in grief does not seek pleasure in an object. Rather, going beyond the pleasure principle by inhabiting such a posture slows one down to recalibrate the measure—understood as the matrix of desire, originary form, or "the cultural contours of the notion of human"—by which loss is adjudicated and confessed as human loss.[52] The result of tarrying with grief does not result in an act of violence to overcome loss or recuperate from it, but is a life-giving destruction of one's own inability to grieve the lost. Squandered life through one's inability to grieve is not recoverable, but from Butler's perspective, what is recoverable is one's ability to grieve moving forward. Many of us

---

50. See also *FW*, 22.
51. Butler, *UG*, 23–25. Butler raises these questions and others.
52. Butler, *UG*, 24.

will not find ourselves in a wedding celebration that is subject to a drone strike by Western armies in an attempt to kill suspected terrorists or fleeing murderous religious zealots or police brutality or "gay bashings," but Butler's desire to tarry with grief is that we will be sensitized not only to their plight and their desire for life, but realize that we are caught up in "forms of social and political organizations" that determine whose life in the end is worth grieving: the family members who lost loved ones in the drone strike, the people living displaced lives due to oppressive governance, the people who fear those who are commissioned to protect them, and finally, the people who endue suffering because they do not or cannot fit into traditional social norms of gender and sexuality.[53]

The Other and Desire

I have uncritically granted Butler's confessed givenness of desire in her gender theory, whether that be her subject of desire or the essential nature of *conatus*.[54] One of the clearest confessions of this is when she asks, "How are we to account for the desire for the norm and for subjectification more generally in terms of *a prior desire* for social existence . . . ?"[55] Butler rejects the notion of a pre-discursive body, but what is this notion of "prior desire"? The ontological nature of Spinoza's *conatus* is a contested notion, but how does Butler treat this anomaly in her otherwise consistently ground-resistant theory of gender?[56] In short, she does not, which is not an error or oversight, but a logical conclusion to which her desire to denaturalize gender is ordered. Instead of ignoring or trying to destroy the historically sedimented notion that bodies were created by God with inherent meaning, Butler takes up the creator/creation mode of relation (being in relation to the other) and reforms it. Therefore, desire and otherness are not produced, and nor do they come out of nowhere, but are *always already*.[57] Desire is given because it emerges, conceptually,

53. Butler, *UG*, 24.
54. Butler, *PLP*, 27–28.
55. Butler, *PLP*, 19 (emphasis mine).
56. For a detailed summary of the pivotal thinkers and their arguments, see Garrett, "Spinoza's *Conatus* Argument."
57. Boer asks the question of Butler how the other is produced, which is framed as a rhetorical question to critique the other who comes out of nowhere. Conceptually, this misses her use of Spinoza to show that the other is not produced but eternal. Boer, *In the Vale of Tears*, 275.

first, as constitutive of the givenness of God. This shows Butler putting into practice her own theory of subjectivity, where she locates society's historic subjection to the desiring, other God of Scripture and populates it with new terms to create a new mode of human subjectivity not in relation to the desire of the Christian God.

Butler's assumed foundation of desire finds its origin in the eternal God, specifically the ancient, confessed belief that God created the world and humanity according to God's good desire. When God is incorporated into Butler's gender theory *via* Spinoza's process of naturalization, nature, along with nature's desire to exist, takes on the divine and eternal materialized form of good desire and thus the assumptive and incontestable ground of reality. What was uncreated and therefore wholly other has been domesticated as creation. Boer critiques the givenness of the other in Butler's thought as a product of ethical discourse. From our investigation of Spinoza's *Ethics*, we see the merit in his claim. Boer describes Butler as someone who is "keen to distance herself from those, like Levinas and Laplanche, who prioritize the 'Other,'"[58] but this claim is true only insofar as the "Other" is "infinite and preontological."[59] Butler must do away with the "Other" while safeguarding the integrity of the dyadic structure that maintains the encounter with another in which responsibility for the other emerges as a call on one's life—a vocation. The task to be accomplished by Butler is to convert further the once transcendent Other (Christian God) from its Spinozan naturalized state into a socialized form. Butler states as much: "For our purposes, however, we will treat the Other in Levinas as belonging to an idealized dyadic structure of social life."[60] This should be taken as an unwitting confession. There is no ethical relation without encountering God and another, which is why Butler describes the ethical scene as comprising myself and "an-other, whether conjured or existing."[61]

Thus, one discovers Butler's assumed prior notion of desire as the result of tracing the trajectory of her reform of humanity's subjection to God. The concept of God with which Butler works begins as *one who* is other to creation (the God of Abraham, Isaac, and Jacob), who is then reformed by Spinoza into *one that* is the unifying principle of the universe

---

58. Boer, *In the Vale of Tears*, 268n47.
59. Butler, *GAO*, 90.
60. Butler, *GAO*, 90.
61. Butler, *GAO*, 21.

AN ETHICS OF GENDER: FINDING HOPE IN DESIRE 157

(God/nature/substance), which is then finally worked by Butler into *one who* constitutes me/us (subject/s of desire). In the end, God is what Butler describes as the socialized "I" (the body-corporate that spans time) which creates and sustains me according to its desires. Butler's "I" reflects Christianity's God and Spinoza's reconceptualization of the Christian God as a paradox of unity and multiplicity. *Conatus*, then, represents a person's individual desire for life and dependence on God, now the socialized "I," for life—a desire to persevere in ourselves as we constitute, and are constituted by, others.

Butler's socialization of Spinoza's materialization of the uncreated God of Scripture results in an assumptive and incontestable ontology that grounds the development of her subject, critique, and ethics. In view of this explanation, consider when Spinoza's materialized *conatus* as a socialized ground of being is recast by Butler as an assumptive ground of being:

> If one accepts Spinoza's notion that desire is always the desire to persist in one's being, and recasts the *metaphysical* substance that forms the ideal for desire as a more pliable notion of social being, one might then be prepared to redescribe the desire to persist in one's own being as something that can be brokered only within the risky terms of social life.[62]

The reform of God through Spinoza's process of domestication has resulted in a God that is manipulable. The new recast eternal mind is "a more pliable notion of social being." This means that Antonio Negri's critique that Butler does not reform oppressive power structures but reiterates them is accurate in one sense, but inaccurate in another.[63] The form of power (unity and multiplicity) undergoes no change through this reform. What changes is the locus of power: it begins as an abstract myth that operates on us from outside creation. Then via Spinoza this power then materializes to be universal truth as nature, which we are as we constitute it, and as it constitutes us. Finally, in Butler's thought, power is an internalized psychical reality that operates, ironically, inside of us from outside of us. The denaturalization of gender is achieved therefore through the internalization of the Christian God in the social psyche, which occurs through processes of naturalization and socialization.

---

62. Butler, *PLP*, 27–28.
63. Casarino and Negri, *In Praise of the Common*, 281n15.

The significance of Butler's early rejection of Foucault's psyche-less subject is revealed. Foucault's theory results in bio-politics, which usurps the traditional sovereign's power, but in so doing reduces life to "birth, death, production, illness, and so on"—a crude form of materialism.[64] This is a fatal theoretical move for Butler as one who understands the force of the foundational beginning and the trans-historical social-psychic. In response, Butler does not disregard the sovereign or seek to strip it of its creative power, but subjects it to processes of deconstitution to harness its (re)creative potential.

One can demonstrate this point by tracing the trajectory of the deconstitution of God. When God is believed to be a personal God who as the creator of the world is other, one is subjectified by God, and so subject to God's commands of embodied life. One can only repudiate this God and disobey the commands, but can never manipulate God to desire one's own mundane desires. Spinoza's God, while immanent, is abstract, not because it is mythical, but because it is a rational explanatory force only. Because this God is not personal, its ordering of the world is static and fixed and so beyond manipulation—everything is deductively necessary. Concerning the final reform of God by Butler, she makes ek-static that which was static, namely, the subject. By virtue of our intersubjective relation to each other, "we" are conceived by Butler "as a more pliable notion of social being." By socializing an already materialized God, Butler develops an ethics of gender that relies on a notion of me that is not wholly me by virtue of us: "a trajectory in desire works in the service of deconstituting the subject, comporting it beyond itself to a possible dissolution in a more general *conatus*. Significantly, it is in the deconstitution and disorientation that an ethical perspective arises."[65] Butler's point is not only that I desire to persevere in being, but that I desire in light of, or as one constituted (and conditioned) by, a more general social "I" that also desires to exist in being. In Butler's estimation, the deconstitution of God leads to the deconstitution of the subject which gives rise to the possibility of an ethical perspective. In terms of Butler's ethics of gender, the disappearance of God leads to the disappearance of the body as a given reality, but also to its subsequent reappearance as a site of political contest. The ground (God and God's desire) that once determined whether mundane desire was moral or immoral is now undermined, thereby recasting

---

64. Foucault, "Society Must Be Defended," 241.
65. Butler, *SS*, 84.

those same desires as political determinations. An ethics of gender, then, is now not only possible, but entirely necessary because morality is disoriented by virtue of the subject's deconstitution.

Democratizing Gender

The Body as Limit

An ontology of desire is the ground on which Butler theorizes an ethics of gender. What value does the universal other-implicating-desire for life have for addressing how we should navigate questions of gender and embodiment in the communities in which we live *and* don't live?[66] Butler addresses this question by developing a latent theme that surfaces briefly when she mentions that the desire to exist was not an unspecified desire, but susceptible to redescription. If *conatus* is subject to description and redescription, then one's desire to exist is caught up in the risky business of negotiating with those who broker the terms that describe a desirable life.[67]

What resources does Butler's ethics of gender have that facilitate a productive engagement with such power brokers? It must first be reiterated that Butler does not have access to transcendent truths about gender and embodiment that she can offer to limit the violent imposition of the incumbent particular description of a desire to live or live well. She has no access to an image of an ideal body that she can promote, and nor does she have any specific biological functions that describe what people desire for life. Second, whatever ethics Butler subscribes to, it must deal with existing gender violence while refusing to install a new description of a desirable life that forecloses other possible desirable lives that might emerge in the future. Drawing on Spinoza again, Butler identifies that the ethical resources at her disposal is God/nature/substance: our material bodies and the body-corporate in which we find ourselves, and which we in part constitute. Butler is explicit: "If the body is what secures singularity, is what cannot be synthesized into a collectivity, but establishes its limit and its futurity, then the body, in its desire, is what keeps the future open."[68] According to Butler, our bodies operate as crude material sub-

---

66. Hull is skeptical and claims it is only of limited value. Hull, "Of Suicide and Falling Stones," 115.

67. Butler, *PLP*, 27–28.

68. Butler, *SS*, 82.

stance to individuate ourselves. Our bodies prevent the body-corporate swallowing us whole.

But what potential does the body have for impacting the body-corporate's monopoly on the description of what is a recognizable life? How does the material body take a seat at the negotiation table to lobby for its own particular desire to live? How might our bodies in Butler's schema keep the future open? Butler continues, "However, for this singularity—conceived as a subject—to be powerful, for it to persevere in its desire and to preserve its own power of perseverance, *it cannot be preoccupied with itself.*"[69] Yet again, Butler's ethics refuses to import a sovereign-I to declare a particular body as the "silver bullet" to solve the problem. The body, despite its individuation, cannot be conceived apart from its subjectivity, which is not fatal if the body is *not* preoccupied with itself, but concerned with the other's life. The individuated body and the body-corporate are therefore once again caught up in each other's life. This *embodied posture* of the individual *and* corporate does not lead to murdering the other, nor does one become suicidally fixated on the self. The body matters because it is thought to matter, and as such, is caught up in the mattering of other bodies.[70]

The mattering of the body is central to Butler's ethics of gender as one of nonviolence. If the body matters only as one participates in others (individuals) and the other (corporate), then one cannot give a full account of oneself. Any self-narration is partial, in the sense that what one knows of the body is mediated socially to me: "My account of myself is partial, haunted by that from which I can devise no definitive story. I cannot explain exactly why I have emerged in this way, and my efforts at narration reconstruction are always undergoing revision. There is that in me and of me for which I can give no account."[71] Paradoxically, that which limits me is not my physical body, but my essential sociality. Earlier Butler states: "It is only in dispossession that I can and do give any account of myself."[72] Butler could use a notion of "opacity" to argue that there are no grounds for accountability and responsibility, yet she does not. Instead, she asks whether one's opacity "gives rise to another *ethical disposition*

---

69. Butler, *SS*, 82.

70. For a nuanced treatment of how matter is mattered in Butler's thought as a theological matter, see particularly ch. 4 in Parsons, *Ethics of Gender*.

71. Butler, *GAO*, 40.

72. Butler, *GAO*, 37.

in the place of a full and satisfying notion of narrative accountability?"[73] This form of accountability focuses instead on one's limit to know one's self by virtue of being bound to another.

Democratizing Gender: A Social and Civic Responsibility

This chapter reveals that Butler, as she confesses, really does struggle to speak about bodies as they exist before our eyes and in the mirror. Just when it seems that Butler is about to speak about the body, it disappears or at least folds into a larger body, obscuring its particularity as it becomes part of a sea of indistinguishable flesh. And so, it is apparent that an ethics of gender in Butler's thought has little to do with bodies, except as an originary *site* of contested ideas and as a personal *call* for epistemic humility toward other narrations of desirable embodiment for others to pursue for life. Butler's ethics of gender is therefore reducible to a mode of responsibility that is not a constructive exhortation, but a consequence that we realize by virtue of a revelation of the nature of things. Responsibility is not, therefore, an imposed ethic from the outside, but a mode of taking up one's life in community.

Refusing to take responsibility for oneself and the other has drastic ethical consequences. Abandoning one's desire to live is suicidal and refusing another's desire to live is murderous. But Butler does not prevent both losses of life by forcibly pulling the person off the edge from which they are about to jump and forcibly restraining the person from executing judgment on the other. Both moments of violence are quelled by requesting each person to give an account of themselves, which according to Butler's gender theory does not confirm either the suicidal person's hopeless life, or the righteous life of the would-be murderer. Both realize the irresponsibility of their action when they take stock of what they know about their respective selves: "Indeed, to take responsibility for oneself is to avow the limits of any self-understanding, and to establish these limits not only as a condition for the subject but as the predicament of the human community."[74] An epistemic catastrophe drives Butler's ethics of gender. When we come to understand ourselves accurately as incoherent and therefore not fully knowable to the self or others, the decision to take one's own life is shown to be an irresponsible act because it is based

---

73. Butler, *GAO*, 40 (emphasis mine).
74. Butler, *GAO*, 83.

on a limited self-understanding. And the decision to take another's life is likewise considered irresponsible because it is unjustifiable given the partial knowledge about oneself and the other to which one has access.

Taking responsibility in this way is not imposed on people, but emerges as a personal response to having the nature of things revealed yet again. Butler does not coax the person off the edge with bombastic claims about pride and self-realization, nor the possibility of an inclusive community or legal reform. And she does not attempt to dissuade the other person from killing with appeals to human rights, sentimental notions of love, or some notion of gender and sexuality needing to be filtered through the lens of the private/public domain. In Butler's ethical paradigm, physical and metaphorical life is not lost because both people confess the reality of the human predicament of limitedness that characterizes themselves and the community in which they live.

Even though incoherence-induced responsibility is not an imposed obligation from the outside but an emergent realization, it is nonetheless obligatory. In this mode of embodied ethical life, I am not *responsible to* someone or something, but *responsible for* someone, which is not a *choice* but a *fact* of our intersubjective existence.[75] The irony of Butler's theorization is that responsibility does not primarily concern how I treat my own or another's body,[76] but rather whether I take responsibility for the other because of our mutual vulnerability. Butler is unusually clear when she states that "responsibility is not a matter of cultivating a will, but of making use of an unwilled susceptibility as a resource for becoming responsive to the Other."[77] Confessing incoherence is a genuine recognition of one's own loss that functions also as a call to the human vocation to be responsible for the other.[78]

In this emergent *state* of realized responsibility, Butler subtly passes a law whereby one is forced to give an account. Butler might have done away with God and God's desires as that which underwrites traditional ethical notions of gender and embodiment, but this does not amount to an eradication of the law and its regulation. Rather, as we have seen, she transforms both into forms of sociality, which are accessible and pliable. The law to which one must submit now and which must be enforced is

---

75. Butler, *GAO*, 87–88.
76. Butler, *GAO*, 88.
77. Butler, *GAO*, 91.
78. Butler, *GAO*, 91.

the *law of desire*. The regulating mechanism of this law is society (the body-corporate). Butler's society manifests the law of desire and regulates it. This is the ultimate collusion: society, which is the body, is a law unto itself. Butler legalizes desire, or to put it in negative terms, Butler has outlawed prohibiting desire. The person who refuses to take up responsibility for the other by desiring their desire to live is a transgressor. This person is one who does not desire life, and by virtue of this transgression, is violent (murderous) and oppressive (inducing suicide).

Evaluating Norms

This book has argued so far that the primary antagonist against which Butler works is a construction of knowledge that *poses* as the limit of gendered possibility. In broad terms, I have explored in Butler's thought the idea that limits imposed by mythical authorities transgress the law of desire and are therefore violent impositions. Regarding gender, limits concern norms that foreclose what one can desire to exist in life. Heteronormativity is one such mythical authority that is purportedly violent.[79] But are limits concerning the body, gender, and sexuality *inherently* violent? Is the heteronormative principle, for example, inherently violent or is it violent for some other reason? Butler argues that limits, even universal limits, are not inherently violent,[80] but can be if they are socially accepted bygone ways of understanding reality that continue to linger in the present. The enduring problem with universality is twofold in that it "fails to be responsive to cultural particularity *and* fails to undergo reformulation of itself in response to the social and cultural conditions it includes within its scope of applicability."[81] Butler's development of an ethics of gender is therefore concerned with individuals whose desires are not catered for by existing and lingering outdated originary terms.

Butler acknowledges the complexity that deconstituted subjectivity poses for developing an ethics of gender. One cannot simply defer to a sovereign-I to lay claim to a new morality. Not only does a sovereign-I not exist due to one's sociality, but one is left with the problem of how "new"

---

79. Butler, *GT*, xxi.

80. Butler, *GAO*, 7. This challenges Mills's reading that "within Butler's account of the normative constitution of the subject . . . norms themselves are inherently violent." Mills, "Normative Violence," 134.

81. Butler, *GAO*, 6 (emphasis mine).

moral claims avoid simply reiterating another inadequate form of moral gendered representation. In response, Butler suggests that by avowing one's loss, one is called to "give an account of oneself."[82] Butler observes that because one is intimately and inescapably bound to the matrix of desire and so is never fully one's own, to give an account of oneself requires that one "as a matter of necessity, become a social theorist."[83] Any account of ethics, Butler suggests, must begin here, which is provoked when one's "'I' is not at one with moral norms" driving one to consider their "social genesis and meaning."[84]

While ethics in Butler's view is a critique of originary structures—genesis (and so Genesis) and the meaning that resides there—the goal of critique is gendered life, which one achieves by reforming originary norms. We might say that rather than constructing an ethics of gender, Butler proposes *the perpetual critique of prevailing norms*, which means they are contingent and therefore open to revision. Butler realizes we cannot do without foundational or originary norms, and so if this is the case, the question is, which norms can be identified for reform or redescription?[85] Social theory, therefore, is a discipline of life—a mode of virtuous living—that interrogates and supports the re-terming of conditions and permits one's desire to persevere and live well.

The task of the ethicist or social theorist, therefore, is to be responsive to the context for which the ethicist formulates answers to the question: what is moral? What is a moral gendered life is decided not by recalling and therefore imposing outdated norms for embodiment, but by observing and describing what is desired for life in the moment. The ethicist, therefore, liberates the human in the present from the "human" of the past, where human implies the originary conditions that allow one to persevere in one's own being. This is what Butler means when she agrees with Emmanuel Levinas that "tethering responsibility to freedom is an error."[86] Butler tethers my responsibility to others in the present as my own subject is bound to them: inasmuch as I am for me, I am for the other.

---

82. Butler, *GAO*, 7.
83. Butler, *GAO*, 8.
84. Butler, *GAO*, 8.
85. Butler, *GAO*, 10.
86. Butler, *GAO*, 88.

In this sense, the traditional task of ethics is violent only as an anachronism.[87] Ethics becomes violent only when "the collective ethos cease[s] to hold sway."[88] Once an ethic has lost its place as the commonly held view "it can impose its claim to commonality only through violence ... to maintain the appearance of its collectivity."[89] Thus, an ethic may hold universal appeal in one era for the precise reason that everyone holds to it. It is not universal because it is universal by nature, but because of its collective appeal. When people begin to move beyond universal ethics, or more accurately, when universal ethics is unable to describe the people in the given jurisdiction, then the ethics can no longer claim universal status. In this way, Butler desires gender norms to be perpetually open to revision to reflect the present social body.

From Butler's viewpoint, an ethics of gender that no longer represents a particular context proceeds in one of three ways: firstly, the outdated gender norms can be imposed continually on the community; secondly, the outdated gender norms can be discarded as redundant; or thirdly, the outdated gender norms can be *reformed* to reflect the present community so that it can again be described as universal.[90] Butler repudiates an ethics of gender that is constituted by old ways of living that must be enforced through violence to maintain its authority. The second perspective is impossible because society cannot exist without norms and no sovereign-I exists simply to reinstate new ones, which only leaves the third option. This means that Butler's ethics of gender is driven by a radical democratic pragmatism that is subservient to the mundane desire of the body-corporate.

One may therefore do the work of a social theorist in our time and observe that the questioning of gender as man and woman is brought to the fore because "the collective ethos cease[s] to hold sway."[91] According to Butler's ethics of gender, where what is man and what is woman continues to be imposed through regulation, whether by law, medicine, religion, custom, or cultural assumption, violence is done: murder and suicide are committed. In the middle of last century, the idea that there were two genders was hardly a matter of dispute. That there are two

---

87. Butler, *GAO*, 4–5.
88. Butler, *GAO*, 4.
89. Butler, *GAO*, 4.
90. Butler, *GAO*, 4–6.
91. Butler, *GAO*, 4.

genders is no longer a given and in some quarters is understood to be a full-blown myth. In this instance, Butler identifies heteronormativity as an ethical principle by which violence is employed to impose an outdated view on present reality. Butler states: "It is important to see that [intersex and transsex] challenge the principle that a natural dimorphism should be established or maintained at all costs."[92] Butler goes on to explain that intersex persons might experience violence through imposed surgery to conform to one gender or the other, while transsex persons are denied surgery to live in a particular sexed state with which they most identify. Ironically, on the account of one having surgery imposed and the other being denied surgery, Butler observes that both are forced to live in realities they potentially do not desire. Thus, Butler shows how a defense of sexual dimorphism can become a violent imposition in an era when it does not describe a universal understanding of gendered existence.[93]

This leads us to the poignant notion that violence forces people to dwell in unlivable conditions. In Butler's ethics of gender, social contexts are obliged to provide the means necessary for all people to live lives that are not just characterized by living or surviving, which Butler describes as being "condemned to a death within life."[94] Rather, social contexts are obliged to facilitate lives in which people are allowed "to breath, to desire, to love, and to live."[95]

Conclusion

This reading shows that Butler's engagement with ethics is patently reluctant. She is cautious not to betray her commitment to a person's intersubjectivity while cognizant of the need for something that demands a reflective ethical posture and response. Butler therefore offers an ontological account of desire that binds us together in an individual quest for life in our bodies. She does not fit into the usual ontologically averse mold of the secular ethicist for the reason that she refuses to fit the mold of the secular philosopher.[96] Breaking the rules that regulate gender in

---

92. Butler, *UG*, 6.
93. Butler, *UG*, 8.
94. Butler, *GT*, xxi.
95. Butler, *UG*, 8. The nature of this obligation and whether this is late or latent throughout her corpus is contested. This is traced by Lloyd in *Butler and Ethics*, 1–6.
96. Butler constantly rejects the title/role of philosopher.

disciplines like philosophy might be "unfair" as far as the "game" goes, but Butler realizes the stakes are far too high for playing games. Butler is not motivated to protect the ideals of liberty and freedom out of a sense of duty, but to protect the lives of those who don't yet matter out of a sense of responsibility for them.

The ontological claim that Butler makes is that we are all subject to a command that I have called *the law of desire*. This could function problematically as an ethical principle that does not have any substantial implications for how we should live our lives as embodied beings. We have seen, however, that this is not the case. Butler's ontological law of desire binds people together in risky union in which negotiation is proposed as the procedural means to deal with the emergence of someone who desires to persist in their particular being for life. Responsibility is driven not by self-care or the projection of one's own desires, but the earnest attempt to seek another's life.

As we turn to the final theological reflection on Butler's gender theory, her ethics of gender gives us several important things to consider, the first of which is the need to resist the seduction of Adam and Eve, which is revealed as a monoprinciple rather than a substantial ethics of gender. Even if Adam and Eve represent a law given by God, which I contend they do (see chapter 4), reducing them to a timeless principle to be enacted is a mistake that Brian Brock identifies as undermining the task of Christian ethics. The mistake concerns the (mis-)translation of one category to another: "the translation of the biblical language of command into the modern ethical language of principle."[97] Like any mistranslation, the result is a product of one's lack of fluency in the language, here, of Christian ethics. As we move forward, we must resist invoking the monoprinciple of Adam and Eve, but instead reflect theologically on what it means to be found in time. Butler provokes us to refuse to install *this* time as *the* time for reflection, instead drawing this time into the light of the concrete originary past and possible future. Specifically, how do we relate to Adam and Eve in the past, and what import does this relationship have for how we consider embodied lives in the present and eschaton? We do not dwell in the beginning, but nor can we ignore it because it is formative for who we are today. Likewise, with regard to the end, we do not live there and we are not privy to what shape embodied life takes there, but

---

97. Brock, "On Generating Categories," 51.

nor can we afford to ignore the end by refusing to properly integrate it into an ethics of gender.

The second point that emerges from Butler's ethics of gender that provokes theological reflection is the question of agency. We have already confirmed a somewhat chastened agency in a Christian theology of gender when we confirmed (in chapter 2) that we are intersubjective beings by virtue of being created by God with "eyes" that recognize the self through the other's eyes, including God's. I am not a sovereign-I, but this chastened agency does not exhibit the epistemic catastrophe that we see in Butler's ethics of gender. Butler confesses to not knowing the beginning or the end, which means giving an account of oneself in the present is always necessarily partial, which undermines the validity of any substantive claim by someone on another. By contrast, we confess Scripture reveals the beginning to us despite our departure,[98] while we confess to not knowing the particularities of embodiment in the end. Agency, moreover, has another point of reference in a Christian theology of gender that Butler's account cannot entertain, namely, the Spirit's power to enable one to image God. In addition to the beginning, we also know the human vocation, and the goal of that vocation, as well as possessing the means to achieve it.

Another significant point raised in this chapter is Butler's construal of the "body." We have seen that Butler does not ignore the physical material body, but grants its functional differentiation. We too can make a similar confession, that bodies possess patterns of functionality, which is a confession that allows us to focus on *concepts* of bodies that dominate a Christian theology of gender, and how the emergence of a non-Edenic body—like the body of a eunuch, even a eunuch by name only, as in the case of Jesus—might impact our collective belief about good embodiment now and in the eschaton.

Finally, Butler raises the idea that gender finds its life in a risky union with others. This is not a theoretical move for Butler but an observation of the nature of things. Union with another, I suggest, is not an option but names the essential and supernatural way we exist in the world. This means that there is no possibility for thinking about embodiment other than within the risky terms of union with another in whom we put our faith to realize our desire for life.

---

98. Bonhoeffer, *Creation and Fall*, 25–37.

Chapter 6

The Vocation of Gender: Vulnerability in Union

Introduction

THIS CHAPTER ADDRESSES PROBLEMATIC Christian attempts to think about gender from the *ethical principle* that this book has narrowed to the Edenic images of Adam and Eve. Where these originary figures take the form of a monoprinciple that demands compliance, I suggest we strip ourselves of the necessary tools to address the current malaise of the body concerning questions about gender. By casting Adam and Eve back into the contexts in which we find them, namely, historical time *and* Scripture, we dispose of the originary figures as a timeless moral principle. In other words, rather than mining Scripture for principles of gender to address questions about gender, I suggest we take seriously our commitment to *Scripture* and its apparent commitment to give an account of *embodied being in time*.[1] This sensitization to the body in time and Scripture has been incited, perhaps regrettably, by Butler, who is a secular queer gender theorist.

Despite her provocation, Butler's ethics of gender has been shown to be problematic for Christians for several reasons. Firstly, human agency is swamped by intersubjectivity such that the human community is reduced to a quagmire of competing desires with no genuine capacity

---

1. This critical methodology takes its impetus from Brock, "On Generating Categories."

to evaluate which desires are worth pursing as a community. Secondly, because what is good is subject to a political contest of debate and negotiation, *every* human desire has the potential to be called good by society. Every desire may not be good at this moment, but every desire beckons society's collective affirming "Yes!" Finally, her account offers us no space for thinking about how the body's functionality has implications for conceiving ourselves as gendered. This final point is not an excuse to lapse at the finish line and import a sovereign-I to introduce a bio-legal standard in the form of Adam and Eve. The question of the functionality of the gendered body haunts Butler's gender theory because she has no means by which to engage with it, without it turning into a bio-legal regulation that undermines her entire work. A Christian account of gender, as I will show, does not fear the functional body or legal threat that Adam and Eve pose, but nor is a Christian theology of gender reducible to them. We have departed the garden of Eden with no hope of reentry; however, we have hope of entry into another place, described in Scripture as a city, in which the form of our future embodiment is uncertain.[2] Human functionality is grounded in the beginning, but this is not definitive of what is good embodiment now, or in the eschaton, despite its claim on our lives.

In what follows, I continue to reform a theology of gender so that it is not grounded in one moment in time. Historically, Christian accounts are grounded in Eden, and we have seen that Butler's account of gender responds to accounts such as these by grounding a notion of gender in the beginning and the present age of anxiety. Her account departs the beginning, revealing that without a dramatic change in circumstances, this age and its social dynamics exhaust the resources at our disposal to think about gender. In contrast to both accounts, I offer a theology of gender that takes it cues from *the beginning, the present*, and also *the eschaton*, which is not a possibility without Jesus Christ whom the apostle Paul boasts saves people from their bodies of death.[3] A body's functionality is not obscured in this account, but is subject likewise to the history-impacting events we find in salvation history. What a body can or can't do is not the starting point of a theology of gender, and nor is it the final port of call. The body, as in Butler's account, supplies us with our individual and body-corporate vocations that call us to perpetually act, not in a particular Edenic manner, nor as a culture prescribes, and

2. Rev 21.
3. Rom 7:24–25.

nor as I desire, but in a way that glorifies God.[4] This reveals that a law of desire is central to reforming a theology of gender, but the object of this law is not Adam or Eve's "heterosexual" desire or bodies, a given culture or subculture's desire, or our own, but *God's* desire.

Considering the previous chapter that explored Butler's ethics of gender, three main themes emerged as important points of theological reflection. The first concerns the full *integration of time* into a theology of gender for thinking about agency and the body. This demands a thorough rejection of the temptation to use Adam and Eve as an ethical mono-principle by engaging in a rigorous inquiry into our relation to them as people in the present who are looking to the future. The second concerns the *vocation of the body* that calls us to act in ways that are faithful to the desire of the one calling us to act. The image of God who is Jesus Christ is brought into view at this point, as well as the Spirit of God, which provides the dramatic change in circumstances for agency that Butler's theory could not accommodate. I do not populate the image of God with Edenic embodiment, but interpret it as an originary yet abiding vocation that God gives to humanity. The third theme concerns the structuring of human lives in *risky union* with another as the means of being recognized, and the hope of life now and in the end.

Resisting Idols, Iconoclasm, and Transcendence

Stumbling Away from Eden

Scripture repeatedly exhorts God's people to smash idols, but when it comes to the idolatrous images of Adam and Eve, what compliance looks like requires further examination than our engagement with the theme in chapter 4. In the first volume of her systematic theology, Sarah Coakley takes up the concept of idolatry, but instead of reiterating the scriptural command she throws doubt on its effectiveness. She warns against the iconoclastic impulse because the strewn debris from violently smashing idols remains potentially dangerous and powerful.[5] The example given much later in the book is Freud's use of the Oedipus complex in which killing the father does not finally do away with him, but rather reaffirms

---

4. 1 Cor 6:20.
5. Coakley, *God, Sexuality, and the Self*, 20.

his rule by keeping the father in place internally despite his absence.[6] Smashing idols does not necessarily do away with their de-animating power, which is why Coakley leans toward an alternative *imaginative* approach of moving away from the idolatrous scene through contemplation of God.[7]

In this ascetic mode of theology and being, concepts of gender and sexuality found in the beginning fade from view. Pursuing participation in the divine is an eschatological turn away from what is known and toward what is unknown. This prayerful and contemplative posture and re-orientation results in chastening fallen desire and obscuring or "darkening" what is regarded as certain knowledge.[8] Apophatic movement beyond the rational desire for control unsettles the status quo and gives rise to troubling possibilities.[9] Darkness has potential, though Coakley clarifies that such darkness[10] is a condition of revelation rather than "absence or 'deferral.'"[11]

Yet despite Coakley's acknowledgment of the inherent dangers associated with the dark (apophatic or negative theology), she does not broach its tendency to "hide" things that the light might adequately reveal.[12] The preference for the dark over the light when it comes to living a life of contemplation raises three important considerations. First, a turn to the dark has the potential to mask a mode of mastery, that is, seeking to affirm what we've known about God and the human all along. When being directed by God's Spirit, what is learned about selfhood in the dark can be viewed as an attempt to avoid a sinful mastery of the world, including the body. But turning the light off in a room does not result in un-mastery of knowledge of the room and its content, but groping about "looking" for what we already know is there. Coakley attempts to foil the critique that systematic theology concerns mastery of God and the world by flicking the light switch, but this is for no apparent reason. If we

---

6. Coakley, *God, Sexuality, and the Self*, 326.
7. Coakley, *God, Sexuality, and the Self*, 20.
8. Coakley, *God, Sexuality, and the Self*, 21–23.
9. Coakley, *God, Sexuality, and the Self*, 22.
10. Coakley, *God, Sexuality, and the Self*, 27. Elsewhere Coakley likens this darkness to a "disconcerting blanking of the mind," where blanking refers to a mind not distracted or operating discursively. See Coakley's engagement with English Benedictine John Chapman in Coakley, *Power and Submissions*, 46.
11. Coakley, *God, Sexuality, and the Self*, 23.
12. Coakley, *God, Sexuality, and the Self*, 19n6.

cannot master the beginning and we cannot master the world in which we live when the light is on, for what reason do we need to step into the dark? Darkness compounds what is already an impossible task.

The second point is an implication of the first, namely, the possibility that the dark hides God's creation which in the light is plain to see. Sometimes appealing to imagination by invoking darkness excuses oneself from grasping what requires little or no imagination at all. I am not suggesting that questions about the body, gender, and sexuality fall into this category of perspicuity, but in line with Butler's critique of mastery, we cannot proceed without that which we seek to know. We need the body we seek to know. Knowing does not equate to mastery any more than saying that knowing my wife is a claim that I have mastered all there is to know about her. Our exploration of wonder in the introduction to this book remains instructive. A posture of wonder before the world we seek to know is not foolish or blind, but wise and open-eyed in our quest to understand how God has spoken in creation. Creation is not a problem to fear and overcome, even if it has been perverted through idolatrous worship. Rather it is an expression of God's desire that is being redeemed and glorified through Jesus Christ.

The third and final point is that darkness is a condition that lends itself to problematic self-revelation. The dark can lead to misunderstanding the thing we experience. We might be grasped by the Spirit who reveals *reality* to us, but we might also be grasped by one's imagination.[13] In the dark we could feel something and conclude that it is something good, which, with the benefit of light, we might avoid touching altogether. Submitting to the dark's demand for imagination might open one to the Spirit's work, but it might also open the door to one's disordered desires or what the apostle Paul calls conforming to the world.[14]

These observations do not seek to undermine God's call on one's life to a vocation of submitting to God's desire to be conformed to the Son by the work of the Spirit. Rather, it draws attention to a traditional notion that knowing God and oneself does not require abandoning that which we can see, but humble attentiveness to the world in which we live, history, the church, Scripture, and our own lives.

---

13. Coakley, *God, Sexuality, and the Self*, 23.
14. Coakley, *God, Sexuality, and the Self*, 325. Rom 12:2.

An Eschatological Distraction

Eschatology is important for thinking about gender and the body, but it should not have the impact of luring humanity into making a wholesale departure from the beginning or the present. Coakley demonstrates this kind of departure in her engagement with Butler's gender theory in her book *Powers and Submissions*. Her critique of Butler amounts to a patristic projection of Gregory of Nyssa's eschatology of the body which inhibits Coakley from rigorously engaging with Butler's emphases on the world in which we live.

In one instance, Coakley notes the uncanny influence of Butler's theory, and asks the question of Butler's theory: but to what end? Instead of going back to Butler's corpus to answer the question, she turns to Gregory of Nyssa, which recalls an introductory claim by Coakley that society's obsession with the body "hides a profound eschatological longing" to overcome the body.[15] The move is swift, yet predictable because the question she asks—to what end?—is punctuated by the word *eschatological* in parenthesis: "But to what (eschatological) end?"[16] The parenthetical insertion all but rules out Butler's texts as a source for answering the question that concerns Butler's theory, but provides Coakley with the opportunity to move to Gregory's eschatological thought. In addition to this, Coakley concludes her Gregory-inspired theological reading of Butler by posing a rhetorical question: "Do we not perhaps detect a yearning for such *completion* in Butler's remorselessly sophisticated and tortured maneuvers?"[17] What began as a question that directed the reader away from Butler to Gregory's desire to transcend the gendered body, now ends in a rhetorical question that similarly hinders returning to Butler's desire to reform the beginning. Whereas the first question was usurped by an eschatological parenthesis and the concluding question stripped of its interrogative status by virtue of its rhetorical nature, in this book we have taken them both at face value: to what end does Butler

---

15. Coakley, *Powers and Submissions*, 153. Elisabeth Stuart problematically follows Coakley's interpretation of Butler's gender theory by looking to the eschatological horizon rather than the beginning to ground her queer theology. Stuart, "Sacramental Flesh," 65. A critique similar to my own is that of Virginia Burrus, who describes Coakley's interpretation as an "extremely disturbing supersessonist positioning of Gregory of Nyssa," which amounts to a "full-blown Christian triumphalism." Burrus, "Queer Father," 160n3.

16. Burrus, "Queer Father," 161.

17. Burrus, "Queer Father," 166 (emphasis mine).

seek to transform gender? And does Butler desire to overcome her body in life? The first question concerns gender violence in the present, and the second question prompts us to reflect on humanity's present relationship to the beginning for thinking about what is a good or transgressive life. Both questions do not allow us to walk away from the beginning or the present, but demand that we interrogate them to take up our proper relation to them.

My reluctance to follow Coakley's imaginative patristic-geared movement away from Eden is like Butler's reluctance to follow Lacan, who also envisages the imagination as the means to resist confronting the law. Here Butler illuminates our theological interaction with Coakley when she (Butler) states: "The imaginary thwarts the efficacy of the symbolic law but cannot turn back upon the law, demanding or effecting its reformulation."[18] Taking Butler's critique of violence seriously requires that something must be done about Adam and Eve. The ideal images that function as a law cannot be smashed, but nor can we turn our back on them as we are swept into an imaginary ideal future. Richard Lints identifies that the only way to truly treat idols is by replacing them with God, but he underestimates their force when he suggests that where knowledge of God has no task to perform, the next best possibility is muting them. I suggest, however, that muting idols is never a possibility as Coakley herself realizes yet inadequately addresses. The images of Adam and Eve must not be smashed, ignored, or muted, but treated with the light of God to reveal their true character.[19]

A theology of gender must not preclude the beginning by being lost in the end or in the pursuit of it. It is oriented to the end, but not before it has appropriately integrated an understanding of humanity's present relationship with God and to humanity in the beginning.

Confused Desire

How should we think theologically about desire and what is its relationship to the beginning? We have seen that for Butler desire is the way we name humanity's inextricable relation to the world which reveals a person's contingency and dependency on that world for life. As an ontological category, desire indicates that personhood is fundamentally

---

18. Butler, *PLP*, 98.
19. Lints, *Identity and Idolatry*, 41.

characterized by loss and lack. If gender and sex are modes of personhood then they too, according to Butler's thought, are manifestations of one's loss and lack. Coakley makes a similar claim that desire is more basic than gender and sex, but this is because desire is an ontological characteristic of God.[20] However, God's desire, unlike that of the person, does not indicate lack or loss and a need for the world to enable God's persistence in being.[21] Desire is essential for human personhood, but only because it is rooted in God.

The main implication of these similar yet contrasting views is that for Butler, desire is a drive for life that puts each person in conflict with the other for persevering in life, while for Coakley, all people find their selves in a common story in which the origin and goal of their desire is God. This is why Coakley states that "'desire' is really about desire for God,"[22] and that "desire is the constellating category of selfhood, the ineradicable root of one's longing for God."[23] Human desire, even when fallen, operates as a divinely instituted reflex that constantly calls the person back to God.[24] A person is a microcosm of humanity and the cosmos that manifests an innate reflexivity—a manifestation of "a ceaseless outgoing and return of the desiring God."[25] In sum, Butler's view of desire leads to an ineradicable material reality wherein originary and mundane desire exhaust the scope of desire, while Coakley's view of desire transcends the material for something she describes as a "holy reality"—the divine life of God.[26]

In view of the previous discussion in which wisdom concerns a posture that sees the world it desires to know, both Butler and Coakley's respective views of desire err. Humanity, in line with Coakley, is not limited by materiality but is open to God, and in line with Butler, cannot transcend the beginning or material reality. I suggest an alternative that humanity's materiality and openness to the divine is better understood as "creation reality," which is both material and holy. This proposal does not merge or unite Coakley and Butler's views, which are not able to modify

20. Coakley, *God, Sexuality, and the Self*, 10, 52.
21. Coakley, *God, Sexuality, and the Self*, 10.
22. Coakley, *God, Sexuality, and the Self*, 9.
23. Coakley, *God, Sexuality, and the Self*, 26.
24. Coakley, *God, Sexuality, and the Self*, 58–9.
25. Coakley, *God, Sexuality, and the Self*, 56.
26. Coakley, *God, Sexuality, and the Self*, 54.

each other—overly materialistic views do not moderate overly transcendent views, and vice versa. Alternatively, creation reality describes the material constitution of people, the world, and universe without forsaking each part's relative openness to God and God's desires.

Creation reality is not "code" for divine in the end, nor is it an attempt to smuggle a queer theorist's desire for mundane desire into a Christian theology of gender. Rather, it is a conviction that desire is an essential aspect of what it means to be a created person, which is not circumscribed by materiality or reducible to God's desire. Desire binds us *both* to creation *and* to God. In the beginning, humanity's desire for God and God's desire for humanity takes the shape of human life. The man and woman manifest their desire for God by desiring God's desire for them to live as a good part of a very good world. Creation reality is not a means to another end, but the mode of being in which a person glorifies God. If there is an imperative in the beginning, it is not to transcend our material selves nor reject our openness to God, but to enjoy what it means to be human and so glorify God with our body. The commands to "fill the earth" and "have dominion" over it describe God's desire for the man and woman, and their offspring, to live into creation by taking up the task of being what they were created to be.[27]

The goodness of creation reality contrasts with Coakley's uncertainty of what to do with the beginning.[28] Specifically, what does God's creation of the man and woman reveal about God's desire for human embodiment? When Coakley describes the ascetic life to be one of purgation and conforming to God's longings, to what are the purging and the longings oriented?[29] The same point can be pressed by asking about disordered desires that characterize our bodies of death. Coakley is right in her insistence on the ascetic aspect of theology as prayerfully transformational.[30] But the very notion of transformation begs the questions: into what, now, and finally? What does it mean "to think, act, desire, and *see* aright"?[31] The Spirit "'breaks' sinful desires," Coakley suggests, "so that they may become one with God's," but she leaves unsaid what God desires, which disordered desires are understood as sinful, and subsequently redressed

---

27. Gen 1:28.
28. Coakley, *God, Sexuality, and the Self*, 8–11.
29. Coakley, *God, Sexuality, and the Self*, 15.
30. Coakley, *God, Sexuality, and the Self*, 19 and 21.
31. Coakley, *God, Sexuality, and the Self*, 20.

by the Spirit.[32] As much as Coakley claims sex and gender do matter,[33] her departure from the beginning to ascend into the triune God leaves human embodiment languishing as that which must be overcome through ascetic purgation. The task is bodily and spiritual, but the originary and mundane body is merely instrumental for experiencing an unarticulated notion of unending delight, even in the present.[34]

Coakley's dependence on Gregory of Nyssa's origin account reveals the source of her reluctance to articulate God's originary desire for human embodiment.[35] Gregory's creation account does *not* conceive of man and woman as the manifestation of God's desire for creation, but as a reaction to God's foresight that asexual creatures would sin and die leading to their extinction.[36] God therefore creates humans with the capacity to procreate and so survive the deleterious end humanity brings on itself due to its rebellion. From Gregory's view, and thus the viewpoint that is impacting Coakley, God's primary desire was for asexual creatures, as demonstrated by their angelic end, which means that God's ultimate desire is for a non-gendered and non-sexual humanity, which is realized in the end by transcending our gender and sexuality through a prayerful ascent into God.[37]

Going by this account, the beginning is inexorably troubled for thinking about gender and sexuality in the present. Both queer *and* differentiated notions of gender are present in the beginning and therefore constitute what can be considered God's originary desire. By subscribing to this creation account that explicitly refuses to grant God's creation of sexual embodiment as the manifestation of God's perfect and eternal will, Coakley is forced to leave behind the troublesome Edenic man and woman for an imagined angelic and therefore "asexual" life in the triune God. Regardless of which comes first—Coakley's conflicted origin account or the claim that all human desire is at root a desire for God—the integrity of creation from the moment of inception is ambiguous and of little use for thinking about what it means to live as God's creatures in the

32. Coakley, *God, Sexuality, and the Self*, 14–15.

33. Coakley, *God, Sexuality, and the Self*, 10.

34. Coakley, *God, Sexuality, and the Self*, 11.

35. The recent turn to patristic sources in Protestant theology tends toward eliding the content in the beginning. Another notable example is Tanner, *Christ the Key*.

36. For a concise account of Gregory's anthropology see Smith, "Body of Paradise," 207–28, and also Harrison, "Male and Female in Cappadocian Theology."

37. Matt 22:30; Mark 12:25; and Luke 20:34–36.

present, since sexual and gendered embodied life is to be finally, even in this life, transcended.

Imagining Another Path

Theological proposals relating to gender are problematic when they rely on an over-determined protology or an over-realized eschatology. The beginning and the end do impact how we conceive gender now, but neither ultimately explains how we experience our bodies now or how we should live, because we live in between these times. As the apostle Paul explains in Romans 8, creation mourns for what is lost, and groans for what is to come, which locates human embodied life in an age of anxiety. As we continue reforming a theology of gender in this chapter, we must consider the continuity and discontinuity between creation and the age of anxiety, between the eschaton and the age of anxiety, and between creation and the eschaton. Such an account inhibits an *over-determined protology*, an *over-realized eschatology*, and an *eternalized age of anxiety*, without downplaying the normative significance and impact of creation, the fall, and redemption on one's life in this present age. My intention is not to hold every age in tension, but to give each its appropriate theological weight for understanding gendered embodiment in the present. In this way, we continue to see the importance of God *and* the concept of time for thinking about ourselves as people with bodies and desires.

Coakley begins her systematic theology by calling theologians to avoid not only mastering the world but also smashing idols. She proposes the need to *transform idols* through imagination and a contemplative theology that reveals an alternative account of a doctrine's development. The account I have offered so far in this book and what I will build on does not resort to idolatry and iconoclasm, nor does it require darkness to imaginatively reconceive the world we seek to know. Furthermore, the door is wide open to engage the Spirit's chastening work as we begin to think about how to conceive of life in our bodies of death. This book models a mode of cataphatic inquiry that has not ended in mastery of God, the world, or the body. The result so far is a theological reform of gender that calls for conviction and confession rather than the imposition of mastered bodies. In this posture and with one eye still on the beginning, we can begin to reflect theologically on the present and future.

A Body of Hope

Desiring Desire's Hope

Laws determine how we can and should live gendered lives in the present. These are codified in civil law and other social regulating mechanisms like medical manuals.[38] Gendered lives can also be codified as norms in society, which compel us to perform in order to fit into the playground, school, workplace, or family, etc. We have seen that Butler does not propose a new set of civil laws, or changes to medical classifications, nor does she offer new norms to redefine gender. Instead, she proposes a law that valorizes the desire of the other. If desire is installed as the mode and means of being man or woman—the ontological reality of personhood—desire replaces the genitals as that which stands synecdochally for a person. One does not love a person when one does not desire their desire: their desire to persevere in being and to live well.

This intended social reform offers hope to those whose desires are not recognized as good by society. For example, a man might not only desire men but also desire that society will recognize such desire as normal and good. The installation of Butler's law accommodates the possible realization of this kind of desire. But notice also that Butler's suggested reform does not afford this without at the same time affording the *possible* normalization of others' desires that some desire for life. One shortcoming of Butler's law is that it has *no limits* as to what desires can be desired. Taboos against polygamous marriage, pedophilia, incest, bestiality, and so on, are immediately threatened by Butler's proposal. This does not mean she necessarily supports the normalization of these things, but it does mean her proposed reform opens the door for society to affirm what is presently deemed morally problematic and even abhorrent. Of course, measures can be installed to limit such possibilities, but where her law of desire is administered justly and universally, taboos that are presently deemed problematic or abhorrent are only provisionally so. Butler's theory provides no means to restrict the normativization of only some desires. Either desire is foreclosed, thereby ruling out some desires, or all desire is essentially contested and so rendered only temporally valid or invalid.

---

38. For example, the *International Classification of Diseases* (ICD), or the *Diagnostic and Statistical Manual of Mental Disorders* (DSM).

Butler's moral law of desire and its implications might seem far removed from a traditional Christian pursuit of a good, embodied life, but the account offered by the apostle Paul in Romans 8 surprisingly runs according to a similar logic. My suggestion is that Paul's correspondence to the church in Rome should *not* be read as supporting a notion of morality that is determined by the law of desire, that in time could be used to justify polygamous marriage, pedophilia, incest, and bestiality—far from it! But where what can be desired is foreclosed by the beginning, one's hope does not reflect a certain departure from the beginning. If human life is utterly regulated by the law of Adam and Eve, then what can be desired for life is limited to what is found in Eden. Paul contradicts this kind of dogged conservative thinking that is fixated on the regulative impact of Adam and Eve for life now and the future when he states: "Now hope that is seen is not hope at all. For who hopes for what is seen?"[39] Hope is exhausted of its potential when what one can hope for is circumscribed by the beginning. If the Christian's eschatological end is not a repristination of the beginning, then Eden is not our hope. If our hope is the coherent, flourishing, embodied lives of Adam and Eve, we live in our bodies of death with no hope at all.

In Romans 8:18–25, Paul speaks about creation and the body as existing in a state of longing. This longing is eschatological, but in contrast to Coakley's desire for the end, Paul's longing is emphatically *embodied*. Paul's emphasis is that he does not desire this body, and nor does he desire the end without this body. He desires to be liberated not from this body but from *death*, here spiritual death (*thanatos* in Rom 7:24), which wracks the body. This does not amount to overcoming or transcending the body, but being released from the effects of death on it. Paul demonstrates his desire for creation and the body's longing by refusing to overcome it, transcend it, or satisfy it. By desiring the body's desire for life, Paul leaves unarticulated what life in the body will look like. He has not seen the hope for which he desires, and this chastens his desire to articulate what it is.

The potential of Butler's law of desire for those who desire life in their bodies comes about because what is good future embodiment is not foreclosed, which parodies the state of the Christian community, which is not privy to the details about future good embodiment. Paul and Butler's respective desire promises that life in the future might stand in contrast

---

39. Rom 8:24.

to what we experience as life now. When people of the Christian community refuse to be determined by their desire for the law of Adam and Eve but instead are captivated by the body's desire for life, new possibilities can be envisaged that, like Butler's desire, will transform what kind of embodied lives can be considered normal and good in the present and the end.

Paul articulates openness to uncertain embodiment when he refuses to articulate specifically what future embodiment will look like. Instead of describing an eschatological humanity that looks like Adam or Eve, or that looks like what he desires for present coherence, Paul uses terms like liberation (v. 21), freedom (v. 21), glory (v. 21), and redemption (v. 23). The temptation to put flesh of a particular form on this future ambiguous humanity must be resisted. It is easy *to dismiss* the law of Adam and Eve in a theology of gender under the guise of eschatological hope, which I've shown describes Coakley's thought, but it is just as easy *to smuggle* the law of Adam and Eve into a theology of gender under the guise of hope. A theology of gender holds to the truth that *humanity's end is not clear*, and that if we are longing to be saved from this body of death, we are left desiring *this* body's desire for a glorious embodied life beyond death.

More poignantly, yet ironically, when we revert to the law of Adam and Eve to satisfy humanity's desire for life, we reject the body's longing for life; the hope of liberation, freedom, glory, and redemption. Not desiring the body's longing is at best a distraction from what is to come, and at worst amounts to withholding the hope the gospel offers for life now and in the end. When Paul desires creation's desire he is not seeking to master desire because a dramatic recalibration of what is desirable has already taken place in his life.[40] The hope that desire for embodied life beyond death expresses is an important theme when it comes to a theology of gender because it not only tames an insatiable, dogged desire to be coherent, or make others coherent through disciplining bodies and minds, but also offers the future event of the redemption of our bodies. The hope of life in *this* body is basic because "for in this hope we were saved."[41]

---

40. 1 Cor 7:29–31.
41. Rom 8:24.

Refining Hope's Desire

Over the millennia, many Christian theologians and philosophers have attempted to bring clarity to Paul's and Scripture's uncertainty concerning the shape of eschatological human embodiment. More recently, as gender and sexuality issues have come to the fore, Christian thinkers have pressed into the doctrine of eschatology to find resources to provide Christians with more clarity on the eschatological body and therefore our present lives. Where clarity can be found, there is the hope of remedying gender discrimination and welcoming those previously cast out for manifesting transgressive gendered lives.

It remains outside the scope of this book to engage Christian theological and philosophical thought on the eschatological body because our theological reflection concerns Butler's emphases, which do not entertain *imaginative speculation* on what will be good in the future. But even if this was not the case, the previous theological reflection has shown that when we seek to satisfy what we long for in the present, we lose the hope for which we have been saved. Butler's perspective is once again helpful: how can imagining future good embodiment avoid reiterating the trouble that wracks the present? How can we avoid developing an eschatological image of human embodiment that is not a statement of our satiated desires? Such an eschatological image, whether embodied or not, gendered or not, sexually active or not, imaging Adam and Eve or not, is not imaginative at all, but exemplary of a stunted imagination that results in foreclosing what a glorious and redeemed body will look like, desire, and do.[42] Sometimes the absence of something does not warrant the use of imagination to make it appear. What is warranted is a patient embrace of the absence. Paul points us in this direction when he concludes his foray into the body's desire and hope: "But if we hope for what we do not see, we wait for it with patience."[43]

Absence of a specific articulation of future eschatological embodiment is arguably different to a revealed articulation of what future eschatological embodiment is not. For example, in Galatians 3:28 we read that "there is no longer male and female." If male and female is not humanity's end, then a degree of clarity is arguably found.[44] Susannah Cornwall is

---

42. For an example of imaginative foreclosing of human desire, see Kamitsuka, "Sex in Heaven?," 261.

43. Rom 8:25.

44. For an overview of how this biblical text might be used to defend various positions regarding gender, see Cornwall, *Sex and Uncertainty*, 69–75.

one theologian who seizes upon this degree of clarity to think through its implications on gender, specifically for people with intersex conditions. Her basic claim is that "the 'no more male-and-female in Christ', then, means no more taxonomies of goodness or perfection attached to the success or otherwise of how a given body meets current criteria for maleness or femaleness."[45] This fits broadly with a theology of gender that is based on the law of Adam and Eve, but Cornwall's theology of gender begins to falter where she snuffs out the uncertain body's hope: "The end—the cessation—of male-and-female is the end—the *telos*—for humanity. This is the crux of reading Gal. 3:28 in a more than future sense, for a realized eschatology is rooted in the *already*, the possibility for the redemption of this present realm."[46] The implication of this over-realized eschatological interpretation of Galatians 3:28 is that God's creation of male and female in the beginning was not good, and what is more, functions as a curse from which humanity (at least some of us) needs redeeming. But in what sense is the originary male and female a curse? The argument unfolding so far in this book is that they themselves are not cursed, but curse, in the sense of condemn to death, those who stand before them.

This is precisely how Paul views the Old Testament law (*Torah*). In Galatians 3:13, Paul speaks of the curse of the law rather than the law as a curse, which recalls his earlier usage in 3:10 in which we read that the curse is a result of not meeting the law's requirements. So the law is not cursed, but it brings to light the cursed state of humanity having realized the law's demands on our lives. We can consider Edenic Adam and Eve similarly, not as cursed, but as revealing *our inability to live up to their righteous lives*. Butler, Cornwall, conservative Christianity, and humanity walk into Paul's sights because too often we assume our own innocence and another's guilt, and where guilt abounds, confidence in our own or another's ability to approximate the law's demands to placate God also abounds. By contrast, Paul maintains the integrity of the law as commensurate with God's promises,[47] and instead of seeking to reform the law to justify his present life, Paul seeks life through God's provision of a rescuer—one who becomes the curse for him.[48]

---

45. Cornwall, *Sex and Uncertainty*, 73–74.
46. Cornwall, *Sex and Uncertainty*, 74.
47. Gal 3:21.
48. Gal 3:13.

THE VOCATION OF GENDER: VULNERABILITY IN UNION   185

Paul's interpretation of our relationship to the law is instructive for developing our understanding of our relationship to the law of Adam and Eve. Instead of seeking redemption from condemnation under the law of Adam and Eve, Cornwall seeks to kill the law by figuring that "the cessation—of male-and-female is the end." But as we saw earlier in Coakley's thought, Adam and Eve do not readily go away because they cannot be killed, defaced, or smashed. Indeed, Cornwall does not turn her back on the beginning, nor suffer a bout of Edenic iconoclasm, but reconstructs the originary images to overcome male and female according to their end so she can justify non-Edenic-conforming bodies in the present.

Cornwall's proposal is different from Coakley's because she (Cornwall) appropriately realizes the enduring vitality of the beginning. Cornwall realizes she cannot allow the male and female in the beginning to operate on the present to condemn only some bodies, and so she uses the eschatological bodies of Galatians 3:28 to undo the force of the controlling normative originary creatures. In explicitly Butlerian fashion, Cornwall seeks to achieve this by getting "access to power—which includes access to God" to change gender norms that reside in the beginning.[49] Those not justified by originary bodies can find respite according to a Butlerian malleable originary form, which can be invested with terms that better reflect present troubled bodies. Cornwall's Christian Butlerian alternative is that the originary terms are reconditioned by investing them with the future eschatological reality (no male or female), which then serves to redeem now those bodies in the present that are not male or female.

What then does Cornwall achieve by virtue of this Butlerian originary re-form that my Butler-provoked though scriptural justification of universally troubled bodies does not? Even though I have demonstrated a desire for the other's desire for life, and moreover, declined to allow my desire to foreclose what that could look like, Cornwall refuses to be hope-filled and patient, instead she enters the originary scene to recreate the beginning to justify people's bodies and desires in the present. What I suggest we hold off as a matter of hope, Cornwall brings close as a matter of justice by doing what we all agree is impossible; accessing the beginning.[50]

Cornwall's decision to use Scripture's neither-male-and-female eschatological body to populate the human on the eschatological horizon is

---

49. Cornwall, *Sex and Uncertainty*, 79.
50. Cornwall, *Sex and Uncertainty*, 236.

troubled by other passages in Scripture. Jesus' words in Matthew 22:30 or Mark 12:25 provide an alternative eschatological human by which we can imagine the present redeemed life, which is more perspicuous than that offered by Galatians 3:28. In these passages, we learn that marriage and sex are limited, arguably extinguished, features in the eschaton.[51] Following Cornwall's method of interpretation, the redeemed state that is ours to enjoy now is angelic: a state that overcomes our bodies and desires. Should we pursue this "human" on the eschatological horizon by remaining unmarried and virgins? One could argue that Jesus desires a similar mode of human existence in Matthew 19:12 concerning those who are eunuchs by their own will for the kingdom of heaven. Paul also expresses such a desire for the believers in Corinth: "I wish that all were as I myself am"—celibate for the kingdom of heaven.[52] Why does Cornwall refrain from projecting these eschatological possibilities into the beginning and thus the present to conceive good bodies, sexuality, and gender?

The trouble hampering Cornwall to make troubled bodies good is the stubborn presence of male and female in Galatians 3:28 that reinforces the trouble that characterizes bodies. Cornwall can bring the future death of male and female to bear on the present, and even subject the beginning to such an end, but the specter of male and female of Galatians 3:28 lingers. These enduring bodies resist vain attempts to reenter the garden to be changed from what God created in the beginning. Reciting Galatians 3:28 *might* function to point to a *future* time when there will be "no longer male or female," but in doing so one simultaneously confesses a time/s—the beginning and in the present—when there was and are male and female. The linguistic form of Galatians 3:28 does not allow itself to be used to purge man and woman from the end *and* the beginning. This should alert us to see that Paul is drawing his readers' attention to the complex dynamic of human continuity and discontinuity between the beginning, the age of anxiety, and the eschaton.

I agree with Cornwall that Paul is drawing on God's redemptive work to bear on how we think about man and woman now and in the future, but she fails to recognize or give credence to what Paul is offering, and how it is realized. She does not need to install troubled bodies in the beginning to justify troubled bodies now, not only because she cannot enter Eden to do so, but primarily because Paul is addressing the precise

---

51. Note the eschatological description does not negate existing marriages, but limits the future possibility of entering into marriage.

52. 1 Cor 7:7.

problem Cornwall is seeking to treat: man and woman as a standard that justifies entry into the community of Christ. What is needed is another means to overcome unjust and discriminatory entry standards, which Paul addresses moments earlier: "for *in Christ Jesus* you are all children of God," not through approximating man or woman through one's desire, body work, or sex work, but "*through* faith."[53] What impacts decisive change in the Christian community is the way Paul thinks of himself and others according to his new identity *in Christ through faith*.

Finally, this should alert us to the possibility that Paul is not obliterating man and woman now or in the eschaton, but is bringing them into question as valid criteria to regulate who can participate in Christ, and therefore the Christian community, now and in the end. I suggest Paul is not commenting on what gender, sexuality, and marriage look like in the present as a reflection of what is found in the eschaton. Rather, Paul is treating the (ab)use of gender as a marker to privilege some over others.[54] In positive terms, Paul is describing who is permitted to participate in the present—not yet revealed—hope of our promised inheritance of life from our bodies of death: "And if you belong to Christ, then you are Abraham's offspring, heirs according to the promise."[55] By reaching back to God's promises to Abraham in Genesis 12:1–3, Paul expresses that the promises are fulfilled in Christ, and that no (gender) marker inhibits one's

---

53. Gal 3:26 (emphasis mine).

54. It is ironic that Paul's explicit treatment of hierarchy and the abuse of power in his context is unsatisfactory for some theologians especially given their own deployment of the same contextual feature to argue for more inclusivity in the church. For example, DeFranza, "Journeying from the Bible to Christian Ethics."

55. Gal 3:29. Laurence Hemming's interpretation of v. 28 hinges on a translation that renders the original Greek as "you are all *singular*"—referencing Jesus' notion of the celibate eunuch for the kingdom of God in Matthew 19:12. This enables Hemming to claim that the "baptized" take on "the *angelic* character of the redeemed state." This interpretation leads Hemming to make the point that neither "sexual difference, nor indeed marriage, carry over into eternity." But this gloss conflates Jesus' words in Matt 22:30 and Paul's words in Gal 3:28. Not only is there scarce textual evidence to suggest that Paul is referring to Jesus' words, but the force of the narratives suggest that they are engaged with different issues. Paul is not seeking to articulate what characterizes the embodied resurrected state, like Jesus (v. 31), but *who can participate in it* and *on what grounds*. The danger of reading Paul in this text as seeking to queer gender and sexuality in the eschaton is that the reading facilitates the eschatological human reality to being read back into the present. Where marriage in the eschaton is arguably "undone," as in Matt 22:30 by Jesus, it does not offer the terms to frame the undoing of gender. Paul is undermining hegemonic forces that seek to limit entry into the redeemed state to a "privileged" few. Hemming, "Undoing of Sex," 65.

participation in Christ and therefore the accompanying blessings. The force of this verse is radical: there is no embodied precondition that one must meet for accepting God's gift of grace by faith.[56] When such a precondition is put in place, Paul is clear: this is a different gospel.[57]

Furthermore, and returning to Galatians 3:13 to reflect imaginatively upon Adam and Eve as a law that curses humanity, the means by which redemption from our bodies of death is found is not through our own re-formation of the beginning—how can it be?—but through participation in Christ's death and resurrection. Paul states that "Christ redeemed us from the curse of the law by becoming a curse for us—for it is written, cursed is everyone who hangs on a tree."[58]

The implication for our inquiry is that redemption of humanity from the curse of the law of Adam and Eve in this moment does not happen by imagining a future gender-less and marriage-less reality, and installing that into the beginning to justify as good present lives that do not manifest God's traditionally conceived originary creatures. Rather, it is through the work of Christ, who becomes the curse for humanity that God rescues a person from their body of death, hence Paul's ecstatic answer to the question, "Who will rescue me from this body that is subject to death? Thanks be to God, who delivers me through Jesus Christ our Lord!"[59] This book's reform of a theology of gender comes into view, whereby one's good yet troubled gendered embodiment in no way bears upon one's right to inherit God's promise of embodied life. Moreover, the means of realizing such a promise is not by imaging or conforming ourselves and others to the beautiful bodies of Adam and Eve, but by participating in the scarred and bloodied *body* of Jesus Christ by faith.

The Eunuch's Hope

Recreating the beginning is not only impossible and ineffectual but also a redundant means of justifying troubled embodiment, especially when Scripture reveals a changing perspective toward troubled embodiment. For example, the changing representation of the eunuch in Scripture

---

56. For a rigorous exploration of this theological concept, see Ferguson, *Whole Christ*.

57. Gal 1:6.

58. Gal 3:13.

59. Rom 7:24b–25a.

THE VOCATION OF GENDER: VULNERABILITY IN UNION   189

reinforces the scope of salvation to which Paul testifies in Galatians 3:14 and 28. In Deuteronomy 23:1, the law teaches that "no one whose testicles are crushed or whose penis is cut off shall be admitted to the assembly of the LORD."[60] In Matthew 19, Jesus, in contrast to the Old Testament law, speaks about the eunuch with compassion, which surely alludes to and develops upon the prophecy about the eunuch in Isaiah 56:1–8. When Jesus turns his attention to these same good yet troubled embodied people in Matthew 19:12, he does not invoke or reinforce the legal reason to exclude them from entering the assembly, but encounters them, and may even identify as one of them:[61] "For there are eunuchs who have been so from birth, and there are eunuchs who have been made eunuchs by others, and there are eunuchs who have made themselves eunuchs for the sake of the kingdom of heaven. Let anyone accept this who can." In this discussion with his disciples, Jesus is speaking specifically about the possibility of a life of singleness in light of the disciples' shocking realization that "it is better not to marry" if divorce laws do not justify discarding an unwanted wife.[62] In this moment, Jesus does *not* identify with Adam in the beginning who loved his wife as God desired, nor with the sinful man who loves himself more than his wife, but with the *eunuch* who has no wife for the benefit of the kingdom of heaven.[63]

What does it mean to identify with the eunuch? It could simply mean that Jesus chooses the single life over what would be expected of a first-century virile Jewish male, that is, to choose a wife (or have a woman chosen for him) and raise a family. Rejecting this expectation, at the very least, means that Jesus is positioning himself in contradiction to Jewish teaching that "any Jew who does not have a wife is half a man."[64] This, however, only accounts for the stigma attached to the Jewish attitude toward singleness. That Jesus is speaking about singleness and celibacy is deduced via his use of the term eunuch, which would have attracted

---

60. See also Lev 22:24–25.

61. Hagner, *Matthew 14–28*, 550; France, *Gospel of Matthew*, 723. It is interesting that most conservative commentators do not ask the question, which classification of eunuch might Jesus identify with? Furthermore, what implications might Jesus' answer have on the discussion about marriage, divorce, and our relation to Adam and Eve in the beginning?

62. Matt 19:10.

63. For a concise overview of the term eunuch in ancient times see DeFranza, "Virtuous Eunuchs," 55–76.

64. R. Eliezer argues this in *Babylonian Tamud Yebamot*, 63a. Cited in Garland, *Reading Matthew*, 203.

its own social characterization within the ancient Roman milieu. Megan DeFranza offers the view that to stand voluntarily in the place of the eunuch (which some physically did)[65] also meant taking on the associated social stigma as "the quintessential foreigners, the epitome of 'other.'"[66] DeFranza describes this otherness as assumed to be "pagan and sexually immoral."[67] If Jesus can be interpreted as counting himself as one who "made" himself a eunuch for the sake of the kingdom of heaven, Jesus is not only laying claim to the goodness of singleness and celibacy as a virtuous life, but doing something much more radical: de-centering marriage and the toxic masculinity that characterized it. Jesus aligns himself with a caste of people who were not unclean and blameworthy, but who were marginalized nonetheless as such. In the context of a discussion about the perversion of Edenic marriage, Jesus troubles the priority of marriage for a flourishing life by refusing it in favor of a life as one who is not a virile man, but one who is "legally other, morally other, sexually other, socially other, religiously other."[68] Jesus sees no shame, embarrassment, or dishonor in being seen as a "eunuch," despite the stigma and social implications of such an existence.

Furthermore, and with direct implications for Jesus' ministry, John Hare, who draws on Talmudic rulings, explains how the eunuch was barred from the priestly role and was not forced into levirate marriage.[69] In "making" himself a eunuch for the kingdom of heaven, Jesus radically re-forms the priesthood and ideal king from being concerned principally with undefiled bodies and patrilineality to being about a broken body that does not cling to an earthly life of virility and legacy. *Jesus re-forms what is considered good "gender and sexuality" into something that is not limited to the marriage that God created in the beginning.* While it sounds rather obvious, it needs to be stated: marriage is not the entry point to "normal," and nor is it the litmus test of orthopraxis.[70] This does not undermine what God created in the beginning because earlier in Matthew 19:4–6, Jesus emphatically reinforces Edenic marriage between a man

---

65. DeFranza, "Virtuous Eunuchs," 56–57.
66. DeFranza, "Virtuous Eunuchs," 62.
67. DeFranza, "Virtuous Eunuchs," 62.
68. DeFranza, "Virtuous Eunuchs," 63.
69. Hare, "Hermaphrodites, Eunuchs, and Intersex People," 85.
70. See Jane Shaw's historical account of the consequences of Martin Luther's theological reaction to the Catholic Church's ideas of marriage and celibacy in Shaw, "Reformed and Enlightened Church," 218–21.

THE VOCATION OF GENDER: VULNERABILITY IN UNION 191

and woman as a paradigm for what God desires as good for marriage now. However, Jesus does bring the "transgressive" body—in terms of the passage, the one not married to a woman, for whatever reason—into the light as the paradigm for thinking about himself, the Son of God, whose concern is on things above rather than ensuring that he is recognizably lawful, acceptable, good, and righteous. The most basic point is that Jesus does not marginalize those whose good yet troubled bodies have been imposed on them by others, or those whose good yet troubled bodies were present at birth, or those who, for the sake of the kingdom of God, have made themselves "eunuchs." Jesus, in fact, appears to inhabit the "strange" and "repulsive" social state, thereby transgressing[71] and therefore displacing marriage and its associated God-ordained blessings (companionship, sex, and children) as *the* locus of human satisfaction and fulfillment.[72] This finds an echo with a similar tone and content in Paul's thought in 1 Corinthians 7:6-7 in which he appeals to discernment rather than a law to adjudicate whether one should "take" a wife (or husband) or not.[73] I do not need to agree with Paul Fletcher's conclusions to concur with his claim that a scriptural "view of marriage is neglected, even elided because it threatens the basis of the modern morality that is resolutely embraced and expounded."[74]

Galatians 3:28 takes its final interpretive nuance when we learn in Acts 8:35-38 that one of the first non-Jews to enter the kingdom of heaven was an Ethiopian *eunuch*, who was presumably made a eunuch by others. Having heard the good news about Jesus explained to him by Philip, the eunuch is baptized. The eunuch who was once unable to enter the temple and who was an alienated caste of human embodiment is not

---

71. Blinzler takes this passage as dealing literally with eunuchs rather than celibacy. At one point he notes that eunuchs at birth or by the hands of people were not to blame for their state, however those who willingly chose to inhabit non-Edenic orders were willingly negligent of, and consciously disobeying God, which he claims Jesus inhabits. Jesus makes himself this kind of transgressor, but for the kingdom of heaven, therefore justifying the "worst" kind of "eunuch" by going "beyond" the law. This notion of going beyond the law is what Jesus persistently teaches in the Sermon on the Mount in Matthew 5-7. Blinzler, "Zur Auslegung von Mt 19:12," 259.

72. Francis Moloney argues that the use of the word "eunuch" in Matt 19:12 is Jesus' way of redeeming the word (and those it represents), commonly spoken as an insult in Jesus' direction because of his unmarried status. Moloney, *"Hard Saying,"* 47-52.

73. See 1 Cor 7:32-35. Garland, *Reading Matthew*, 203.

74. Fletcher, "Antimarriage," 259-60.

barred from participating in the Christian community or the kingdom of heaven and the blessing that accompanies it. Here we meet an example of ambiguous embodied life that could not be realized if the body's longing is not desired. The eunuch *cannot* inhabit Edenic created orders, but as one who has placed faith in Christ *can* inhabit the Christian community, now and in the end.

In sum, the force of Paul's claim in Galatians 3:28 must not be watered down by eschewing what Douglas Campbell describes as an "irreducibly radical, abolitionist, and therefore also political and liberational text."[75] Despite the radicality of the text, Campbell goes on to argue that it "contains implicit warnings against extrapolating Paul's positive views of creation . . . and on the degree of eschatological realization."[76] Thus the moral concern of Galatians 3:26–29 is not to promulgate gendered embodied possibilities in the present that reflect the eschaton (in which male and female "pass away") or the beginning (to reify inaccessible Edenic embodiment).[77] Paul is not drawing on the past or future to reorder God's creation of humanity in the present. Rather, in this moment, Paul is morally sensitized to the sinful discriminating entry standards that some might use to rule out and rule in who can participate in the community of the promise and hope of God, that is, Jesus Christ. Jesus Christ invites all good yet troubled embodied existence to enter the kingdom of heaven by faith to enjoy the hope of glorified bodies now.

The Image of God: A Vocation of Conformity

Deferring the Image

Male and female and the doctrine of the "image of God" are often connected due to their proximity in Genesis 1:26–27.[78] Humanity's certain departure from God's originary creatures, however, casts some doubt on such a connection. Moreover, we have recently traveled the redemptive historical journey with the eunuch who transgresses the originary couple while living up to what it means to be created in the image of God. This transgressive yet good example of embodiment is reinforced by Jesus

---

75. Campbell, "Logic of Eschatology," 69.
76. Campbell, "Logic of Eschatology," 71.
77. Cornwall, *Sex and Uncertainty*, 73.
78. References to the image of God are found also in Gen 5:1–3 and 9:6.

who *chooses* not to identify with, or conform himself to, the man in Eden. This reveals that one cannot confidently assume that the image of God is the final bulwark against present efforts, like Butler's, to undermine what it traditionally means to be a man or woman.

The contested nature of the image of God is well documented and its relationship to male and female is equally explored.[79] For example, in the first chapter of an influential compilation of essays about manhood and womanhood, the nature of the image of God is first shown to be contested, but then assigned with male and female, which is further tightened when the image of God as man and woman is defined along complementarian lines.[80] Elsewhere, Anthony Hoekema articulates that the image of God is broadly a vocation that is directed toward God, one's neighbor, and creation.[81] He narrows his view significantly in his concluding observation when he abruptly says that "male and female is an essential aspect of the image of God."[82] For Coakley, the image of God is a human role that is directed toward God, which one cannot take up without one's gender, understood as *"differentiated, embodied relationships."*[83] As we explored earlier in the chapter, the gendered aspect of the role is not essential but added to humanity by God as it moved toward the fall which is lost in the end.[84] Then there is Karl Barth's famous claim that the image of God concerns "existence in confrontation."[85] The I/thou confrontation between the man and woman is an analogy of relation that reflects God and humanity.[86] This view has come under strong criticism due to its analogous hierarchical relational asymmetry between God and humanity and therefore man and woman.[87] In contrast to these accounts, I have resisted what might look like an obvious starting point for an exploration of gender, instead deferring taking up the doctrine until now. This is justifiable on the grounds that the content of the originary doctrine and what it means to be a person today is contested and lacks

---

79. For example, Middleton, *Liberating Image*, ch. 1; Clines, "Image of God in Man," 53–103; and Bray, "Significance of God's Image in Man," 195–225.

80. Ware, "Male and Female Complementarity."

81. Hoekema, *Created in God's Image*, 75–82.

82. Hoekema, *Created in God's Image*, 97.

83. Coakley, *God, Sexuality, and the Self*, 53.

84. Coakley, *God, Sexuality, and the Self*, 281–82.

85. Barth, *Church Dogmatics*, III/1, 195.

86. Barth, *Church Dogmatics*, III/3, 203.

87. Bodley-Dangelo, *Sexual Difference, Gender, and Agency*.

clarity. If there is any validity in Gerhard von Rad's observation that "the declaration about God's image is indeed highly exalted, but it also remains intentionally in a certain state of suspense," then temporary deferral is warranted.[88] Also, if we have been listening carefully to Butler, then caution should characterize one's handling of an originary condition like the image of God. The doctrine of the image of God should be treated like a transcendent law that is susceptible to an investment of terms that some might use to inappropriately justify their own sinful gendered lives, while inflicting hurt on others for transgressing it.

The decision to defer an explicit engagement with the image of God has been fruitful because it has created the space to establish an originary notion of man and woman that does not evade the impact that time has on our relation to them. This certain departure from the beginning chastises Christian engagement about gender and the body that does not account for the events of the originary creatures' rebellion and the redemptive work of Christ with a view toward the eschaton. The task of making (creating) *and* remaking (re-creating) the body belongs to God, and the originary doctrine of the image of God is the theological key to understanding both divine acts, but not by undermining the certain departure from the beginning and uncertain end that we have affirmed.

Locating the Image of God

In *Christ the Key*, Kathryn Tanner interprets Genesis 1:26–27 as posing a question and task, rather than giving an answer and description: if the man and woman were created in the image of God, what is the image of God that the man and woman were created to image? The assumption is that the originary man and woman, even as a part of God's very good world, do not image God directly as they find themselves, but indirectly through participating in the image of God.[89] Humanity's *task*, therefore, is to image God, but only after identifying *what* the image of God is, which Tanner identifies as the second person of the Trinity. The Word of God does not participate in God, but *is* God and so represents

---

88. Von Rad, *Genesis*, 59.
89. Tanner, *Christ the Key*, 1.

God perfectly.[90] By *participating* in the Word of God incarnate—Jesus Christ—humanity accomplishes the task of imaging God.[91]

This accomplishment, however, occurs by passive participation in virtue of the Word's attachment to humanity in the incarnation.[92] The introduction of participation as the means of enjoying the fullness of God comes in weak and strong forms: a weak participation in God "means nothing more than being a creature of God,"[93] while humanity's strong form of participation is "in virtue of the gift to them of what remains alien to them, the very perfection of the divine image that they are not, now having become their own."[94] The weak form is not God's desired end for humanity, but the created condition whereby humanity can realize its ultimate good by attaching to the Word of God by the Spirit.

This very brief reading of Tanner's account of the image of God as a task to be accomplished, and weak and strong participation as modes of imaging God, reveals what Tanner means by imaging God in the present. If the image of God *is* the Word of God, and if humanity realizes God's good through participation *in* the Word of God, then a strong participation occurs when the Word takes on humanity via incarnation. Imaging God is not something I am or do, but something Christ *is* and in which I participate, and that is realized through my attachment to Christ by the Spirit.

One strength of this account is that the image of God is not reducible to a set of criteria that one must perform to be what God created humanity to be in the beginning. This means that the image of God does not undermine humanity's certain departure from Adam and Eve nor impose the need to approximate Adam and Eve for life or to please God. In short, the image of God is not reducible to capacities like rationality, reason, decision making, or the will, nor exhibiting originary qualities like desiring or marrying someone of the other sex or binary bodies.

Another strength of Tanner's account is that the image of God is located within God's plan of redemption. This reconciles the Old Testament's relative silence and the New Testament's articulation of the

---

90. Tanner, *Christ the Key*, 1, 5–7; Heb 1:3.
91. Tanner, *Christ the Key*, 8.
92. Tanner, *Christ the Key*, 58.
93. Tanner, *Christ the Key*, 8.
94. Tanner, *Christ the Key*, 12.

theme.⁹⁵ Jesus Christ, who *is* the image of God,⁹⁶ is not a sideshow to the main event of the Edenic man and woman who were made in the image of God. Tanner brings into view the vital scriptural and patristic emphasis that if Jesus Christ is the image of God, then humanity's creation in God's image in the beginning involves Jesus Christ in some sense. Approaching the image of God from this perspective not only invests a theology of gender with a christological orientation from the beginning, but also renders the image with a certain measure of uncertainty, which chimes well with the previously developed notion of an uncertain eschatological body. Who the image of God is in the beginning was still to be revealed, and the vocation to locate that image and fulfill the originary calling to image God's revelation was irrevocable.⁹⁷

The upshot of Tanner's account of the image of God is that it recalibrates overly anthropological accounts by setting it within salvation history and the theological locus of Christology. While this corrective has scriptural and theological grounds, the assumptions that ground her subsequent constructive notions of weak and strong modes of imaging God are more speculative and require attention. I suggest that such a distinction relies on an underestimation of the goodness of the beginning, which includes the creaturely mundane vocation of the man and woman to image God with their lives. Tanner argues that in the beginning the man and woman do not lack God but had "the gifts of God's Word and Spirit," which, she affirms, "allowed us to live well."⁹⁸ We learn from this that it was only because of sin that humanity loses these gifts (God), which reveals the fundamental human predicament to be overcome. It is not their loss of God, or the sin and its consequences that precipitated this loss, but their "poor initial capacities" that hindered them from receiving God properly and fully. Humanity is a weak image of God in the beginning because it can *lose* God.⁹⁹ This is what requires redeeming.

95. Image of God language in the Old Testament is only found in Gen 1:26–27; 5:1–2; and 9:6. There is arguably an allusion to it in Pss 8 and 17:15.

96. 2 Cor 4:4 and Col 1:15. For an exploration of these texts, see Grenz, "Jesus as the *Imago Dei*," 618–20.

97. The vocation to conform to Jesus Christ as the image of God is a strong New Testament theme that is found in passages like Rom 8:29; 1 Cor 15:49; 2 Cor 3:18; Col 3:9–11; and Eph 4:17–24. Grenz, "Jesus as the *Imago Dei*," 621–24.

98. Tanner, *Christ the Key*, 34.

99. Tanner, *Christ the Key*, 34. There is no space here to integrate the claim, but it would stand to reason that Tanner's account of the image of God cannot justify a place where people are separated from God for eternity.

THE VOCATION OF GENDER: VULNERABILITY IN UNION 197

Jesus Christ is Tanner's suggested remedy for humanity's originary immaturity. Christ is the key because he manifests the "unloseability" of God for humanity wherein God—the Word—is united with humanity. Tanner states it plainly:

> Lost through sin, the gifts of Word and Spirit that made humans the image of God at their creation would need to be restored to humanity by Christ in some new way that improves upon the original situation that permitted their loss. . . . Although we were images of God in the strong senses of both having the divine image within us and being shaped into a human version of it through the power of the Spirit, we were not yet at our creation images through those gifts in the strongest possible fashion because of some immaturity in *our reception of them*.[100]

This passage exhibits a certain frustration with our God-given creatureliness. Tanner's perspective resembles the discontent in the man and woman when the serpent tempts them to desire more.[101] Their fall is set in motion when they seek to overcome their creatureliness: they do not desire to participate in God's willed creation as God desired, but to participate in creation like God. Speaking of the fruit God commanded them not to eat, the serpent says: "You will not die; for God knows that when you eat of it your eyes will be opened, and you will be like God, knowing good and evil."[102] This is not a divine invitation to take up one's vocation to live into God's desire for man and woman to image God but a parody that preys upon their capacity to desire more than what God has given them to desire, which rebels against God's expressed desire for humanity to image God through faithful participation in God's manifest expression of desire in creation.

Tanner is captivated by the originary humans' *capacity* to lose God, rather than their God-ordained *capacity* to *function* to image God.[103] She is also concerned that "the divine simply cannot be imitated very well in what is not divine,"[104] but as creatures this is surely to be expected at some level, especially in light of God's voiced estimation that everything

---

100. Tanner, *Christ the Key*, 33–34 (emphasis mine).
101. Gen 3:1–6.
102. Gen 3:4–5.
103. This notion of structure and function in the image of God relies on Hoekema, *Created in God's Image*, 68–73.
104. Tanner, *Christ the Key*, 12.

is "very good."[105] Originary creation is not a poor version of something better that God has in mind, whereby that something better comprises new "hands" that cannot fumble the good gift of Godself. I suggest such an account does not stem from the originary inability of the man and woman to properly image God, but a lack of belief in God's expressed satisfaction with humanity imaging God in this way.

A Creaturely Vocation

A distinction can be made between traditional *linear* evangelical approaches to the image of God, Tanner's *nonlinear* offering, and a third way that values both approaches, but concludes with valorizing God's glory rather than our own. Evangelical theologians are inclined to reduce the doctrine of the image of God to an originary anthropological condition with little or no christological import.[106] This is a linear approach because the image of God does not point forward to a time when the image of God will be revealed. Rather, the image of God is rooted in the beginning to articulate what humans are, which is then subject to the fall, and finally redeemed by Christ's redemptive work on the cross. In short, Jesus Christ is the means by which we can be the image of God that we cannot be on our own due to sin. Despite the usual evangelical claim of scriptural faithfulness and exegetical clarity, this fully linear approach elides the nonlinear and indisputable witness of the New Testament that Jesus Christ *is* the image of God. Where the evangelical impulse is to stay in the beginning, Scripture presses us to depart, and to focus on Jesus Christ.

Tanner, on the other hand, errs in the other direction by stripping the doctrine of any originary anthropological importance, instead preferring to find the means for interpreting the beginning in an unspecified future christological realization of God's image. This exclusively nonlinear approach minimizes any originary anthropological claim the doctrine may have. Humanity's relationship with God, however, is not an otherworldly reality, but takes specific shape in human creatureliness, which means that humanity images God according to what they have

105. Gen 1:31.

106. For example, see Grenz's description of the influential evangelical systematic theologies of Millard Erickson, Wayne Grudem, and even his own in Stanley Grenz, "Jesus as the *Imago Dei*," 624–25. Notable exceptions include Richard Lints, *Identity and Idolatry*, and Bird, *Evangelical Theology*, 740–44.

been created to be in relation to God. We cannot imagine what it means to have a relationship with God other than as the creatures God created. Where Tanner desires to move on from the beginning, Scripture presses one to look back.

For example, in Psalm 8:4–8, the author meditates on the creation account to describe the human's creaturely vocation in relation to God. The passage reveals that God glories in the majesty of creation in which humanity finds especial significance. Humanity's existence is not assumed but takes the shape of "a son of man"[107] which is described as "crowned with glory and honor" and enthroned as the king to rule everything in the world. It is hard not to reflect upon the God-given Edenic vocation to rule over the world when one reads in the psalm about the animals in the wild, birds in the sky, and fish in the sea.

Of significance in this psalm is the reinforcement of humanity's vocation to live as God's creatures according to God's desire in the world, but note that sonship is a vital theme that connects the image of God to other passages in Scripture. For example, in Genesis 5:1–3 there is a clear intended connection between God creating humanity in the likeness of God in verse 1 and Adam having a son in his own likeness in verse 2. In addition to this and of less renown is the notion of likeness in terms of sonship where Adam is described as God's son in the genealogy of Jesus in Luke 3:38. The genealogy makes the remarkable claim that, in some sense, Jesus is the son of God because Adam was the son God. Where the image of God is exclusively linked to Jesus Christ as God incarnate, the image fails to account for the anthropological significance Scripture ascribes to it in familial terms. Thinking about humanity as the image of God within a father/child relationship meets Tanner's desire for a relational emphasis, but by giving this emphasis particular creaturely shape enables us to avoid overlooking our creatureliness and God-given ongoing vocation that applies to ourselves as well as Jesus.[108]

Instead of assuming that man and woman were created in lack and in need, being attached to God to attain fullness, I suggest we confess that the beginning was created by God and that their originary state was characterized by desire for the world, yet nonetheless with wholeness, satisfaction, full life, and, as Tanner suggests, with the *vocation* of

---

107. The NRSV translates "*ben adam*" as "mortal" but acknowledges in the footnotes that a literal interpretation is "son of man." The author of Heb 3:6 cites this part of Ps 8, which renders the Hebrew literally as "son of man."

108. Ortlund, "Image of Adam, Son of God."

imaging God that is ultimately expressed in Jesus Christ. What Tanner depreciates as "nothing more than being a creature of God," I want to hold up as *the* manifestation of God's desire of humanity imaging God in a strong sense. The vocation of imaging God should be seen as the originary man and woman living out their lives as a part of God's world in relation to God as God desires. This vocation to image God does not only imply their work, but also as people found in an inextricable and complex dynamic of relationships. While they had not yet completed the tasks God had given to them, they did *not* need to be conformed to God's desires because they already imaged God in the lives they lived with each other, in the world, and with God.

This is *part* of the historical context in which we come to learn about Jesus as the image of God. The beginning is not an unfortunate mixture of divine will and human reality to be transcended (Coakley), or the unjust beginning in need of reform (Cornwall), or the start that must be left to get to a better end (Tanner). I suggest we take the beginning as Butler does, as a literal, inaccessible, indispensable, and irrepressible foundation that conditions what it means to live in the world. God created man and woman in the image of God, and it is this image or vocation that continues to haunt humanity, even after it is expelled from Eden.

We are in a position to see that the image of God is a creaturely reality that is continuous between the beginning and the age of anxiety. It is not, however, a transcending law that we can populate with images (like man or woman) or capacities (like rationality or speech) against which humanity is measured or to which it must conform. The image of God describes people insofar as they have the ineradicable vocation of imaging God with their lives. The originary man and woman were the image of God not merely because they lived (functioned) in a way that was in harmony with God's expressed desires, but because they had the *capacity* to do so. In other words, the image of God is the God-given *structure* to *function* in the world according to God's desire, where *structure* pertains to what is needed to *function* in the world according to God's desires. This means that while one will always have the image of God in a structural sense (the ability to hear the call of God and the necessary capacity to respond to it by living in harmony with God's desires), one may reject the call to image God and instead use the God-imaging capacity to function in the world for one's own or another's desires.

A Body Not My Own: Gender as Becoming

Discerning the Vocation

The image of God is the principal and ineradicable human vocation, which concerns every aspect of being human, including what it means to be a man or woman. When a theology of gender is properly oriented to the doctrine of the image of God, the originary man and woman do not populate the image, but are subject to it. The implication is that wherever a person finds themselves, whether in the Edenic garden or outside, and however a person conceives themselves as gendered, one cannot evade the call to image God. This becomes complex in the age of anxiety where it is our good yet troubled bodies of death that are to image God. We have already seen that the image to which one is to be conformed is not Adam or Eve or the uncertain future glorified body, because we cannot enter Eden and nor are we privy to the glorified body. The vocation is therefore one of discernment that is lived out each day by faith, which means that man or woman are not particular things, but modes of faithful embodied living according to God's desires.

Discernment requires *freedom*, which has the potential to stray into *license*, but this is not a reason to curb the exercise of freedom for which Christ has set us free.[109] Indeed, as Bonhoeffer presses, there is no life without freedom.[110] Indeed, without freedom Jesus could not use Adam and Eve to uphold God's *vision* for marriage (Matt 19:4–6), present them as a bygone *righteous standard* to condemn the Pharisees in their sin (Matt 19:8), or count himself as an *exception* by becoming a eunuch for the kingdom of heaven (Matt 19:12). The call to discern interrupts the tendency to fixate on the beginning, the present, or the end to negotiate sinful sex lives, troubled bodies, or patterns of the world. Jesus was *not* oriented to Eden, the age of anxiety, or the eschaton, but to *all three* eras and in *different ways* as needed to make sense of the different questions of embodied life that were raised. When a certain departure has not been made from the beginning, imaging God with our embodied lives requires no discernment but pure compliance to the law of Adam and Eve, which, as we have already seen, is often administered unjustly and is unable to bring life. Where a wholesale departure has occurred, as the Pharisees demonstrate, there is no recourse to God's expressed

---

109. Gal 5:1.
110. This a persistent theme in Bonhoeffer, *Creation and Fall*.

originary vision for the man and woman. And where the eschatological body is populated with Adam and Eve or a queer body as opposed to an uncertain redeemed, liberated, and glorified body, discernment tends to be quickly overrun by self-justifying desire. Imaging God with our bodies is a vocation of *discernment* that does not turn its back on Eden, takes seriously the reality of troubled embodied life in the age of anxiety, while looking in hope to the final glorification of our bodies.

The result of Jesus' exercise of discernment in Matthew 19 is not therefore the stale reiteration of religio-cultural hegemony, but several surprising conclusions that were otherwise impossible to conceive in that milieu. Jesus uses his freedom to discern how to consider marriage, how to treat a woman's body in light of the prevailing cultural patterns, and how non-binary bodies in that time could be considered good socially and within the kingdom of heaven. Jesus did not crassly appeal to the beginning, this age, or the end to respond to the Pharisees, to teach his disciples, or describe himself, but rather, models sensitivity to the complex dynamics that structure each scenario. He demonstrates awareness of the resources at his disposal, and he draws upon these to discern what is good, embodied life in the present.

Contingent Agency

The freedom to discern good embodied life broaches the theme of agency, which for Butler is conflicted. While exploring Butler's subject, we have seen that a person is swamped by intersubjectivity, which undermines their capacity to freely discern what is good. They cannot avoid exercising the terms that give rise to what can be considered good. And where the same person is not able to perceive themselves apart from that which forms them, which is also inaccessible, they find themselves in a quagmire of opacity. This universal mode of intersubjectivity and self-unknowing drives Butler to proffer a law of desire whereby our lack of access to the beginning or end, and ourselves, results in a hopeless collapse of time and existence into an eternal age of anxiety. The point at which Auden calls for help having scoured the body only to find he could not enter Arcadia, Butler resigns, concluding there is no vantage point from which we can discern a course to find life in our bodies of death. She stops the search, rendering each person vulnerable in the face of the vulnerable other. Butler takes us back to the originary scene in Hegel's master/slave dialectic where two self-conscious people face-off. Instead of allowing the scene to develop wherein one submits to the other resulting in the master and slave dynamic, the stand-off is enshrined by the law of desire. Where there is no means of being saved from our bodies of death, calling a cease-fire in the pursuit of what *is* good is not only logical but ethically imperative. Butler, followed by those who install her subject into their theology of gender, does not merely reform gender, but reforms the human vocation of imaging God. It is no longer characterized by discerning God's desires, but obeying Butler's desire: desiring the other person's desire.

The Christian theology of gender being developed in this book, on the other hand, has doggedly refused to allow a collapse of the present into either the beginning or the end. In contrast to Butler, I have held the beginning and end in their respective places while maintaining the intersubjective nature of being human. Our physical bodies are not crass material objects that have meaning without the world in which they are found, which includes each other's and our own desires. This is why human agency as discernment is therefore never pure autonomy, but a mode of meaning-making as "subject-bodies."[111] A person, therefore, has the capacity to discern what is good, but the discerned good is always underscored by the Christian confession that we see only in part.[112] To see in part is another way of saying that we live good, embodied lives not by sight but faith.[113] I diverge significantly from Butler at this point. In order to mitigate violence and not foreclose future possibilities of gendered life, Butler renders the foundation contingent and agency essentially thwarted. In contrast, I observe and treat violence by conceiving the foundation as certain, yet departed and inaccessible, and the future as uncertain, yet temporally inaccessible, which renders human agency in the present contingent. The vocation of imaging God with our bodies requires discernment because we have resources at our disposal: we find ourselves outside of Eden and the eschaton, but in an age of anxiety with vision that recognizes ourselves and others, but only indistinctly.[114] This

---

111. Daniell, "Spiritual Body," 12.

112. 1 Cor 13:12.

113. 2 Cor 5:7; Heb 11:3.

114. Paul uses the word *ainigmati* in 1 Cor 13:12, which connotes that of a riddle or what is figurative, which renders the thing in view as indistinct. Fee, *First Epistle to the Corinthians*, 647n42.

does not equate to a catastrophic epistemic failure, but a chastened notion of agency.

For Butler opacity implies an epistemic catastrophe, which induces a law of desire, whereas seeing indistinctly for the Christian implies faith, hope, and love.[115] Faith and hope signify absence, drawing one's vision to the past and future, while love is a mode of living in community now that is grounded and therefore characterized by the signified absence. The Christian alternative to what Butler offers is again on show as the distant past and the future come into play for thinking about discerning how to image God with our subject-bodies. Faith and hope are the final nail in Adam and Eve's coffin because they reveal the true image of God to which humanity is to be conformed: Jesus Christ. Faith and hope do not reveal Adam and Eve or our mundane desires as that to which we must be conformed, but the image of God who is Jesus Christ, who by the power of the Spirit transforms our minds away from the mundane patterns, or desires of the world, to those of God.

Exercising our freedom to discern how we should live in God's world as subject-bodies is also contingent because we are not our own.[116] If nothing else, Butler's theory presses the Christian to reflect on how intertwined we are in terms of the means and content by which we conceive ourselves and others as gendered. She has sensitized the Christian to the reality that we are not gendered bodies with minds or bodies with gendered minds, but subject-bodies that have the God-created facility to unite with another for death and life. Like the metaphor of the rider's mind entering the dressage horse by which the horse's actions conform to the rider's desire, we glimpse, however inadequately, what happens when the Spirit of God enters the subject-body. The body is possessed by God and becomes an instrument for the honor of God, which is another way of saying that the person honors God with their body by submitting to the desires of God for their body. Again, Butler is not far off the mark when we learn that the apostle Paul describes the body as a dispossession: "you are not your own."[117] God's Spirit enters the person and in doing so takes possession of them. Discerning how to fulfill the vocation of honoring God with our bodies is not an act of sovereign agency because it is done under the influence of the Spirit.

---

115. 1 Cor 13:13.
116. 1 Cor 6:19.
117. 1 Cor 6:19.

In fact, one's body is recast as a temple in which God not only dwells, but is honored through participating in and being a part of God's very good world. As Richard Lints describes, "creation is 'built' for worship" and here in the age of anxiety we see the "rebuilding" of the desecrated originary creation/temple/body by faith in Christ through the power of the Spirit for the worship and honor of God.[118] The import of creation as a doxological entity picks up on humanity's liturgical instinct that, when it comes to the body, can be directed to God, the images of Adam and Eve, or our own desires that we install as images in the beginning or on the eschatological horizon. This stunning array of possible objects that humanity glorifies indicates our originary enslavement, or ineradicable vocation, to lift things up for praise and thus our "doxological fragility."[119] The state of this fragility is revealed when one psalmist states that creation declares God's praises, but in the next stanza confesses his willful straying from God's desires and the tragedy that sin rules him.[120] Sin does not merely inhibit one from fulfilling the God-given vocation to honor God, but authorizes other unworthy replacements. Sin is parasitic, taking up residence in the body, dwelling in each part, demanding the body's allegiance to follow its own desires.[121] Sin is a law unto itself, dominating the natural body such that humanity demonstrates what Paul confesses, "with my flesh I am a slave to the law of sin."[122]

Butler's resignation to the body of death and law of desire is shown to be, in theological terms, a capitulation to the law of sin. The remarkable claim is that the law of sin dominates those who live in their flesh or natural orientation (*sarx*), which is a warning for those who appeal to the claim that "whatever is natural is good."[123] We have already seen that justifying one's desire of the other *or* same sex on the grounds that it is natural is fallacious. There is *no* mode of human embodiment that is "naturally" good because *all* sex, sexuality, and gender is under the influence of this age of anxiety from which we need to be rescued. Moreover, and in line with the thrust of this book, the Christian does not escape being owned by the flesh despite being spiritual. Paul describes the Christians

---

118. Lints, *Identity and Idolatry*, 53.
119. Lints, *Identity and Idolatry*, 42.
120. Ps 19.
121. Rom 7:17, 23.
122. Rom 7:25.
123. Fee, *Epistle to Romans*, 453–54.

in Corinth as "spiritual" (*pneumatikois*) yet "fleshly" (*sarkinois*),[124] which also resonates with the assumption behind Paul's exhortation to the Roman Christians not to conform to patterns of the world.[125] The body is a glorifying agent because it is a subject-body, which is why it can glorify God once again by the power of the indwelling Spirit.

In line with Butler's pessimistic resignation to the law of sin, being rescued by Christ from one's body of death is *not* into a life of sovereign agency where the mind exceeds the world it seeks to know. The turn to the mind is significant because this is the contested site where the vocation to image God is waged daily by the power of the Spirit, which Paul points out when he says that "the mind controlled by the Spirit is *life and peace*."[126] Hence Paul's conclusion, having reflected on the work of Jesus Christ, in Romans 7:25: "So then, with my mind I am a slave to the law of God, but with my flesh I am a slave to the law of sin." The work of the Spirit is to set one's mind free from its preoccupation with its own desires, which is to be set free "from the law of sin and death."[127] So, Butler rightly notes that the body is a contested site wherein the body is not a crass material object, but a subject-body that, once again in theological terms, is ripe for possession by sin or the Spirit. However, where her theory seeks to normativize mundane desire that not only permits, but encourages people to "have their minds set on what nature desires" by installing a feedback loop from the mundane to the originary scene, Paul exhorts those who find their lives in Christ to "have their minds set on what the Spirit desires."[128]

The vocation to image God with our subject-bodies, therefore, requires the discerning treatment of three intersecting operative laws: the law of Adam and Eve, the law of desire, and the law of God.[129] We have exposed the function of the law of Adam and Eve as revealing our bodies of death and need for life, and we have explored the law of desire in Butler's thought as resignation to fleshly desire (the law of sin), which condemns us to bodies of death, while confessing the uncertainty of the body in the eschaton. Now we come to the law of God, which the Spirit

---

124. 1 Cor 3:1.
125. Rom 12:2.
126. Rom 8:6 (emphasis mine).
127. Rom 8:2.
128. Rom 8:5.
129. Rom 7:22, 25; 8:7.

desires and which Paul commends to his readers.[130] But what is the law of God that the Spirit desires, and on which those in Christ should set their minds?

In Romans 7, Paul reveals the content of the law of God by contrasting it with the law of sin. A further point of clarification is made when Paul identifies these laws as mutually exclusive: one is *either* a slave to the law of sin *or* a slave to the law of God.[131] But Paul contrasts sin and God, which does not elucidate the content of the law, but positions the law of God in opposition to the law of sin. In chapter 6, Paul makes another contrast, but this time he makes a distinction between sin and righteousness, and death and righteousness. It is worth citing the passage at length because toward the end Paul alludes to the ethical implications of desiring the Spirit's desire of God's law:

> For sin will have no dominion over you, since you are not under law but under grace. What then? Should we sin because we are not under law but under grace? By no means! Do you not know that if you present yourselves to anyone as obedient slaves, you are slaves of the one whom you obey, either of sin, which leads to death, or of obedience, which leads to righteousness? But thanks be to God that you, having once been slaves of sin, have become obedient from the heart to the form of teaching to which you were entrusted, and that you, having been set free from sin, have become slaves of righteousness. I am speaking in human terms because of your natural limitations. For just as you once presented your members as slaves to impurity and to greater and greater iniquity, so now present your members as slaves to righteousness for sanctification.[132]

The talking point that should be at the center of discussions about gender is not what *is* a male or female, but *whether what enslaves our subject-bodies leads to death or righteousness*. The famous claim of Jesus that one cannot serve two masters at the same time is relevant here: one is either a slave to sin and death or a slave to obedience and righteousness.[133] Butler's call to obey the law of mundane desire signals her slavery to death, whereas Paul's call to obey the law of God leads to righteousness. Notice, however, that obedience in Paul's mind is not a willed action

---

130. Rom 8:5.
131. Rom 7:25.
132. Rom 6:14–19.
133. Matt 6:24.

toward the other person, as in the case of Butler's call for obeying desire, but a disposition of the heart toward God's desire for righteousness. The great flaw in Butler's theory is that even her law of desire is unable to achieve what she desires because the law of sin inevitably leads to action that serves one's own desires and not another's. Indeed, her proposed law of desire is an instantiation of her desire for her own desire to be desired by society. Without a radical change of the heart, her ethics amounts to another futile human attempt to displace human desire as the controlling desire. The angst that Paul narrates is that we do what we don't want to do, and we don't do what we know we should do.[134] No amount of willing will tear the self away from pursuing one's own desires because we are enslaved, not to another's desires, but our own. The reason someone can obey righteousness is because it flows from a heart that *is* able to choose. This is why discernment is needed: within a state of grace, we are set free from our slavery to the law of sin and death and released into a new form of slavery of freedom to pursue righteousness.

Embracing one's freedom in Christ to discern how to image God with our subject-bodies reveals the contingent nature of human agency, which means that the vocation is not a self-help exercise, nor does it amount to availing oneself of the need to participate actively in the vocation of imaging God. The concluding thoughts in the above passage reveal that one's role, which is to "present one's members," has a measure of personal "responsibility" to carry out this role. Moreover, even one in slavery to sin is responsible for rehearsing the sacrifice of their bodies on the altar of impurity. The Spirit *or* sin is at work in us, but each of us participate in our respective desires by performing what we desire: lives of death or righteousness. Elsewhere, Paul captures this coworking arrangement when he describes one's own salvation as being continually worked out by God, wherein God is the agent moving the person's will and action to fulfill God's desires.[135] To *will* and to *act* are both works of God, which when applied to the vocation to image God with our subject-bodies reveals that glorifying God—the desire and the act—are a divine work. The synergistic nature of this act is realized when Paul gives the imperative "to work."[136] While many are hesitant to use the word synergism to describe Christian agency, living in our bodies as God desires is

---

134. Rom 7:15.
135. Phil 2:12–13. See also 1 Thess 5:23.
136. See also Rom 12:1; 2 Cor 7:1; 1 Thess 4:3; Heb 12:14; 2 Pet 1:5.

a work of God and ourselves, which only ramps up the complex nature of embodiment and a theology of gender. The vocation to image God with our subject-bodies is not therefore characterized by sovereign agency and therefore self-construction, nor is it utter subjection to God thereby rendering gender as something given and not susceptible to reform. Without God at work in us, patterns of the world would flourish untouched, and without our own work, any form of one-sided formation would look like yet another moment of gender violence.

Faithful and Vulnerable Bodies

Aligning my will with God's to glorify God with my body, takes theological shape in Ephesians 5:31–32. Here, once again, Paul exhorts the reader to offer their body to another based on one's willing participation in a covenant relationship, which he explicitly grounds theologically in the originary marriage covenant that we read about in Genesis 2:24. The parents' eyes are no longer the gaze that defines how one understands their self, but by uniting with another, one comes to understand one's self as a new creation in the eyes of that other. The Edenic person is not freed from their parents to realize their own life, but is released to offer their bodies and selves to be desired by a new constitutive gaze, which in this age of anxiety is distorted, thereby causing anxiety and fear despite our deep love for the one with whom we are united.

The re-creating (as distinct from pro-creating) capacity of the marriage covenant is also in view when Paul exhorts the Roman and Corinthian Christians to surrender control of their bodies. The first call is to offer the body to the other by virtue of being united to Christ in his death and resurrection (Rom 6:5). The second is in view of God's mercy (Rom 12:1), but later oriented to being one body in Christ (Rom 12:5), and the third, again by virtue of being united to the Lord (1 Cor 6:17). The reason one gives one's body over to the desires of Christ is because one is united to Christ in covenant relationship. In union with Christ, I do not lose but willingly forgo "ownership" of my body, which is why I can resist the other's desire for my body. The implication is that the marriage covenant is not a conditional (if/then) contract—I will offer my body to Christ only if he satisfies my desires—but a covenantal willing relinquishing of my body to the other: both *take* the willing other.[137] This idea of covenant

---

137. 1 Cor 7:4.

marriage in which I willingly give over my body to the other's desires renders me utterly vulnerable to the other's desire.[138]

Butler's conclusion that vulnerability in union with the other is the ineradicable human lot is perceptive. However, there is a radical divergence from Butler where vulnerable union with another is understood by the Christian first through the lens of participation in the church's union with Christ. This union is the mystery that Paul claims marriage between a man and woman both manifests and explicates.[139] It is within this relationship (between church and Christ) that I confess that my body is not my own, thereby relinquishing control of my body to the desires of Christ. In a time when society is trying to claw back the right to do as we please with our bodies, Scripture continues to exhort me to hand over my body to be subject to another's desires, namely Christ's. It does *seem* utterly foolish, which Paul does not deny, but if we take seriously our discussion with Butler, and our previous inquiry into our slavery to sin or God, we cannot avoid the human reality that our bodies are always subject to another's desire. I cannot escape vulnerability in union, which means that risk always accompanies the vocation of gendered and sexual life. The question is not whether I will give over my body to the desires of another, but whether I will willingly entrust my body to Christ's desires, or resist him?

In his essay "The Body's Grace," Rowan Williams explores the notion that union with another is characterized by a loss of control. In one provocative moment, Williams suggests, "Sexual 'perversion' is sexual activity without risk," which flips the usual Christian narrative that risky sex is to be avoided.[140] Risk-free sex puts me at a safe distance from the peril associated with uniting with another. Safe sex is cast also by society as responsible sex, which finds its ultimate manifestation in the popular quip "no-strings-attached sex." The strings represent the risky reality of being known that comes with uniting with another, which pornography, likewise, enables one to avoid. Accordingly, pornography is the safest sex because there is no possibility of uniting literally with the other who is

---

138. This is the reason why *all* relationships, and not only those that are supposedly Christian, are susceptible to domestic violence. I emphatically reject the idea that this justifies counselling people to stay in abusive relationships. In fact, it should sensitize the church to the very real possibility that some are taking advantage of this vulnerability to satisfy their own sinful desires.

139. Eph 5:31–32.

140. Williams, "Body's Grace," 47.

in view or even being seen by them. In all forms of risk-free sex, the possibility of pain and hurt that another person can inflict is minimized or even negated. Unfortunately, within a risk-free sex-life the possibility of the life-giving grace of the body is also obliterated. In commercial fashion, whatever grace the other body might offer me, giving myself to another in covenant to be subject to their desires and perception is often a risk simply not worth taking.

In response to this fearful approach to uniting with another, we should be careful not to proffer marriage between a man and a woman as the God-given locus in which one can enjoy the safest sex and avoid risk. Williams guides his readers to understand that a faithful union "is not an avoidance of risk, but the creation of a context in which grace can abound."[141] That is, marriage is the place where the risky business of learning to become God's creatures as gendered and sexual beings can be explored. In union with another, one is vulnerable before the other's gaze, which is the willing and humble positioning of the self to be remade according to the other's desire. Humbly positioning myself in the other's gaze enters into the vocation of Jesus' glorification which is captured by his utterance, "Not what I want but what you want."[142] I will die to myself to be remade by my wife. I find myself in the eyes of the one whom I love and in whom I am united, which happens only when I am released from my own will that desires to create myself in the "safety" of my isolation. Williams goes on to say:

> I cannot make sense of myself without others, cannot speak until I've listened, cannot love myself without being the object of love or enjoy myself without being the cause of joy.... We are led into the knowledge that our identity is being made in the relations of bodies, not by the private exercise of will or fantasy: we belong with and to each other, not to our "private" selves (as Paul said of mutual sexual commitment), and yet are not instruments for each other's gratification.[143]

Notice that in the thinking of Williams, my will and fantasy is displaced in the formation of self-understanding. I cannot learn who I am without the world in which God created *us*, which draws us back to God's utterance that "very good" does not describe any individual's particular

---

141. Williams, "Body's Grace," 50.
142. Matt 26:39.
143. Williams, "Body's Grace," 51–52.

existence and accompanying desires, but one's participation in God's world, as a part of God's created world as God desires. I come to learn about myself as God's creature when I am utterly disposed to the complex relations of bodies.

What grace does the body offer if we don't have an operative notion of grace? Williams asks this question,[144] but I want to be more explicit than Williams by saying that one cannot learn about who one is as God's creature in relation to/with other bodies without experiencing the grace of Christ's body via the marriage *par excellence*. It was Auden who, toward the end of *The Age of Anxiety*, motioned in the direction of marriage as the way out of his body of death. He saw that suffering the risk of union with another was the means of God's grace and that through which life was grasped. We must remember, however, that for Auden, in line with Williams, earthly marriage did not have the power to save him (or society, I might add). He was aware that marriage with a woman was not God's power for salvation because no one was more aware than Auden that a woman's body lacked the grace he desired *and* needed to overcome his body of death. Auden appropriately qualifies marriage as a means of grace, as a "noble symbol," which surely alludes to Ephesians 5:30–32, in which Paul explains how God's creation of marriage in the beginning and lived out through this age between a man and a woman bears witness to, and is a shadow of, the mystery and ultimate human reality of the union between Christ and the church. In a moment of irony—which, in keeping with the argument of this book, should not be redeployed to re-invest the creation account with new terms—it was only as one in risky union with Christ that Auden found the grounds to refuse to desire his mundane same-sex desire. He longed "in times of war"—the age of anxiety—for "peace and forgiveness" through the noble symbol of marriage, which finds its reality in union with, and grace of, Christ's body.[145]

Learning to be God's creature in union with Christ is God's desire, but it is not risk free for the reason that in this union, like any earthly marriage, I hand over my body *and* my desires to another. By offering my body to Christ, I deny myself the illusion that I know myself fully and reject the myth of self-mastery. Instead, I move into a union of wonder to learn to be who I am in relation to Christ. In light of my union with Christ I confess that "it is no longer I who live, but it is Christ who lives

---

144. Williams, "Body's Grace," 52.
145. Auden, *Age of Anxiety*, 88.

in me."[146] In other words, "I live," but this "I" is not mine, as Butler has sensitized us to see, but Christ's with whom I am united *and* whom I image by conforming to his desires. The previous theme of the image of God here finds flesh: I do not therefore live by imitating Christ's life, but through living in Jesus Christ and his Spirit living in me. I do not seek to master my desire, but be mastered by God's desire. This is not a question about ontological transformation, but spiritual transformation, which is a glorified corporeality.[147] This is why the risen Jesus not only exemplifies this possibility, but as one united to him by the Spirit, Jesus is also my life through my participation in his death and resurrection.[148] As Grant Macaskill states: "the Spirit who inhabits us is not an energizing infusion of power; he is very specifically Christ's Spirit, who makes his goodness a reality in our limbs."[149] This view stands in contrast to Tanner's view that Jesus Christ and the Spirit take advantage of our "inputs" to provide me with the injection of divine power I need to move my lacking creatureliness divine-ward. My goal is not to be a better person who is more virtuous and moral but to be the person Jesus Christ desires of me. The climax of this book, therefore, is not to incite better versions of ourselves by accruing symbolic (social or religious) capital that justifies my salvation through approximating the images of Adam and Eve in the eyes of those regulators of pure religion.[150] The purpose, rather, is to shed light on the transformative impact on our subject-bodies of death by being united to Christ and participating in his death and resurrection life by the Spirit.

For some, however, the level of risk of uniting with Christ is unacceptable: how can I be sure that Christ will desire my desire for life, or that Christ will desire what is ultimately good for me? Will Christ withhold goods from me that I desire for my satisfaction as a gendered and sexual being? Will I come to see myself in Christ's gaze as I desire to see myself? And if I am re-created according to Christ's gaze in such a way

---

146. Gal 2:20.

147. 1 Cor 15:42–44. Glorified embodiment is also central to Rom 8:18–30, with particular emphasis on vv. 23 and 29–30.

148. Eph 3:20–21. I agree with Macaskill that such a notion of uniting with Jesus Christ does not threaten the creator/creature divide, Macaskill, *Living in Union with Christ*, 66n4.

149. Macaskill, *Living in Union with Christ*, 56.

150. Phil 3:8–9. For a theological exploration of "social capital" and "incorporated identity," see Macaskill, *Living in Union with Christ*, 43–51.

that it conflicts with my mundane desire, will it result in a life of death in life?[151]

This raft of cascading questions gives voice to our doubts about the goodness of union with Christ, and the basic truth that I cannot help at times (even most times) desiring my own desires. This unrelenting desire for God to desire my desires locates me precariously in a world outside of my control. Returning to the risky sexuality account of Williams, his comment toward the vocation of singleness is apt for the general Christian human vocation of offering our bodies in union to Christ: "finding a bodily/sexual identity through trying to expose yourself first and foremost to the desirous perception of God is difficult and precarious in a way not many of us realize."[152] This book is an attempt to explicate this difficulty and precarity. Offering myself to God's desires is to place deep trust in Christ, that he will love me and desire me as a husband ought. This marriage between Christ and the church is like every marriage: it is a covenant based on faith, that is, the faithfulness of the other, in this case, Jesus Christ.

Desiring to understand my body according to Jesus Christ's body is a posture of faith-filled wonder into which I am saved and empowered to maintain by the power of the Spirit. This means that to be a man or woman is not a crass fact that one is or is not, because we do not assume that our embodied experiences reflect Christ's desires. Being a man or a woman is a life-long pursuit of coming to *see* oneself through the eyes of Christ as participating in God's work of creation *and* re-creation. We come to understand what matters now by hearing afresh God's Word speak into the darkness in the first instance when God created man and woman, *and* finally and decisively when the Word of God—Jesus Christ—speaks into our darkness revealing God's desire to restore us through participation in his body. Therefore, to be a man or a woman is always a faith-, hope-, and love-filled mode of being in willing covenant relation to Jesus Christ, of seeing myself as Jesus Christ sees me, of learning to desire Jesus Christ's desire for me, in order to become the holy and spotless subject-body that Christ desires of me as a part of his creation and bride.

What theological resources provide an alternative to Butler's resigned humanistic treatment of our bodies of death? With Butler, I concur that our hope lies not in our own bodies, but only in the body of the

---

151. Lints, *Identity and Idolatry*, 81.
152. Williams, "Body's Grace," 53.

other and their desires. But where Butler socializes the God of Scripture via Spinoza to co-opt divine power to re-create the beginning to justify troubled bodies now, I suggest that a reforming Christian account of gender hold the view that since God created man and woman in the beginning, God alone has the power to re-create humanity by providing us with another body in and through which I come to understand myself justified as God's creature. This body that brings life to bodies of death is not a retrospective re-creation of the originary body to justify my body of death, but the resurrected body of Jesus Christ that vindicates the goodness of troubled bodies. To understand how Christ's body transforms our body we must explore the theological concept of marriage, which cannot be done without first reflecting on how God made man and woman in the image of God in the beginning. I contend that the image of God is *not* man and woman, but the vocation of glorifying God with our bodies in union with the image and glory of God, namely, Jesus Christ. In this light, gender is a human vocation of becoming what I am not yet.

Conclusion

The decision to engage Butler's gender theory has not resulted in a theology of gender that is stripped of its creaturely and functionally differentiated goodness. Nor is gender reformed in such a way that the body is immaterialized, which we must conclude is indicative of Butler's thought. The risky conversation with Butler has, however, been redemptive in that we have been provoked to locate where idolatry and self-justification has crept into our use of Adam and Eve for thinking about gender. In so doing, we have also been able to differentiate where Butler's thought diverges from a confessional Christian account of gender.

In this final chapter we have seen that when we integrate time and Scripture into our thinking about gender, the conversation is drastically reoriented from the seductive bodies of Adam and Eve to the disgraceful eunuchized body of Jesus. Ironically, this mode of embodiment is revealed to the reader only after Jesus chastises powerful men who saw fit to use the holy law to justify their own and others' sinful embodiment. By locating himself outside of Eden, the Jewish customs, and the cultural appetites of the time, Jesus confirms our departure from Eden and the futility of returning to Eden to find embodied life. The question of where to find a life from our bodies of death is not answered by uniting with another person of the other sex, as the moralizing principle of Adam and Eve suggest, nor the same sex, as is often argued by people who have turned their back on the beginning, but *by uniting with Jesus Christ by faith*. Such a risky union is not a means to get back into Eden, nor to have our mundane desires recognized as good, but to a groaning body of life in the Spirit.

The theology of gender developed in this book has been provoked by Butler to mimic in many ways the apostle Paul's struggle in his letter to the Galatians with those who sought to smuggle aspects of the law into the gospel. Having decried those who would offer the gospel *and* law hand-in-hand for life,[153] Paul's letter narrates an unrelenting pursuit of embodied life from beginning to the end apart from the law.[154] Most striking for our purposes is his piercing question: "Are you so foolish? Having started with the Spirit, are you now ending with the flesh?" A theology of gender does not do away with the law of Adam and Eve temporarily in order to attain life through faith in Jesus Christ only to reintroduce the law of Adam and Eve in order to reach the righteous embodied lives for which we are ultimately called. Conservative evangelical theology, praxis, and cultural engagement reek of human death where the family, heterosexual marriage, and procreation are an unwitting façade behind which stands the originary law of man and woman that reveals humanity's need for life from bodies of death. Even when he must "flesh out" the gospel to describe the Christian life, Paul refuses to reinstate a law to direct one's life, opting instead to describe the *fruit* of the Spirit and that the works of the flesh are *obvious*.[155] Paul is confident that one simply "knows" the sinful desires that if acted upon contradict one's vocation to glorify God with the body with fruit of the Spirit that blossoms "naturally." We find ourselves in a death trap when we have been convinced that we need the law of Adam and Eve at any stage of the redemptive journey for life. One does not begin or end with the law of Adam and Eve for life.

The theology of gender developed in this book reveals that the legal moralizer who appeals to the law of Adam and Eve for life demonstrates a lack of faith in God's plan to bring life to bodies of death. Despite their claim of faith, they demonstrate their alienation from Christ, and forsake

---

153. Gal 1:7; 3:2.
154. Gal 3:3.
155. Gal 5:19, 22.

the grace of God.[156] The dilemma facing the moralizing ensnared mind is that they cannot comprehend how a person or society's transgression of Adam and Eve will be curbed *without* imposing the law. But Paul is clear also on this point: is one even righteous if one performs the law? Paul's response is that doing or not doing the law has no value. What counts is faith that is being worked out in love.[157] A theology of gender is not caught up in developing a model of gender that limits, hinders, or reforms embodied transgression but rather draws human embodiment into the realm of the gospel, which is God's powerful means to save bodies of death by glorifying them.

This realm, as we have seen, is where the originary vocation to glorify God with our bodies is captivating. By returning to Jesus' embodied vocation that transgresses Edenic orders, we see that Jesus's life was not determined by the physical ability (or lack thereof) of his body, nor the direction of his mundane desires, nor the cultural climate that sought to devour him. Despite his physical ability (or lack thereof), desire for his own desires for life, and pain he would endure, Jesus is "so taken over by the urgent presence of the kingdom that he could do no other than give himself entirely to it."[158] This vocation of glorifying God as subjective-bodies is never easy, as Adam and Eve and Jesus experienced on different occasions and in different gardens, but one that leads to embodied life now and in the end.

---

156. Gal 5:4.
157. Gal 5:6–7.
158. Moloney, "*Hard Saying*," 51.

Bibliography

Alliaume, Karen Trimble. "Disturbingly Catholic: Thinking the Inordinate Body." In *Bodily Citations: Religion and Judith Butler (Gender, Theory, and Religion)*, edited by Ellen T. Armour and Susan M. St. Ville, 95–119. New York: Columbia University Press, 2006.

Althaus-Reid, Marcella. *Indecent Theology: Theological Perversions in Sex, Gender and Politics*. London: Routledge, 2000.

Armour, Ellen T., and Susan M. St. Ville, eds. *Bodily Citations: Religion and Judith Butler (Gender, Theory, and Religion)*. New York: Columbia University Press, 2006.

Auden, W. H. *The Age of Anxiety: A Baroque Epilogue*. Princeton: Princeton University Press, 2011.

Augustine. *The City of God against the Pagans*. Edited by R. W. Dyson. Cambridge: Cambridge University Press, 2016.

———. *The Confessions*. The Works of Saint Augustine: A Translation for the 21st Century. Edited by John E. Rotelle. Translated by Maria Boulding. New York: New City, 1997.

———. *Expositions of the Psalms 1–32; Vol. 1*. Translated by Maria Boulding, edited by John E. Rotelle. New York: New City, 2000.

———. *Sermons on the Psalms 99–120*. Translated by Maria Boulding. The Works of Saint Augustine: A Translation for the 21st Century. New York: New City, 2003.

Barth, Karl. *Church Dogmatics*, III/1. Edited by G. W. Bromiley and T. F. Torrance. Translated by J. W. Edwards et al. Edinburgh: T. & T. Clark, 1958.

Barzun, Jacques. "Workers in Monument Brass." *Harper's* magazine, September 1947.

Behr, John. *The Mystery of Christ: Life in Death*. New York: St. Vladimir's Seminary Press, 2006.

Benhabib, Seyla. "Feminism and Postmodernism: An Uneasy Alliance." In *Feminist Contentions: A Philosophical Exchange*, edited by Seyla Benhabib et al., 17–34. London: Routledge, 1995.

Bird, Michael F. *Evangelical Theology: A Biblical and Systematic Theology*. 2nd ed. Grand Rapids: Zondervan, 2020.

Black, David A., and Jacob N. Cerone, eds. *The Pericope of the Adulteress in Contemporary Research*. Library of New Testament Studies. London: Bloomsbury, 2016.

Blinzler, Josef. "Zur Auslegung von Mt 19:12." *Zeitschrift für die Neutestamentliche Wissenschaft* 48 (1957) 254–70.

Blocher, Henri. *In the Beginning*. Leicester, UK: InterVarsity, 1984.

Blomberg, Craig L. *Matthew: An Exegetical and Theological Exposition of Holy Scripture*. New American Commentary 22. Nashville: Broadman & Holman, 1992.

Bodley-Dangelo, Faye. *Sexual Difference, Gender, and Agency in Karl Bath's Church Dogmatics*. London: T. & T. Clark, 2019.

Boer, Roland. *In the Vale of Tears: On Marxism and Theology V*. Chicago: Haymarket, 2014.

Bonhoeffer, Dietrich. *Creation and Fall: A Theological Exposition of Genesis 1–3*. Edited by John W. de Gruchy. Translated by Douglas Stephen Bax. Dietrich Bonhoeffer's Works 3. Minneapolis: Fortress, 1997.

———. *Sanctorum Communio: A Theological Study of the Sociology of the Church*. Edited by Clifford J. Green. Translated by Reinhard Krauss and Nancy Lukens. Dietrich Bonhoeffer's Works 1. Minneapolis: Fortress, 1998.

Boucher, Geoff. *The Charmed Circle of Ideology: A Critique of Laclau and Mouffe, Butler and Žižek*. Melbourne: Re-press, 2008.

———. "Judith Butler's Postmodern Existentialism: A Critical Analysis." *Philosophy Today* 48 (2004) 355–69.

Bounds, Christopher T. "Augustine's Interpretation of Romans 7:14–25, His Ordo Salutis and His Consistent Belief in a Christian's Victory over Sin." *Asbury Journal* 64 (2009) 20–35.

Brady, Anita, and Tony Schirato. *Understanding Judith Butler*. Thousand Oaks, CA: Sage, 2011.

Bray, Gerald "The Significance of God's Image in Man." *Tyndale Bulletin* 42 (1991) 195–225.

Breen, Margaret S., and Warren J. Blumenfeld, eds. *Butler Matters: Judith Butler's Impact on Feminist and Queer Studies*. Abingdon, UK: Routledge, 2005.

Brintnall, Kent L., et al., eds. "Queer Disorientations: Four Turns and a Twist." Introduction to *Sexual Disorientations: Queer Temporalities, Affects, Theologies*, edited by Kent L. Brintnall et al., 1–44. Transdisciplinary Theological Colloquia. New York: Fordham University Press, 2018.

Brock, Brian. "Jesus Christ the Divine Animal: The Human Distinctive Reconsidered." In *Christ and the Created Order: Perspectives from Theology, Philosophy, and Science*, edited by Andrew B. Torrance and Thomas H. McCall, 2:55–75. Grand Rapids: Zondervan, 2018.

———. "On Generating Categories in Theological Ethics: Barth, Genesis, and the Ständelehre." *Tyndale Bulletin* 61 (2010) 45–67.

———. *Singing the Ethos of God: On the Place of Christian Ethics in Scripture*. Grand Rapids: Eerdmans, 2007.

Brown, Callum. *The Death of Christian Britain: Understanding Secularization 1800–2000*. London: Routledge, 2001.

Brownson, James V. *Bible, Gender, Sexuality: Reframing the Church's Debate on Same-Sex Relationships*. Grand Rapids: Eerdmans, 2013.

Bulgakov, Mikhail. *Master and Margarita*. Translated by Diana Burgin and Katherine T. O'Connor. London: Picador, 2019.

Burrus, Virginia. "Queer Father: Gregory of Nyssa and the Subversion of Identity." In *Queer Theology: Rethinking the Western Body*, edited by Gerard Loughlin, 147–62. Oxford: Blackwell, 2007.

Butler, Judith. *Antigone's Claim: Kinship between Life and Death*. New York: Columbia University Press, 2000.

———. *Bodies That Matter: On the Discursive Limits of "Sex."* Abingdon, UK: Routledge, 2011.

———. "Contingent Foundations: Feminism and the Question of 'Postmodernism.'" In *Feminists Theorize the Political*, edited by Judith Butler and Joan W. Scott, 3–21. London: Routledge, 1992.
———. *Excitable Speech: A Politics of the Performative*. London: Routledge, 1997.
———. "Foucault and the Paradox of Bodily Inscriptions." *Journal of Philosophy* 86 (1989) 601–7.
———. *Frames of War: When Is Life Grievable?* Radical Thinkers. Reprint, London: Verso, 2016.
———. *Gender Trouble: Feminism and the Subversion of Identity*. 2nd ed. Reprint of anniversary edition. London: Routledge, 2007.
———. *Giving an Account of Oneself*. New York: Fordham University Press, 2005.
———. *Notes toward a Performative Theory of Assembly*. Cambridge: Harvard University Press, 2015.
———. *Precarious Life: The Powers of Mourning and Violence*. London: Verso, 2006.
———. *The Psychic Life of Power: Theories in Subjection*. Redwood City, CA: Stanford University Press, 1997.
———. "Response." *Political Theology* 16 (2015) 392–99.
———. *Senses of the Subject*. New York: Fordham University Press, 2015.
———. "Sexual Inversions." In *Discourses of Sexuality: From Aristotle to AIDS*, edited by Domna C. Stanton and Ann Arbor, 344–61. Ann Arbor: University of Michigan Press, 1992.
———. *Subjects of Desire: Hegelian Reflections in Twentieth-Century France*. 2nd ed. Reprint, New York: Columbia University Press, 2012.
———. *Undoing Gender*. London: Routledge, 2004.
———. "What Is Critique? An Essay on Foucault's Virtue." In *The Political: Readings in Continental Philosophy*, edited by D. Ingram, 212–26. London: Blackwell, 2002.
Cahill, Lisa Sowle. *Sex, Gender, and Christian Ethics*. New Studies in Christian Ethics. Cambridge: Cambridge University Press, 1996.
Campbell, Douglas A. "The Logic of Eschatology: The Implications of Paul's Gospel for Gender as Suggested by Galatians 3:28a in Context." In *Gospel and Gender: A Trinitarian Engagement with Being Male and Female in Christ*, edited by Douglas A. Campbell, 58–81. Studies in Theology and Sexuality. London: T. & T. Clark, 2003.
Campbell, Jan, and Janey Harbord. "Playing It Again: Citation, Reiteration or Circularity?" In *Performativity and Belonging*, edited by Vikki Bell, 229–40. London: Sage, 1999.
Casarino, Cesare, and Antonio Negri, eds. *In Praise of the Common: A Conversation on Philosophy and Politics*. Minneapolis: University of Minnesota Press, 2008.
Chambers, Samuel A. "Normative Violence after 9/11: Rereading the Politics of Gender Trouble." *New Political Science* 29 (2007) 43–60.
———. "Subjectification, the Social and a (Missing) Account of the Social Formation: Judith Butler's 'Turn.'" In *Butler and Ethics*, edited by Moya Lloyd, 193–218. Critical Connections. Edinburgh: Edinburgh University Press, 2017.
———. *Untimely Politics*. Edinburgh: Edinburgh University Press, 2003.
Clines, D. J. "The Image of God in Man." *Tyndale Bulletin* 19 (1968) 53–103.
Coakley, Sarah. *God, Sexuality, and the Self: An Essay "On the Trinity."* Cambridge: Cambridge University Press, 2013.

———. *Power and Submissions: Spirituality, Philosophy and* Gender. Oxford: Blackwell, 2002.

———. "Visions of the Self in Late Medieval Christianity: Some Cross-Disciplinary Reflections." In *Philosophy, Religion and the Spiritual Life* 32 (1992) 89–103.

Cornwall, Susannah. *Controversies in Queer Theology*. Controversies in Contextual Theology. Norwich, UK: SCM, 2011.

———. *Sex and Uncertainty in the Body of Christ: Intersex Conditions and Christian Theology*. London: Equinox, 2010.

Curley, Edwin. Introduction to *A Spinoza Reader: The Ethics and Other Works*, edited by Edwin Curley, ix–xxxiv. Princeton: Princeton University Press, 1994.

Daniell, Anne. "The Spiritual Body: Incarnations of Pauline and Butlerian Embodiment Themes for Constructive Theologizing toward the Parousia." *Journal of Feminist Studies in Religion* 16 (2000) 5–22.

DeFranza, Megan K. "Journeying from the Bible to Christian Ethics in Search of Common Ground." In *Two Views on Homosexuality, the Bible, and the Church*, edited by Stanley N. Gundry, 69–101. Grand Rapids: Zondervan, 2016.

———. *Sex Difference in Christian Theology: Male, Female, and Intersex in the Image of God*. Grand Rapids: Eerdmans, 2015.

———. "Virtuous Eunuchs: Troubling Conservative and Queer Readings of Intersex and the Bible." In *Intersex, Theology, and the Bible: Troubling Bodies in Church, Text, and Society*, edited by Susannah Cornwall, 55–76. New York: Palgrave Macmillan, 2015.

Derrida, Jacques. *The Death Penalty*. Vol. 2. Translated by Elizabeth Rottenberg. Chicago: University of Chicago Press, 2017.

———. *Of Grammatology*. Translated by Gayatri Chakravorty Spivak. Baltimore: John Hopkins University Press, 1976.

———. *Positions*. Translated by Alan Bass. Chicago: University of Chicago Press, 1972.

Dolezal, Luna. "Shame, Vulnerability and Belonging: Reconsidering Sartre's Account of Shame." *Human Studies* 40 (2017) 421–38.

Edelman. Lee. *No Future: Queer Theory and the Death Drive*. Durham, NC: Duke University Press, 2004.

Eribon, Didier. *Insult and the Making of the Gay Self*. Translated by Michael Lucey. Durham, NC: Duke University Press, 2004.

Fee, Gordon, D. *The First Epistle to the Corinthians*. New International Commentary on the New Testament. Grand Rapids: Eerdmans, 1987.

Ferguson, Sinclair B. *The Whole Christ: Legalism, Antinomianism, and Gospel Assurance—Why the Marrow Controversy Still Matters*. Wheaton, IL: Crossway, 2016.

Fletcher, Paul. "Antimarriage." In *Queer Theology: Rethinking the Western Body*, edited by Gerard Loughlin, 254–66. Oxford: Blackwell, 2007.

Foucault, Michel. *Discipline and Punish: The Birth of the Prison*. Translated by Alan Sheridan. 2nd ed. New York: Vintage, 1995.

———. *The History of Sexuality: An Introduction*. Vol. 1. Translated by Robert Hurley. New York: Vintage, 1990.

———. *Security, Territory, Population: Lectures at the Collège de France 1977–1978*. Translated by Graham Burchell. New York: Palgrave Macmillan, 2007.

———. *Society Must Be Defended: Lectures at the Collège de France 1975–1976*. Translated by D. Macey. New York: Picador, 2003.

France, R. T. *The Gospel of Matthew*. New International Commentary of the New Testament. Grand Rapids: Eerdmans, 2007.
Friedan, Betty. *The Feminine Mystique*. New York: Norton, 1963.
Fuller, John. *W. H. Auden: A Commentary*. Princeton, NJ: Princeton University Press, 1998.
Garland, David E. *Reading Matthew: A Literary and Theological Commentary of the First Gospel*. Macon, GA: Smyth and Helwys, 2013.
Garrett, Don. "Spinoza's *Conatus* Argument." In *Spinoza: Metaphysical Themes*, edited by Olli Koistinen and John Biro, 127–58. Oxford: Oxford University Press, 2002.
Gillingham, Susan. *A Journey of Two Psalms: The Reception of Psalms 1 and 2 in Jewish and Christian Tradition*. Oxford: Oxford University Press, 2013.
Gregory of Nyssa. *St. Gregory: Ascetical Works*. Translated by Virginia Wood Callahan. Fathers of the Church 58. Washington, DC: Catholic University of America Press, 1967.
Grenz, Stanley J. "Jesus as the *Imago Dei*: Image-of-God Christology and the Non-Linear Linearity of Theology." *Journal of the Evangelical Theological Society* 47 (2004) 617–28.
Grudem, Wayne. *Evangelical Feminism: A New Path to Liberalism?* Wheaton, IL: Crossways, 2006.
———. *Evangelical Feminism and Biblical Truth: An Analysis of More Than 100 Disputed Questions*. Wheaton, IL: Crossway, 2012.
———. "The Key Issues in the Manhood-Womanhood Controversy, and the Way Forward." In *Biblical Foundations for Manhood and Womanhood*, edited by Wayne Grudem, 19–68. Wheaton, IL: Crossway, 2002.
Guenther, Lisa. "Shame and the Temporality of Social Life." *Continental Philosophy Review* 44 (2011) 23–39.
Guest, Deryn. "Troubling the Waters." In *Transgender, Intersex, and Biblical Interpretation*, edited by Teresa J. Hornsby and Deryn Guest, 21–44. Atlanta: SBL, 2016.
Hagen, Kenneth. "*Omni homo mendax*: Luther on Psalm 116." In *Biblical Interpretation in the Era of the Reformation*, edited by Richard A. Muller and John L. Thomson, 85–102. 1996. Reprint, Eugene, OR: Wipf and Stock, 2020.
Hagner, Donald A. *Matthew 14–28*. Word Biblical Commentary 33b. Dallas: Word, 1995.
Hare, John. "Hermaphrodites, Eunuchs, and Intersex People: The Witness of Medical Science in Biblical Times and Today." In *Intersex, Theology, and the Bible: Troubling Bodies in Church, Text, and Society*, edited by Susannah Cornwall, 79–96. New York: Palgrave Macmillan, 2015.
Harrison, Glynn. *A Better Story: God, Sex, and Human Flourishing*. Nottingham, UK: InterVarsity, 2016.
Harrison, Verna E. F. "Male and Female in Cappadocian Theology." *Journal of Theological Studies* 41 (1990) 441–71.
Hauerwas, Stanley. *After Christendom? How the Church Is to Behave If Freedom, Justice, and a Christian Nation Are Bad Ideas*. Nashville: Abingdon, 1999.
———. *The Peaceable Kingdom: A Primer in Christian Ethics*. Notre Dame, IN: University of Notre Dame Press, 1983.
Hegel, G. W. F. *Phenomenology of the Spirit*. Translated by A. V. Miller. Oxford: Oxford University Press, 1977.

Hemming, L. "The Undoing of Sex: The Proper Enjoyment of Divine Command." *Studies in Christian Ethics* 23 (2010) 59–72.
Hoekema, Anthony A. *Created in God's Image*. Grand Rapids: Eerdmans, 1986.
Honeysett, Marcus. *Meltdown: Making Sense of a Culture in Crisis*. Leicester, UK: InterVarsity, 2002.
Hornsby, Teresa J. "The Annoying Woman: Biblical Scholarship After Judith Butler." In *Bodily Citations: Religion and Judith Butler*, edited by Ellen T. Armour and Susan M. St. Ville, 71–90. New York: Columbia University Press, 2006.
Hull, Gordon. "Of Suicide and Falling Stones: Finitude, Contingency, and Corporeal Vulnerability in (Judith Butler's) Spinoza." In *Between Hegel and Spinoza*, edited by Hasana Sharp and Jason E. Smith, 151–69. London: Bloomsbury, 2012.
Irigaray, Luce. *An Ethics of Sexual Difference*. London: Continuum, 2004.
Isherwood, Christopher. *Christopher and His Kind*. London: Vintage, 2012.
Jacobs, Alan. *What Became of Wystan: Change and Continuity in Auden's Poetry*. Fayetteville, AK: University of Arkansas Press, 1998.
Jantzen, Grace M. "'Promising Ashes': A Queer Language of Life." In *Queer Theology: Rethinking the Western Body*, edited by Gerard Loughlin, 245–53. Malden, MA: Blackwell, 2007.
Jones, Peter R. "Sexual Perversion: The Necessary Fruit of Neo-Pagan Spirituality in the Culture at Large." In *Biblical Foundations for Manhood and Womanhood*, edited by Wayne Grudem, 257–73. Wheaton, IL: Crossway, 2002.
Kamitsuka, Margaret D. "Sex in Heaven? Eschatological Eros and the Resurrection of the Body." In *The Embrace of Eros: Bodies, Desires, and Sexuality in Christianity*, edited by Margaret D. Kamitsuka, 261–74. Minneapolis: Fortress, 2010.
Karhu, Sanna. "Judith Butler's Critique of Violence and the Legacy of Monique Wittig." *Hypatia* 3 (2016) 827–42.
Kirsch, Arthur. *Auden and Christianity*. New Haven, CT: Yale University Press, 2005.
Kotsko, Adam, "The Failed Divine Performative: Reading Judith Butler's Critique of Theology with Anslem's *On the Fall of the Devil*." *Journal of Religion* 88 (2008) 209–25.
Kuby, Gabrielle. *The Global Sexual Revolution: Destruction of Freedom in the Name of Freedom*. Translated by James Patrick Kirchner. Kettering, UK: LifeSite, 2015.
Kuehne, Dale S. *Sex and the iWorld: Rethinking Relationships beyond the Age of Individualism*. Grand Rapids: Baker, 2009.
Latour, Bruno. "What Is Iconoclash? Or Is There a World beyond the Image Wars." In *Iconoclash: Beyond the Image Wars in Science Religion and Art*, edited by Bruno Latour and Peter Weibel, 14–37. Cambridge: Massachusetts Institute of Technology Press, 2002.
Lewis, C. S. *Mere Christianity*. New York: Macmillan, 1952.
Lints, R. *Identity and Idolatry: The Image of God and Its Inversion*. Downers Grove: InterVarsity, 2015.
Lloyd, Moya, ed. *Butler and Ethics*. Edinburgh: Edinburgh University Press, 2015.
———. "The Ethics and Politics of Vulnerable Bodies." In *Butler and Ethics*, edited by Moya Lloyd, 167–92. Edinburgh: Edinburgh University Press, 2015.
Lord, Beth. *Spinoza's Ethics*. An Edinburgh Philosophical Guide. Edinburgh: Edinburgh University Press, 2010.
Loughlin, Gerard. *Alien Sex*. Malden, MA: Blackwell, 2004.

Macaskill, Grant. *Living in Union with Christ: Paul's Gospel and Christian Moral Identity.* Grand Rapids: Baker, 2019.
Macherey, Pierre. *Hegel or Spinoza.* Translated by Susan M. Ruddick. Minneapolis: University of Minnesota Press, 2011.
MacIntyre, Alasdair. *After Virtue: A Study in Moral Theory.* Notre Dame, IN: University of Notre Dame Press, 1981.
Magnus, Kathy Dow. "The Unaccountable Subject: Judith Butler and the Social Conditions of Intersubjective Agency." *Hypatia* 21 (2006) 81–103.
Marchal, Joseph A. "Queer Approaches: Improper Relations with Pauline Letters." In *Studying Paul's Letters*, edited by Joseph A. Marchal, 209–27. Minneapolis: Fortress, 2012.
Mawson, Michael. "Subjectivity and Embodied Limits: Deborah Creamer's *Disability and Christian Theology*." *Journal of Religion, Disability and Health* 17 (2013) 409–17.
Mendelson, Edward. *Later Auden.* London: Faber and Faber, 1999.
Middleton, J. Richard. *The Liberating Image: The Imago Dei in Genesis 1.* Grand Rapids: Brazos, 2005.
Miller, Richard B. "Evil, Friendship, and Iconic Realism in Augustine's 'Confessions.'" *Harvard Theological Review* 104 (2011) 387–409.
Mills, Catherine. "Normative Violence, Vulnerability, and Responsibility." *Differences* 18 (2007) 133–56.
Moloney, Francis. J. *"A Hard Saying": The Gospel and Culture.* Collegeville, MN: Liturgical, 2001.
Moo, Douglas J. *The Epistle to the Romans.* New International Commentary on the New Testament. Grand Rapids: Eerdmans, 1996.
Morris, Leon. *The Epistle to the Romans.* Pillar New Testament Commentary. Grand Rapids: Eerdmans, 1988.
Murphy, Edwina, and David Starling, eds. *The Gender Conversation: Evangelical Perspectives on Gender, Scripture, and the Christian Life.* Eugene, OR: Wipf and Stock, 2016.
Nietzsche, F. W. *Beyond Good and Evil / On the Genealogy of Morals.* Translated by Adrian Del Caro. Complete Works of Friedrich Nietzsche 8. Redwood City, CA: Stanford University Press, 2014.
———. *Thus Spoke Zarathustra.* Edited by Adrian Del Caro and Robert B. Pippen. Translated by Adrian del Caro. Cambridge Texts in the History of Philosophy. Cambridge: Cambridge University Press, 2006.
O'Donovan, Oliver. *Finding and Seeking.* Ethics as Theology 2. Grand Rapids: Eerdmans, 2014.
———. "Know Thyself! The Return of Self-Love." In *The Authority of the Gospel: Explorations in Moral and Political Theology in Honor of Oliver O'Donovan*, edited by Robert Song and Brent Waters, 268–84. Grand Rapids: Eerdmans, 2015.
———. *The Problem of Self-Love in St. Augustine.* New Haven, CT: Yale University Press, 1980.
Ortlund, Gavin. "Image of Adam, Son of God: Genesis 5:3 and Luke 3:38 in Intercanonical Dialogue." *Journal of Evangelical Theology Society* 57 (2014) 673–88.
Parsons, Susan F. *The Ethics of Gender: New Dimensions to Religious Ethics.* New Dimensions to Religious Ethics. Oxford: Blackwell, 2002.

———. *Feminism and Christian Ethics*. New Studies in Christian Ethics. Cambridge: Cambridge University Press, 1996.
Patterson, Daniel R. "The Law of Adam and Eve." In *1968: Culture and Counterculture*, edited by Daniel Matthys and Thomas V. Gourlay, 292–309. Eugene, OR: Wipf & Stock 2020.
Plato, *Phaedo*. In *Plato, Complete Works*, translated by G. M. A. Grube, edited by John M. Cooper and D. S. Hutchinson, 49–100. Indianapolis: Hackett, 1997.
Post, Stephen G. "Love, Religion, and Sexual Revolution." *Journal of Religion* 72 (1992) 403–16.
Rae, Murray. "Jesus Christ, the Order of Creation." In *Christ and the Created Order: Perspectives from Theology, Philosophy, and Science*, edited by Andrew B. Torrance and Thomas H. McCall, 2:23–34. Grand Rapids: Zondervan, 2018.
Rees, Geoffrey. *The Romance of Innocent Sexuality*. Eugene, OR: Cascade, 2011.
Riedl, Anna Maria. *Judith Butler and Theology*. Leiden: Brill, 2021.
Rogers, Eugene F., Jr. "Bodies Demand Language: Thomas Aquinas." In *Queer Theology: Rethinking the Western Body*, edited by Gerard Loughlin, 176–87. Malden, MA: Blackwell, 2007.
Rudy, Kathy. *Sex and the Church*. Boston: Beacon, 1997.
Sanlon, Peter. *Plastic People: How Queer Theory Is Changing Us*. London: Latimer, 2010.
Sartre, Jean-Paul. *Being and Nothingness: An Essay on Phenomenological Ontology*. Translated by Hazel E. Barnes. London: Routledge, 2003.
Scruton, Roger. *Sexual Desire: A Philosophical Investigation*. Phoenix: London, 1986.
Sedgwick, Eve Kosofski. *Touching Feeling: Affect, Pedagogy, Performativity*. Durham, NC: Duke University Press, 2003.
Sharp, Hasana. *Spinoza and the Politics of Renaturalization*. Chicago: University of Chicago Press, 2011.
Shaw, Jane. "Reformed and Enlightened Church." In *Queer Theology: Rethinking the Western Body*, edited by Gerard Loughlin, 215–29. Malden, MA: Blackwell, 2007.
Smith, J. Warren. "The Body of Paradise and the Body of the Resurrection: Gender and the Angelic Life in Gregory of Nyssa's 'De hominis opificio.'" *Harvard Theological Review* 99 (2006) 207–28.
Song, Robert. *Covenant and Calling: Towards a Theology of Same-Sex Relationships*. London: SCM, 2014.
Spinoza, Benedict. *A Spinoza Reader: The Ethics and Other Works*. Edited by Edwin Curley. Princeton: Princeton University Press, 1994.
Stone, Ken. "The Garden of Eden and the Heterosexual Contract." In *Bodily Citations: Religion and Judith Butler*, edited by Ellen T. Armour and Susan M. St. Ville, 48–70. New York: Columbia University Press, 2006.
Stuart, Elizabeth. "Sacramental Flesh." In *Queer Theology: Rethinking the Western Body*, edited by Gerard Loughlin, 65–75. Oxford: Blackwell, 2007.
Sverker, Joseph. *Human Being and Vulnerability: Beyond Constructivism and Essentialism in Judith Butler, Steven Pinker, and Colin Gunton*. Stuttgart: Ibidem, 2020.
Tanner, Kathryn. *Christ the Key*. Cambridge: Cambridge University Press, 2010.
Thiem, Annika. *Unbecoming Subjects: Judith Butler, Moral Philosophy, and Critical Responsibility*. New York: Fordham University Press, 2008.

Tilling, Chris. "Paul, Christ, and Narrative Time." In *Christ and the Created Order: Perspectives from Theology, Philosophy, and Science*, edited by Andrew B. Torrance and Thomas H. McCall, 2:151–66. Grand Rapids: Zondervan, 2018.

Timmins, Will N. *Romans 7 and Christian Identity: A Study of the "I" in Its Literary Context*. Society for New Testament Studies Monograph Series. Cambridge: Cambridge University Press, 2017.

Tonstad, Linn Marie. *Queer Theology: Beyond Apologetics*. Eugene, OR: Cascade, 2018.

Trible, Phyllis. *God and the Rhetoric of Sexuality*. Overtures to Biblical Theology. Philadelphia: Fortress, 1978.

Trueman, Carl R. *The Rise and Triumph of the Modern Self: Cultural Amnesia, Expressive Individualism, and the Road to Sexual Revolution*. Wheaton, IL: Crossway, 2020.

Velleman, J. David. "The Genesis of Shame." *Philosophy and Public Affairs* 30 (2001) 27–52.

Von Rad, Gerhard. *Genesis: A Commentary*. Translated by John H. Marks. Philadelphia: Westminster, 1973.

Wannenwetsch, Bernd. "The Desire of Desire: Commandment and Idolatry in Late Capitalist Societies." In *Idolatry: False Worship in the Bible, Early Judaism and Christianity*, edited by Stephen C. Barton, 315–30. London: T. & T. Clark, 2010.

Ware, Bruce A. "Male and Female Complementarity and the Image of God." In *Biblical Foundations for Manhood and Womanhood*, edited by Wayne Grudem, 71–92. Wheaton, IL: Crossway, 2002.

Ward, Graham. "Adam and Eve's Shame (and Ours)." *Literature and Theology* 26 (2012) 305–22.

———. *Cities of God*. Abingdon, UK: Routledge, 2000.

Watson, Francis. *Agape, Eros, Gender: Towards a Pauline Sexual Ethic*. Cambridge: Cambridge University Press, 2003.

Wenham, Gordon J. *Genesis 1–15*. Word Biblical Commentary. Waco, TX: Word, 1987.

Williams, Rowan. "The Body's Grace." In *Christianity*, edited by Stephen Hunt, 41–58. Library of Essays on Sexuality. London: Routledge, 2010.

Wirzba, Norman. "Creation *through* Christ." In *Christ and the Created Order: Perspectives from Theology, Philosophy, and Science*, edited by Andrew B. Torrance and Thomas H. McCall, 2:35–53. Grand Rapids: Zondervan, 2018.

Wittig, Monique. *The Straight Mind and Other Essays*. Boston: Beacon, 1992.

Woolhead, Linda. "Sex and Secularization." In *Queer Theology: Rethinking the Western Body*, edited by Gerard Loughlin, 230–39. Oxford: Blackwell, 2007.

Yarhouse, Mark A. *Understanding Gender Dysphoria: Navigating Transgender Issues in a Changing Culture*. Downers Grove: InterVarsity, 2015.

Subject Index

Abraham, 187–88
accountability, 114, 160–61
Adam and Eve
   and Brownson, 62
   Christian theology of gender, 54–55, 169–71
   and Cornwall, 184–85
   discernment, 201–2
   faith and hope, 204
   image of God, 195
   images of, 128–35, 175, 205, 213
   innocent sexuality, 126–28
   law of, 2, 117–18, 135–37, 184–85, 188, 206
   master/slave dialectic, 32
   politicization of sexuality, 120–22
   and Rees, 116–20, 122–23
   sexual revolution, 123–25
   and shame, 69–70
   and Stone, 57–60
   theological critique of gender violence, 116
   vocation in relation to God, 199
   wonder, 6
agency, 22, 47–48, 49, 51, 53, 62, 110, 113, 202–3, 204
agent-self theory, O'Donovan, 47–55
The Age of Anxiety (Auden), 81–90, 81n133, 212
agonism, 34, 121
agreed concept (norms), 142
All Souls, 82
Althusser, Louis, 112

androgyny, 58n51, 59, 61–62
Antigone's Claim (Butler), 56
anxiety, age of, 81–89, 179, 186, 200, 201–3, 205, 209, 212
apophatic movement, 172
Armour, Ellen, 11
ascetic aspect of theology, 172, 177–78
asexual creatures, 178
assimilation, 31, 103
attachment, 37–39, 41, 152, 195
attentiveness, 173
Auden, W. H., 45, 81–90, 81n133, 127, 202, 212
Augustine of Hippo
   and Auden, 81, 84, 86–87, 89
   danger of desire, 25
   experience of self, 77–80
   and idolatry, 131, 132–34
   and lust, 72n98
   and Rees, 117, 120, 125–26
   and righteousness, 137
   and shame, 68–69
Austin, J. L., 111, 112n74
authority, 26, 28, 125–26, 163–65
authorship, 113
autonomy, 28, 28n48, 33, 36, 54, 113–14, 203

babies, 50, 102, 104, 112–13
Barth, Karl, 2n3, 43, 56, 193
Barzun, Jacques, 81
Beauvoir, Simone de, 102, 103–4
becoming process, 15–17, 18, 37–40, 102, 103–4, 108, 201–15

SUBJECT INDEX

beginning
    and Butler, 15–17, 200
    and Cornwall, 184–85
    and desire, 175–79
    gender reform, 15–17
    image of God, 194–96, 198–99, 200
    innocent sexuality, 121
    morality, 181
binary conception of gender, 45, 101, 104–6
bio-legal demands, 142–43, 170
bio-logic functions, 109, 142
biology, 9, 101–3, 142
bio-politics, 19, 158
bio-power, 18, 120
bodies
    agency, 202–9
    Butler's ethics of gender, 141–44
    Butler's reading of Foucault, 18–23, 107–10
    desire for life, 161–63, 181–82
    discernment, 201–2
    eschatological, 174–75, 183–88
    eunuchs, 188–92
    and fear, 7–8
    gender and sexuality, 117–18
    image of God, 194
    law of man and woman, 103–5
    as limit, 159–61
    mundane desire, 177–78
    reforming a theology of gender, 179
    rescue, 85–90
    in time, 169–71
    and trouble, 74–76
    union with Christ, 209–15
    violence, 105–6
    and wonder, 4–7
    See also embodiment
Bodies That Matter (Butler), 38, 110, 113
body-corporate, 141–44, 149–50, 157, 159–60, 163, 165, 170
"The Body's Grace" (Williams), 210–14
Boer, Roland, 149–50, 155n57, 156
Bohemia, 83–85

Bonhoeffer, Dietrich, 67–68, 201
Boucher, Geoff, 32
Brock, Brian, 6, 65–66
Brownson, James, 62–63, 62n72, 72, 73n102
Bulgakov, Mikhail, 83
Butler, Judith
    agency, 202–8
    beginning, 15–17, 200
    and the body, 141–44
    and Christians, 85, 169–70
    and Coakley, 174–77
    contextual landscape, 9–10
    conversation, 10–12
    and Cornwall, 184–85
    critique of mastery, 173
    danger of desire, 25–29
    desire for recognition, 29–34
    desire in gender theory, 23–25, 44–45, 76–80, 155–59
    desire to depart the human, 46–48, 54–55
    and embodiment, 73
    eschatological embodiment, 183–85
    ethics of gender, 141–44, 149–51, 159–63
    evaluating norms, 163–66
    and fear, 8–9
    and Foucault, 107–10
    and Freud, 40–42
    gender performativity, 110–13
    gender theory introduction, 1–3
    gender violence, 93–97, 100–105
    image of God, 193–94
    images of the originary man and woman, 130, 135
    incoherence, 88
    and inscription, 107–10, 107n54
    law of desire, 180–82
    law of man and woman, 100–105
    loss-induced desire, 151–55
    and O'Donovan, 53–55
    originary scene, 37–42, 55, 79, 152, 206
    physical body, 75–76, 105–6
    and power, 18–23

recognizing gender, 34–36
and Rees, 118, 119, 120, 127
and shame, 71, 98
sociality of the body and intersubjectivity, 55–61, 67
Spinoza's God, 144–46
and Stone, 56–60
subjectivity, 93
supernatural foundation, 146–48
union with Christ, 214–15
vulnerability in union, 210
and Ward, 2n3

Cahill, Lisa Sowle, 125n24
call of wisdom, 46–48, 52–53
Campbell, Douglas, 92
Campbell, Jan, 12n26
canon and a canonical approach, 73–74
categories of gender and sex, 59, 100–103
celibacy, 189–90
Chambers, Samuel A., 17n6, 94n9, 96
The Charmed Circle of Ideology (Boucher), 32
Christianity
   agency, 208–9
   ethics of gender, 142, 154
   gender theory, Butler, 3, 8–9
   idolatry, 128–32
   image of God, 194
   law of desire, 181–82
   mundane desire, 23
   participation in Christ, 187
   and Rees, 116–17
   and rescue, 85
   and shame, 68
   and Spinoza, 148
   subject-bodies, 205–6
   subjectivity, 156–57
   theology of gender, 44–45, 54–55, 65–66, 75–76, 116–17, 169–70, 177, 203–4
   union with Christ, 209–15
   See also creation
Christology, 146, 196

Christ the Key (Tanner), 194–98
church and Christ, 7, 210, 212, 214
The City of God (Augustine), 68–69, 72n98, 120
civil laws, 180
closeting, 97–99
Coakley, Sarah, 4n8, 171–79, 172n10, 181–82, 185, 193, 200
coherence
   coherent body, 88
   deception of, 31–32
   desire for sexual coherence, 128
   and grief, 80
   hope, 137
   and identity, 119
   innocent sexuality, 117
   and lack, 20
   memory of, 126–28
   moral subjectivity, 29
   originary innocence, 126–27, 136
   and Paul, 182
   psyche, 21
   and Stone, 59–60
   through sex, 126
   traditional notion of gender and sex, 120–22
   and women, 100
community, 63, 72, 145, 149, 161–62, 165, 169–70, 204. *See also conatus*, Spinoza; kinship
compulsory heterosexuality, 56–58, 96
conatus, Spinoza, 143, 145–46, 148–51, 154, 155–59
concept (second form of body), 142
conditions, originary, 27, 30–31, 35, 38, 107, 164
Confessions (Augustine), 25–26, 77–79, 86
conservative Christianity, 184
conservative church, Rees, 125
conservative theological view of gender, 54–55, 117, 123, 126, 128–29, 136
constitutive gaze, 71, 73, 91, 209

232 SUBJECT INDEX

constructed body, 108–10
constructivist theory, 46–48, 50–51,
    54–55, 126–27
contemplative theology, 172, 179
contingency of desire, 35, 37
contingent agency, 202–4, 208
contraception, 123
conversation, 10–12
Cornwall, Susannah, 183–87, 200
covenant marriage, 209–11, 214
creation
    creation order, O'Donovan, 54
    creation reality, 176–79
    danger of desire, 25–26
    and darkness, 173
    embodiment, 66–74
    God's view of, 64–65
    and Lints, 205
    objectification of, 132–33
    originary form, 31
    and participation, 197–98
    and Paul, 181–82
    in Psalms, 199
    and Rees, 119, 121, 123, 126–27
    relation, Butler, 155–56
    Spinoza's doctrine of God,
        146–48
    and Stone, 57–61
    troubled embodiment, 61–63,
        74–76
    and wonder, 4–5
    See also Adam and Eve
Creation and Fall (Bonhoeffer), 67
creatureliness, 48, 65–66, 70, 131,
    197, 198–200
critique of constructivist theory,
    47–48, 50–51, 54–55
cross-disciplined theology of gender,
    9–10
crude material body, 141–42,
    159–60
culturally constructed body,
    Foucault, 107–10

danger of desire, 25–29
Daniell, Anne, 1n2
darkness, 65, 85–90, 172–73, 179,
    214

death, bodies of, 6, 81, 85–90, 106,
    117–18, 126, 127, 133, 135,
    137, 177, 179, 181–82, 187–
    88, 201–9, 212–13, 215
death drive, 152, 154
death in life, 34, 94, 111–13, 166,
    214
death of society, 123–26
deception of coherence, 32
declaration of God, 61–65
deconstitution process, 158–59
deconstruction, 19, 42, 130. *See also*
    double reading
DeFranza, Megan, 190
democracy and inclusion, 36
democratic pragmatism, 165
democratization of gender, 36, 144,
    159–66
denaturalization of gender, 94–96,
    142–44, 155–57
denied sexuality, 39
departure, 16, 44–45, 55, 101, 116–
    17, 127, 136–37, 152, 174,
    192–94, 195, 201–2
Derrida, Jacques, 34, 38, 56
desire
    and Auden, 81–85, 127
    and Augustine, 72n98
    confused desire, 175–79
    contingent agency, 202–8
    and creation, 197
    danger of, 25–29
    and darkness, 172
    desire-induced incoherence, 25,
        37, 41, 44, 77, 80, 83, 85,
        120, 126, 152
    ethics of gender, 163–66, 169–70
    and fulfillment, 129
    gender theory, Butler, 16–17
    of God, 6, 77, 125, 133, 162,
        173, 176–77, 199–200, 201,
        203–5, 208, 212–14
    good embodiment, 76
    and hope, 183
    law of, 163, 171, 180–82, 202–4
    law of nature, 109
    to live, 141–44, 148–51, 161
    master/slave dialectic, 29–34

SUBJECT INDEX 233

mundane fact of, 23–25, 34–36, 135
originary scene, Butler, 40–42
and the other, 155–59
between the primeval creatures, 57
and recognition, 23, 29–37, 41, 71, 103
Rees' employment of Butler's queering strategy, 120
rescue from, 85–90
for sexual coherence, 122–26, 128
and shame, 71
Stone's Butlerian reading of the second creation narrative, 60–61, 71
and subjectivity, O'Donovan, 45
as teacher, 76–80
vulnerability in union, 209–15
to wonder, 4–6
Deuteronomy, 129, 189
discernment, 47, 85, 144, 191, 201–9
Discipline and Punish (Foucault), 19, 107n56
discursive "I," 112–13
discursive violence, 102
disordered desires, 76, 173, 177
distrust, Spinoza, 144
divorce, 135–36, 189
doctrine of the image of God, 5–6, 192–94, 198, 201
Dolezal, Luna, 70n94
domestication process, Spinoza, 157
domination, 22–23, 58
double reading, 38, 56
drag, 110
dressage horse metaphor, 20–21, 30, 40–41, 78, 98, 204
dyadic structure of social life, 156

Eden
age of anxiety, 83
and Coakley, 175
and Cornwall, 186
desire in, Augustine, 72n98
discernment, 201–2
Edenic marriage, 190–91

ethics of gender, 170
image of God, 193, 200, 203
innocent sexuality, 123–24, 126–27, 129
location, 61–65
moral law of desire, Butler, 181
originary innocence, 136–37
reforming a theology of gender, 116–18
returning to, 2–3
self in, 135
social structuring, 69
embodiment, 66–74
Christian ethics of gender, 142
embodied existence, 63–65, 76, 81
embodied experiences, 109, 214
embodied posture, 160
embodied reality, 64, 87
embodied relationality, 67
embodied sexual coherence, 121
image of God, 192–93
norms for, 164
originary man and woman, 63
participation in Christ, 188
responsibility, 162
subject-bodies, 209
subjective experience of, 76
trouble, 74–76
vulnerability, 154
emergence of desire, 31, 34, 36, 37–39
encounter, 148–50, 156
enslavement, 79, 205
epistemic catastrophe, 161–62, 168, 204
epistemic humility, 43, 46, 161
Eribon, Didier, 96–99, 111
eschatological bodies, 183–86, 196, 202
eschatology, 174–75, 179, 183–86
eschaton, 5, 53, 170, 179, 186–87, 192, 194, 201, 203, 206
Ethics (Spinoza), 27, 144–48, 151, 156
ethics of gender, 141–43, 149–51, 154, 158–59, 159, 160, 161, 163–65, 166, 169

eunuchs, 186, 188–92, 201
evangelical theologians, 198
evil, 78–79
Excitable Speech (Butler), 31, 47, 113
existentialism, Auden, 86–87

faith, 46, 187–88, 192, 201, 203–4, 214
fall, 64, 66, 74–76, 79–80, 117, 119, 120, 123–25, 197, 198
false man, Augustine, 131
false redemption, Rees, 133–34
false unity, 135
false worship, 135
family, 99, 125, 199
Faustian pact, 123–24
fear, 7–9, 24, 211
feedback loop, 31, 135, 206
feminism, 16, 93, 100
fictive/non-fictive subjectivity of desire, 24, 41–42
Finding and Seeking (O'Donovan), 45, 52–53, 52n35, 68
Fletcher, Paul, 191
Foucault, Michel
　and Butler, 28n51, 36, 107–10, 150, 158
　culturally constructed body, 107–10
　and Eribon, 98
　productive power, 18, 22–23, 109
　and Rees, 120, 123, 124, 128–29, 132
　theory of power, 17, 18–23
"Foucault and the Paradox of Bodily Inscriptions" (Butler), 107–10
fragility, 205
Frames of War (Butler), 55–56, 150
freedom, 47–48, 167, 182, 201–2, 204, 208
freeze-framing, 130
Freud, Sigmund, 17, 32, 37–40, 112, 127, 171–72
fulfillment, 129, 131, 136, 191
Fuller, John, 82

"The Garden of Eden" (Stone), 56
gay insults, 97–98
gay self, 97–99, 111
gaze, 51, 53, 69–71, 108, 116, 118, 121, 128–29, 209, 211. *See also* idolatry
gender
　as becoming, 103–4, 215
　binary, 104
　Butler's reading of Foucault, 107–10
　Christian theology of, 44–45, 54–55, 65–66, 75–76, 116–17, 169–70, 177, 203–4
　conservative theological view of, 54–55, 117, 123, 126, 128–29, 136
　democratization, 36, 144, 159–66
　denaturalization of, 94–96, 142–44, 155–57
　discrimination, 183
　dysphoria, 99–100
　embodiment, 66–67
　embodiment in the present, 179
　eschatology, 174–75, 179, 183
　ethics of, Butler, 150–51, 154, 165, 169
　Foucault, Butler's reading of, 21–22
　and Freud, 37–40, 127
　God's originary desire, 178
　and grief, 151–55
　and hope, 81
　identity disorder, 59
　law of Adam and Eve, 136–37
　law of desire, 180
　law of man and woman, 100–105
　master/slave dialectic, 33
　mind/body question, 146
　norms, 32, 34, 56, 59–61, 94–95, 96, 101, 163–66, 185
　originary scene, 37–40
　originary scene, Butler, 41
　participation in the divine, 172
　and performativity, 110–14
　personhood, 176

physical body, 105–6
psychic framework, 38
questioning of, 7–8
recognizing, 34–36
reform of, Butler, 44–45
and shame, 71
and Spinoza, 145–46
subject-bodies, 207
theology of, Cornwall, 184
theory of, Butler, 1–3, 15–17, 26–27, 40, 41–42, 75–76, 85, 93, 95–96, 101–2, 104–5, 142, 151, 155–56, 170, 174–75, 203
trouble, 74–76
violence, 92–96, 97, 100, 106, 116, 129, 153, 159, 175, 209
voluntarist notion of, 110–13
Gender Trouble (Butler), 20, 32, 93–95, 100, 110
genealogy of Jesus, 199
genealogy of the body, 18
genitalia, 57–58, 103
glory/glorification, 2, 182, 198–99, 202, 211, 215
God, imaging of, 192–204, 208, 213, 215
God, Spinoza's uncreated, 144–48, 157–58
good
 constructed body, Foucault, 108–9
 contingent agency, 202–5
 creation, 61–68, 177
 desire, 156, 170
 embodiment, 74–76, 143, 144–45, 170
 imaging God, 194–95
 innocent sexuality, 117–18, 121
 law of Adam and Eve, 135–37
 law of desire, Butler, 180–82
 mundane sexuality, 37–39, 60
 physical body, 106
 Rees's queer theology of sexuality, 119, 120
 troubled bodies, 186–88, 189–92, 201–2

grace of God, 116, 120, 128, 137, 188
grace of the body, 210–12
Gregory of Nyssa, 174, 178
grief, 40, 79–80, 152–55
ground of being, 157
Guest, Deryn, 10n23

Harbord, Janey, 12n26
Hare, John, 190
Harper's magazine, 81
Hauerwas, Stanley, 6, 8
Hegel, Georg, 17, 23, 27–34, 81, 112, 148–51, 149n34, 202–3
heteronormativity, 32, 59, 163–66
heterosexuality
 compulsory heterosexuality, 56–58, 96
 hetereosexualization of social bonds, 111
 heterosexual marital sex, 117, 122–25
 heterosexual matrix, 18, 100–103
 normative violence, 96
 original heterosexual form, 15–16
 and Rees, 119
 and shame, 98–99
 and Stone, 57–59
heterosexual marital sex, 120
historical Christianity, 120
history of bodies, Butler, 107
The History of Sexuality (Foucault), 120
Hoekema, Anthony, 193
homophobic discourse, 97–98
homosexuality, 39, 40, 82, 84, 87, 89, 97–99, 212
Honeysett, Marcus, 12n27
hope, 46, 60, 80n132, 81, 151, 180–87, 204, 214
human agency, 169–70, 203, 208
human community. *See* community
human desire, 30–31, 76, 148, 170, 176, 178, 208
human embodiment, 72–73, 74, 179, 183, 191–92, 205

human existence, 27, 51, 59, 62, 71, 74, 81, 85, 186
hypersexuality, 72–73

iconoclash, 130
iconoclasm, 130, 179, 185
ideal body, 159–61
identifications, 33, 38–39
identity, 9, 34, 59, 97, 100, 113, 119
identity politics, 10n23, 100, 113
idolatry, 6, 116, 126–29, 131–35, 171–75, 179
illegitimacy, 99
images
    of Adam and Eve, 128–35, 175, 205, 213
    imaging God, 192–204, 208, 213, 215
imagination, 173, 175, 179, 183
imago Dei, 6, 56, 66
impact of the fall, 64, 74–76, 124
imprisonment, 19
incarnation, 146, 195
incoherence
    and anxiety, 84
    Auden and Butler, 88
    and desire, 23–25, 27–28
    desire-induced, 41, 44, 77, 83, 85, 90, 120, 126, 152
    and gender, 35, 38
    and grief, 80
    and responsibility, 161–62
individual and societal coherence, 117, 120, 127
individual constructed society, 46–47
innocent sexuality, 116–33, 137
inscription, 105–14, 107n54
Insult (Eribon), 97–100
internalization of the Christian God, 157
internal relations, 31–32
international relations, 152–53
interpellation, Althusser, 112
intersex persons, 166, 184
intersubjectivity, 30, 32–34, 66–67, 74–75, 158, 162, 169, 202–3
is/ought fallacy, 26–27

I/thou confrontation, 193–94

Jacobs, Alan, 81–85
Jesus Christ
    Christology, 146, 196
    and creation, 5–7, 173
    discernment, 201–2
    embodiment, 192–93
    eschatological bodies, 186
    and eunuchs, 189–91
    gender theory, Butler, 2
    genealogy of, 199
    image of, 130
    imaging God, 195–96, 198–200, 204
    law of Adam and Eve, 135–36, 188
    and Tanner, 197
    and transgression, 118n3, 191n71
    union with, 209–15
judgment, 61, 82, 111–12, 134, 150n34, 161
Jung, Carl Gustav, 81n133, 82, 84

Kallman, Chester, 82
Kant, Immanuel, 27–28
Karhu, Sanna, 95
kinship, 56, 62n72, 63, 72
knowledge, 4, 26–27, 31, 49–50, 52

Lacan, Jacques, 175
lack, 20, 24–25, 35, 37–38, 76, 80, 81, 83, 87–88, 127, 176
Latour, Bruno, 130
law
    of Adam and Eve, 2, 117–18, 135–37, 184–85, 188, 206
    of desire, 162–63, 171, 180, 181–82, 203, 204, 205, 206, 208
    of gender, 103
    of God, 206–7
    legal precedents in modern law, 112
    of man and woman, 100–105, 106
    of nature, 108–10
    righteous law, 116–17

of sin, 207, 208
  unjust, 103, 117, 119, 135
lesbians, 32, 105, 154
"Letter to the Bishops of the Catholic Church" (Ratzinger), 56
Levinas, Emmanuel, 81n132, 156, 164
liberation, 182
lifeless idol, 132
limit, Bonhoeffer, 67
Lints, Richard, 175, 205
Lloyd, Moya, 33
location and embodied existence, 63–65
longing, 181–82, 183, 192
Lord, Beth, 145, 147
loss, 37–38, 40, 42, 76, 79–80, 81, 83, 87–88, 99, 127, 151–54, 162, 176
loving, Augustine, 78–79

Macaskill, Grant, 213
male and female, 59, 106, 129, 136–37, 183–85, 192–93. *See also* gender
male dominance, 58
marriage
  in Auden, 89–90, 212
  covenant marriage, 209–11, 214
  discernment, 201–2
  Edenic, 190–91
  embodiment, 73
  innocent sexuality, 117, 121
  originary, 76
  and Rees, 119, 120–21
  and risk, 211
  in Scripture, 186–87
  sexual revolution, 123
  speech act, 111–12
  union with Christ, 214
Massacio, 69
Master and Margarita (Bulgakov), 83
master/slave dialectic, 17, 29–34, 203, 207
material body, 19, 108–9, 141–42, 160

materiality, 109, 176–77
materialization of the uncreated God of Scripture, Spinoza, 157
materialized God, 158
medical treatment, 6–7, 102, 109
melancholic identification, 38
melancholy, 37–40, 99, 127, 152
messianic figures, 133–34
mind(s), 67, 71, 73, 75–76, 103, 106, 146, 182, 204, 206–7
monoprinciple, 143, 167, 169
morality, 26–29, 64–66, 78, 85, 126, 131, 158–59, 163–64, 181, 191–92
Moses, 135–37
mundane
  agency, 111
  body, 177–78
  desires, 76
  experience of shame, 98
  gendered and sexual life, 60, 118
  gender violence, 93
  humanity, 103
  mundane desires, 24–25, 29, 30–31, 34, 36, 37–42, 61, 79, 85, 135, 158–59, 165, 176–77, 204, 206–7, 212, 214
  and the originary, 44–45, 95–96, 108, 111
  originary scene, 152
  vocation of imaging God, 196
murder, 154, 161–63, 165
myths, 46–47

narration of human subjectivity, O'Donovan, 48–55
narration of the originary scene, Butler, 37–40
naturalization, 33, 105, 146, 154, 156. *See also* denaturalization of gender
nature, law of, 108–10
The Nature and Destiny of Man (Niebuhr), 83–84
Negri, Antonio, 157
neighbor, O'Donovan, 49–50

SUBJECT INDEX

New Testament, 195–96, 196n97, 198
Niebuhr, Reinhold, 83–84
Nietzsche, F. W., 110
non-binary bodies, 45, 202
nonviolence, 93, 151–66
normalization, 180
normativization, 95–96
norms, gender, 32, 34, 56, 59, 94–95, 96, 101, 163–66, 185. *See also* heteronormativity
notion of the self. *See* self
nuclear family, 125

obedience, 19, 86, 207–8
objectification of God's creation, 132–33
objective gaze, 51, 53
objectivity, 49–53
O'Donovan, Oliver, 45, 46–54, 52n35, 68, 71
Oedipus mechanism, 38–39, 152, 171–72
Old Testament law *(Torah)*, 184, 189
ontology of desire, Butler, 41–42, 159–61
opacity, 160–61, 202–4
oppressive transgressor, 163
originary desire, 24–25, 30–31, 38, 176, 178
originary embodiment, 66–67
originary form, 16n2, 30–31, 55, 60, 151, 154, 185
originary images of Adam and Eve, 126–27
originary innocence, 118, 126–27, 136
originary loss, 42, 81–85
originary man and woman. *See* Adam and Eve
originary marriage, 76
originary marriage covenant, 209
originary scene, Butler, 37–42, 55, 79, 152, 206
originary scene, Freud, 37–40
originary scene, Hegel, 202–3
originary scene, Stone, 58–60
originary structures, 164

originary violence, 94
originating principle, 20–21
other
    body-corporate, 141–44, 160
    and *conatus*, 148–50
    and desire, 155–59
    desire of, 180
    embodiment, 67–73
    master/slave dialectic, 32–34
    responsibility for, 65–66, 143, 150, 161–64
    vulnerable union with, 209–11
    See also eunuchs

Parsons, Susan F., 13n28
participation in the divine, 172, 187–88, 194–95, 197, 205, 212–14
Paul (apostle)
    ainigmati, 203n114
    and Augustine, 81, 84, 86
    and the body, 204–6
    and Butler, 1n2
    conforming to the world, 173
    and desire, 76–78
    discernment, 191–92
    epistemic humility, 46
    eschatological embodiment, 183–88
    primeval man and woman, 57, 72
    rescue, 85–88
    in Romans, 52–53, 76–77, 179, 181–82
    salvation, 189
    and sin, 207–8
    union with Christ, 209–10, 212
perception, 69, 105–6, 211. *See also* gaze; shame
perfection, 61, 65–66, 124, 133, 144–45, 195
performativity, 9, 21, 47, 110–13
perseverance, 148–50, 154, 157–58, 160, 164, 176, 180
persistence, 143–44
personhood, 175–76, 180
Pharisees, 118n3, 136, 139n53, 201–2

Phenomenology of the Spirit (Hegel), 17, 32
Philip, 191
philosophical knowledge, 23, 25–27
physical bodies, 66–67, 75, 105–6, 203. *See also* embodiment
Plato, 27, 61
politics, 10n23, 100–103, 105, 113, 120–22, 123, 152–55
pornography, 210–11
postlapsarian era, 13n28, 65, 71, 83, 89
post-structuralism, 28n48
power, 17–20, 22–23, 96–97, 110–13, 125, 130–33, 157–58
Power and Submissions (Butler), 174
power of the Spirit, 6, 204–6, 213–15
practical knowledge, 26–27
pre-discursive body, 107–8, 155
prelapsarian era, 61–62, 68, 125
pre-man-and-woman figure, 59–62
present. *See* mundane
pre-social sovereign-I, O'Donovan, 51–53
pre-woman man, 57–59, 64
prior desire, 155
privacy, 69–71, 69n91
private Christian schools, 7
private/public differentiation, 121, 162
productive power, Foucault, 18, 22–23, 109
prohibition, 16n2, 37–40, 42–43, 152
psalmist, 64–65, 131–34, 205
psyche, 19, 19n12, 21–22, 37–38, 157–58
Psychic Life of Power (Butler), 20, 38, 47, 151
psychoanalysis, 19–20, 22, 32, 37–38
public government schools, 7

queer, language of, 110
queer body, 202
queer figure, 59–61
queer gender politics, 10n23, 105
queer notions of gender, 178
queer theology of gender and sexuality, Stone, 63
queer theology of sexuality, Rees, 119
queer theory, Butler, 8–9, 10–11, 105

racism, 92–93
rational agency, O'Donovan, 47
Ratzinger, Joseph, 56
reading, Derridean strategy of, 38–39, 56
reality, Spinoza, 145
reality effect, 95, 106, 110–11
recognition, 23, 29–36, 41, 70–71, 103–4, 149–50n34
recognizable "I," 112–13
redemption, 77, 89, 120, 128, 133–34, 137, 182–88, 195–96
Rees, Geoffrey, 8, 116–29, 132–33, 136–37
reflexivity, 24–25, 49–51, 53, 74–75, 176
reform
    conception of gender, 10
    and desire, 24, 155–56, 171, 180
    of gender and sex in Butler's gender theory, 15–16, 44–45, 102, 104–5, 165, 203
    of God, Spinoza, 146–48, 157–58
    law of Adam and Eve, 2
    of originary structures, 164
    theology of gender, 116–18, 129–30
    unjust law of gender, 103
    vocation to image God, 209
regulation, 8, 95, 110, 162, 165, 170
Reidl, Anna, 9n22
relationality
    of bodies, 212
    embodied, 67
    between gender and sex, 103
    between God and creation, 146
    and intersubjectivity, 34, 158
    and shame, 68, 70
repentance, 128
representational politics, 100–103

rereading of the second creation account, 56, 59–60
rescue, 85–90, 184, 188, 205–6
resistance, 20, 22, 104, 110, 129
responsibility, 47, 64–66, 120, 127, 141, 143, 150–51, 160–64, 208
resurrection, 188, 209, 213–15
righteous law, 116–17
righteousness, 125, 135–37, 184, 201, 207–8
risk, 210–14
The Romance of Innocent Sexuality (Rees), 116, 118

safe sex, 210–11
salvation, 106, 128, 133, 137, 170, 189, 196, 208, 212–13
same-sex attraction. *See* homosexuality
Sanlon, Peter, 10n23
Sartre, Jean-Paul, 70, 94n7
Scripture, 4–5, 55, 56, 88, 130, 169, 183, 185–86, 188–89, 198–99, 210
Scruton, Roger, 68–69
second creation account, 56, 59–61, 66
The Second Sex (de Beauvoir), 102
self
    discursive "I," 113
    in Eden, 135
    experience of, 75–77
    O'Donovan, 48–55, 67
    self-awareness, 50–53, 202
    self-desire-induced incoherence, 41
    self-discovery, 49
    self-government, 28
    selfhood, 51, 65, 172
    self-knowledge, 48, 54
    self-love, 49–50, 54
    self-mastery, 80, 212
    self-naming, 113
    self-narration, 160–61
    self-perception, 69, 70
    self-preservation, 98
    self-reflection, 45
    self-revelation, 173
    self-serving, 143
    self-understanding, 162, 211
    self-unknowing, 202
    theorization of, 50–54
    ungrievable, 153–54
Senses of the Subject (Butler), 150
sexuality
    age of anxiety, 205
    and Butler, 15–17, 162
    Christian theology of gender, 54–55, 76, 116, 128, 136–37
    and darkness, 172–73
    de-naturalization of gender, 95
    and desire, 80
    embodiment, 72–74
    eschatology, 179
    and hope, 81
    innocent sexuality, 116–33
    integration of originary story into gender theory, Butler, 55–61
    law of man and woman, 100–105
    master/slave dialectic, 32
    material body, 108–9
    originary desire, 178
    and power, 18
    sexual ethics, 8
    sexual prohibition, 38–40
    sexual revolution, 123–25
    and shame, 67–71, 70n92, 75, 98–99, 111, 119, 120–22
    sinful sexuality, 119–22, 123, 125, 136–37
    and Stone, 63
    violence, 96–100
shame, 67–71, 70n92, 75, 98–99, 111, 119, 120–22
sin, law of, 205–8
sin, temptation of, 84–85, 89
sinful sexuality, 119–22, 123, 125, 136–37
Singing the Ethos of God (Brock), 65
singleness, 189–90, 214
slavery, 92–93, 92n1, 207–10. *See also* master/slave dialectic
smashing idols, 171–72, 179

sociality
- of the body and intersubjectivity, 67
- Butler's ethics of gender, 160–61, 162
- deconstitution of God, 158
- embodiment, 66–74
- otherness, 190
- reform, 180
- sexual revolution, 123–24
- social constructivism, Butler, 48
- social constructivism, O'Donovan, 47
- social contexts, 166
- socialized "I," 157
- social norms, 35–36, 155
- social structuring, 68–69, 93
- social theory, 164
- social union of bodies, 142
- sovereign-I, 163

sonship, 199
soul(s), 19–21, 28, 41, 128–29
sovereign agency, 13, 54, 204–9
sovereign-I, 48, 51–53, 110–14, 160, 163, 165, 170
speech act, 111
Spinoza, Baruch, 8–9, 27, 143–48, 150–51, 153–59, 215
Stone, Ken, 45, 56–63, 71, 88
structure and function in the image of God, 197n103, 200
structures, originary, 31, 41, 56, 164
subject-bodies, 203–13
subjectification, 33, 97, 120
subjection, 18–19, 41, 73, 151, 156, 209
subjectivity
- and the body, 160
- coherent moral subjectivity, 29
- critique of gender violence, Butler, 93, 100
- and desire, 27, 156
- and embodiment, 76
- ethics of gender, Butler, 163–64
- gender theory, Butler, 40, 101
- Hegelian metaphor, 32–33
- and O'Donovan, 45, 48, 49

- originary desire, Butler, 30, 41–42
- as production of power, Foucault, 17, 19, 20–22
- and shame, 67, 98
- social norms, 36

subject/object relation, 108
Subjects of Desire (Butler), 29–30
suicide, 160–61, 163, 165
supernatural, 146–48
symbolic capital, 213
Symposium (Plato), 61
synergism, 208–9
systematic theology, 171–72, 179
systematization, 29

taboos, 39, 180–82
Tanner, Kathryn, 194–200, 213
tarrying with grief, 152–55
task of ethics. *See* ethics
temptation to sin, 84–85, 89. *See also* sin
thematization of gender, Butler, 41
theology of gender
- agency, 62
- age of anxiety, 179
- beginning, 175
- Christian, 44–45, 55, 65–66, 203
- and desire, 76
- embodiment, 73
- gender reform, Butler, 44–45
- gender violence, 116
- image of God, 196, 201
- images of Adam and Eve, 128, 129–30
- innocent sexuality, 136–37
- law of Adam and Eve, 118, 182, 184
- law of desire, 170–71, 203
- queer, 63
- and shame, 67
- synergism, 209

troubled gendered embodiment, 188
theology of sex, 127
theorization of self, 50–54
Thiem, Annika, 10n23
third gender, 105

time, 9, 17, 18, 54–55, 74, 108–9, 127, 169, 179
toxic masculinity, 190
tradition. *See* norms, gender
transformation, 80, 132, 177, 179, 213
transgender persons, 96, 100, 153–54
transgression, 27, 103, 142–43, 163, 183, 191, 192–94
trans-historical social-psychic, 158
transsex persons, 166
Trible, Phyllis, 56, 58, 58n51, 61n66, 63
trouble
    and desire, 26
    Edenic man and woman, 178
    troubled embodiment, 61, 66, 74–76, 81, 117–18, 185–89, 191–92, 201–2, 215
Trueman, Carl, 3n7, 146n20
truth, 26–27
two genders, 165–66

uncreated God of Scripture, 144–48, 156–57
Undoing Gender (Butler), 29–30, 35, 79, 93, 145, 150, 152
ungrievable self, 153–54
union, 121, 122, 142, 144, 209–15
unity
    of body and mind, 17, 19
    and coherence, 122
    embodied relationality, 67
    false unity, 135
    and marriage, 120–21
    moral unity, 29
    and multiplicity, 157
    primeval marriage, 72
    and Rees, 127
    return to, 137
universal disorder, 82–83
universal ethics, 165–66
universality, 152–54, 163
unjust law, 103, 117, 119, 135
unlivable conditions, 166

Velleman, J. David, 69, 69n91

violence
    Butler's critique of, 101–2, 114, 175
    constructed body, Foucault, 108
    desire to live, 159–61
    domestic, 210n138
    and Eribon, 96–100
    ethics of gender, 163–66
    gender violence, 92–96, 97, 100, 106, 116, 129, 153, 159, 175, 209
    and grief, 153–54
    vocation of imaging God, 203
vocation
    of discernment, 201–2
    and gender, 104
    of honoring God with our bodies, 204
    of imaging God, 199–200, 203, 206
    responsibility for the other, 156
    of submitting to God's desire, 173
    vulnerability in union, 210
voice of desire, 31, 78
voluntarist notion of gender, 110–13
von Rad, Gerhard, 194
vulnerability, 71, 151–54, 162, 210–11

Wannenwetsch, Bend, 134–35
Ward, Graham, 2n3, 70
Watson, Francis, 62
weak and strong modes of imaging God, 195–96
Williams, Rowan, 210–12, 214
wisdom's call, 46–48, 52, 176
Wittig, Monique, 56n42, 95, 101–2, 104–5
women, 37–39, 62–63, 72, 100, 124n23, 135–36
wonder, 4–7, 173, 212–14
Word of God, 194–95, 197, 214
World War II, 82

Yahwist, 57–60

Scripture Index

OLD TESTAMENT

Genesis

1:1—2:3	61
1:26–27	61n63, 192, 194, 196n95
1:28	177n27
1:31	55n39, 61n64, 198n105
2:1–20	66
2:4	61
2:17	25n37, 74n106
2:18	61n65
2:21	66
2:21–22	62
2:22–24	67
2:23	71–72
2:24	72n97, 72n100, 209
2:25	67–68, 75n108
3:1–6	197n101
3:4–5	197n102
3:6	25n37
3:7	4n9, 74
3:7–8	75n107
3:11	75
3:16	57, 76n109
3:24	89n164
5:1–2	196n95
5:1–3	192n78, 199
9:6	192n78, 196n95
12:1–3	187

Leviticus

22:24–25	189n60

Deuteronomy

4:15–16	129
23:1	189

Isaiah

56:1–8	189
64:6	137n52

Psalms

1:2	14n31
8	196n95
8:4–8	199
17:15	196n95
19	205n121
115:2	2n6
115:4–7	131n34
115:8	133

Proverbs

8:1	46n3
9:17	77n112

NEW TESTAMENT

Matthew

6:24	207n133
19	189
19:3–12	135n46
19:4–6	114, 190–91, 201
19:7	136n47
19:8	136n49, 201
19:10	189n62
19:12	186, 187n55, 189, 191n72, 201
22:30	178n37, 186, 187n55
26:39	211n142

Mark

7:1–23	118n3
12:25	178n37, 186

Luke

3:38	199
6:31	49n26
20:34–36	178n37

John

1:3	5n14
8:2–11	139n53

Acts

8:35–38	191

Romans

1:25	134
3:19–20	136n48
6:5	209
6:14–19	207n132
6:23	123n20
7:14–25	77n113
7:15	77n111, 78n116, 208n134
7:17	205n121
7:22	206n129
7:23	205n121
7:24	14n29, 76–77, 181
7:24–25	170n3
7:24b–25b	188n59
7:25	205n122, 206, 206n129, 207n131
7:25a	14n30
8:2	206n127
8:3	14n32
8:5	206n128, 207n130
8:6	206n126
8:7	206n129
8:18–25	181
8:18–30	213n147
8:23	213n147
8:23–25	2n5
8:24	182n41
8:25	183n43
8:29	130n30, 196n97
8:29–30	213n147
12:1	208n136, 209
12:2	52, 173n14, 206n125
12:3	50, 52
12:5	209

1 Corinthians

3:1	206n124
6:17	209
6:19	204n116, 204n117
6:20	2n4, 171n4
7:4	209n137
7:6–7	191
7:7	186n52
7:29–31	182n40
7:32–35	191n73
8:6	5n14
13:12	4n10, 46n5, 203n112
13:13	204n115
13:14	203n114
15:42–44	213n147
15:49	196n97

2 Corinthians

3:18	196n97
4:4	196n96

5:7	203n113	4:17–24	196n97
7:1	208n136	5:29–32	72n97
		5:30–32	212
Galatians		5:31–32	209, 210n139
1:6	188n57		
1:7	216n153	**Philippians**	
2:20	213n146	2:12–13	208n135
3:13	184, 184n48, 188	3:8–9	213n150
3:14	189		
3:2	216n153	**Colossians**	
3:3	216n154	1:15	196n96
3:10	184	1:16	5n12
3:13	188n58	3:9–11	196n97
3:21	184n47		
3:26	187	**1 Thessalonians**	
3:26–29	192	4:3	208n136
3:28	183–86, 187n55, 189, 191–92	5:23	208n135
3:29	187n55	**Hebrews**	
3:31	187	1:2–3	5n14
5:1	201n109	1:3	195n90
5:4	217n156	3:6	199n107
5:6–7	217n157	11:3	203n113
5:19	216n155	12:14	208n136
5:22	216n155		
		2 Peter	
Ephesians		1:5	208n136
3:20–21	213n148		

www.ingramcontent.com/pod-product-compliance
Lightning Source LLC
Chambersburg PA
CBHW030824230426
43667CB00008B/1361